Monkey
Business

Grand Central Publishing
Hachette Book Group
1290 Avenue of the Americas
New York, NY 10104

www.HachetteBookGroup.com

Printed in the United States of America

Originally published in hardcover by Hachette Book Group.
First Trade Edition: April 2001
Reissued: September 2009
20 19 18 17

Grand Central Publishing is a division of Hachette Book Group, Inc. The Grand Central Publishing name and logo are trademarks of Hachette Book Group, Inc.

The Hachette Speakers Bureau provides a wide range of authors for speaking events. To find out more, go to www.hachettespeakersbureau .com or call (866) 376-6591.

The publisher is not responsible for websites (or their content) that are not owned by the publisher.

The Library of Congress has cataloged the hardcover edition as follows:

Rolfe, John
    Monkey business : swinging through the Wall Street jungle / John Rolfe and Peter Troob.
      p.   cm.
    ISBN 978-0-446-52556-5
    1. Rolfe, John.   2. Brokers—United States—Biography.
3. Donaldson, Lufkin & Jenrette, Inc.   4. Stock exchanges—United States.   5. Stocks—United States.   I. Troob, Peter.
II. Title.
HG4928.5.R655   2000
332.6'2'092—dc21
[B]   99-3960
                                        CIP

ISBN 978-0-446-67695-3 (pbk.)

Cover design by Tom McKeveny

When we started writing this book, we ran into a dilemma. We had lots of stories we wanted to tell, but we also had lots of friends who didn't necessarily want their names associated with those stories. We knew that a story without people isn't much of a story, though, so we decided to make some changes.

The stories in this book are true. However, we've modified the identities and certain details about the people and companies and divisions we've written about. All the names except our own, DLJ's, and those of Dick Jenrette and John Chalsty, have been changed. The dialogue has been reconstructed to the best of our memory. After all, we didn't spend our days as investment bankers wired up like a couple of CIA guys.

Hopefully, we've managed to protect the innocent and embarrass only ourselves. We're OK with that. We hope this keeps our friends friendly and ensures that neither of us will ever wake up with a horse's head under our bedsheets.

Truth is indeed stranger than fiction.

Contents

Acknowledgments

There are a whole bunch of people we need to thank.

First of all, we'd like to thank the lovely ladies who've promised to spend the rest of their lives putting up with us. We're two very lucky guys, although we might not tell you that quite as much as we should. Your support and encouragement are priceless. We love you.

Second, we'd like to thank our entire families. Moms, dads, stepparents, grandparents, brothers, sisters, in-laws, and the rest of the gang. We're just happy that we're not the only dysfunctional ones in the crew. You make us proud. If it weren't for you, we'd have no one to thank for our deviance.

We'd like to thank our editor, Amy Einhorn, for great editorial advice and for making this entire process as easy as it could have possibly been. Thanks for helping us relax when we just got too damned hyper. You're an angel.

We'd like to give special thanks, for both reading the early drafts and providing other invaluable advice, to Lisa Cohen, Susie-Q Silva, Julie Wurm, Mike Marone, Nick Day, Deion Oglesby, and Lou Wallach.

We'd like to thank everybody else who read the early drafts of the book and told us that we needed to try a little harder . . . Climpedy Ballbag, John McGuire, P Rowan, Dan Shore, All- Sports & Kelley Day, David Hillman, David

ACKNOWLEDGMENTS

Jackson, and Jon Bauer. One day perhaps we can repay you—like with a cookout or something. We'll even buy the beer.

We'd like to thank the entire crew at Time Warner Trade Publishing, especially Sandra Bark—without all of you, it wouldn't have happened.

We'd like to thank simian artist extraordinaire, Larry Keller. You draw the best monkeys of anyone we know. May your life be full of bananas.

We'd like to thank our counselor, Bob Stein, for providing good advice and helping us chart a safe course through the sometimes uncertain waters of publishing legalese. We like you lots and would love to spend more time shooting the shit with you, but that damned business of getting charged by the hour is standing in the way.

And, of course, we'd like to thank all our other pals who were in the trenches with us at DLJ, without whom we wouldn't have had anything to write about. You know who you are. We hope that every single one of you finds what you're looking for.

Caution: Cape does not enable user to fly.
—Batman costume warning label

Introduction

*I never could understand how two men can write a
book together; to me that's like three people getting
together to have a baby.*

—**Evelyn Waugh**

A few years ago, Rolfe and I stood on the edge of what
we thought was a desert. Across the desert we believed
we saw a lush, green oasis. We hoped that the pleasures
of that oasis would one day be ours. The more we thought
about the oasis, the more convinced we were of the untold pleasures that lay within its luxuriant borders. There
was only one problem. The desert.

When we first started out as investment banking associates, the oasis was represented by a coveted appointment as a managing director of the firm. We were willing
to cross those hot burning sands, the interim years as investment banking associates and vice presidents, in order
to one day bask in the shade of a palm frond. A few
months after beginning our journey, though, we began to
suspect that the original oasis that we had seen might be
a mirage. For a time we became lost, delirious in the hot

sun, but eventually we regained our bearings. It became clear to us that whatever oasis lay out there for us, to get there we were going to have to cross more sand than we could ever have imagined.

We reasoned that many careers have a painful rite of passage attached to them. The medical profession has med school and residencies. The legal occupation has clerkships and the years of initial grunt work. The investment banking business is no exception. Young investment bankers must pay their dues in order to be able one day to grab hold of the brass ring. Most, if not all, senior bankers paid these dues and took these lumps. Some of them are better off for having done so. If they had to do it, then so did we. Those were the rules.

Are we better off for having subjected ourselves to the associate ranks of investment banking? Yes. Was it all miserable? Absolutely not. We experienced lots of good and lots of bad while on the dues-paying highway, most of it without much sleep. But at one point along that highway we decided to pay the exit toll and get off. We both still work in the world of Wall Street, and we'd be lying if we told you that money doesn't matter to us. When it came to investment banking, though, the costs and the benefits seemed way out of whack. So we don't work as bankers anymore, and now we enjoy walking into work every day.

This is the story of our rite of passage. It's the story of two investment banking associates and our long journey from eagerly competing to enter the world of investment banking to even more eagerly scrambling to get out of it. This book is our catharsis. Banking is what we did—investment banking associates were who we were. Like virgins defiled, we can't possibly rid ourselves of the scourge to which we knowingly submitted. It strengthened us and it toughened our hides. That was good and that was bad. If there was a pumice stone for the soul, we would have scrubbed ourselves raw. There isn't.

Investment banking is a profession characterized by extremes. Whether it's money, booze, food, sex, or work hours, the typical banker believes that more is better. We experienced our fair share of these extremes, and have recounted some of our adventures within these pages. Excess and debaucherous pursuits are only half the story, though. The other side of the coin for us was our realization that being anointed investment bankers didn't make us the big-shot advisers to corporate directors we thought we were going to be. Instead, it turned out that we spent most of our work time as mindless paper processors. And even though we were paid mighty well to push that paper around, the unwavering devotion to the job that was required of us just wasn't worth it. We've tried to convey our path to these realizations within these pages as well. We don't have a lot of regrets. There aren't many jobs, after all, that could have given us the opportunity to live like hedonists and come to the realization that the emperor has no clothes, all before our thirtieth birthdays.

We worked at Donaldson, Lufkin & Jenrette (DLJ). This story isn't just about DLJ, though. This story is about the dues that all junior investment bankers have to pay. We have lots of friends at other investment banks. Same shit. Investment bankers spend 50 percent of their time trying to convince potential clients that their bank is different than the other guy's bank, but for a junior banker, at the end of the day, they're all the same. Any young investment banker, regardless of the bank he works at, can tell the same stories about working for three days straight with no sleep, getting screamed at for messing up the page numbers in a pitch book, or aging before one's time like a block of cheddar cheese left out of the refrigerator. The older bankers may have had better lives, they may have had more fun, but we wouldn't know this because we were junior bankers. As junior guys, our lives sucked.

For some, hopefully, this story may provide a fresh window into the world of investment banking. Without being one, no one can really know what a banker does. Before we started, all we knew was that bankers, traders, and egregious salaries were always mentioned in the same breath. Understanding what a trader does is a little more intuitive than understanding what a banker does, because everybody's traded for something in their life. It may have been something as simple as a rookie Ron Guidry baseball card for an All-Star Reggie Jackson card, but the concept of an exchange for relative value is as old as humankind itself. Investment banking has no such intuitive counterpart in real life. It took our mothers six months to realize that we weren't stockbrokers, working the phones to sell crappy public offerings to unsuspecting investors. It took *us* another six months after that to realize that we were, in fact, selling crappy public offerings to investors. The only difference was that we weren't selling them over the phone, we were doing it in person, and the investors weren't unsuspecting individual investors, they were the Fidelitys, the Putnams, and the T. Rowe Prices of the world.

The closest most people have ever come to understanding what an investment banker does may have been on October 24, 1995, when they heard the outrageous special interest story of the day. The wire services released the story first. It was quickly picked up and parroted by almost every major media outlet in the country as a classic example of Wall Street excess. A fifty-eight-year-old frustrated managing director from Trust Company of the West, on an airplane trip from Buenos Aires to New York City, downed an excessive number of cocktails, got out of his seat in the first-class cabin of a United Airlines flight, dropped his pants, and took a crap on the service cart. There you have it. That's what bankers do: consume, process, and disseminate.

In general, the only way for a young associate to survive the investment banking gauntlet is either to buy into it hook, line, and sinker or to maintain some sense of humor about what it is that he or she is doing. Keeping one foot grounded in reality, though, doesn't necessarily dictate the maintenance of any mental equilibrium. After all, if you've got one foot on a block of dry ice and the other on a red-hot stove, the average temperature may be pretty comfortable but you'll still end up with two blistered feet at the end of the day.

Our first full-year compensation after signing on full-time at DLJ following business school was about eight times what the average college graduate earns at his first job, and we could expect that compensation to double every two years. We traveled the country by private jet, stayed in the best hotels, and ate in the best restaurants. Eventually, though, we realized that the compensation levels and the perks weren't in place because being an associate in investment banking was a great job. They were in place because the job sucked. The one immutable truism that exists for bankers is that any problem can be solved by throwing enough money and time at it. The implication? The banker's greatest enemies are those people whose souls are not for sale, and those who realize that time is a nonrenewable commodity.

Our intent here is not to judge. Lots of our friends are still bankers. They're still out there crossing that burning-hot sand with the sun beating down on their heads, and some of them really like what they're doing—just like a throng of wandering Bedouins. As some malcontent once said, it's a dirty job but someone's got to do it.

When we talked about writing a book about our time as associates in investment banking we asked each other, "What will we say?" And then we immediately answered, "How we got there. What we did and how we got out. How we lost our balance. Everything, man."

Well, as our favorite boxing referee, Mills Lane, always proclaims, "Let's get it on!"

Recruiting:
The Seeds of a
Dream

In the middle of Times Square, at the intersection of Broadway and Forty-third Street, sits what was once the United States Armed Services' premier recruiting office. The office, built almost fifty years ago, was conceived as a shining testament to the unlimited promise of a military career, positioned as it was in the middle of the Crossroads to the World. Today, though, it is only a vague reminder of what it once was. Vagrants use the back of the building to provide some relief from the summer sun, and occasional relief from a bottle of Boone's Farm. On a good day, a few listless teenagers may wander in to find out exactly how much they'll get paid to be all they can be.

With the decline of the military's once-venerable institution, however, has come a concomitant rise in another recruiting institution: the Wall Street Investment Banking Machine. From lower Manhattan to midtown, the well-oiled device hums around the clock and around the calendar. Its serpentine tentacles are rooted in nearly every well-regarded undergraduate institution in the country and all of the top business schools. The machine's sole objective: to fill the conduit with as many analysts and associates—the serfs and indentured servants of the investment banking world—as it can find.

Ultimately, as we would find out, a large part of any investment bank's success becomes a function of how many bodies it can throw at a given piece of business, or, even more important, a potential piece of business. The effort to fill the pipeline with these bodies, therefore, is never-ending.

The Analysts

At the lowest level of the investment banking hierarchy are the analysts. To find this young talent, the I-banks send their manicured young bankers out to the Whartons, Harvards, and Princetons of the world to roll out the red carpet for the top undergraduates and begin the process of destroying whatever noble ideals these youngsters may still have left. For the recruiting banker, the ideal analyst candidate is somebody with above-average intelligence, a love of money (or the capacity to learn that love), a view of the world conforming with that of the Marquis de Sade, and the willingness to work all night, every night, with a big grin on his face, like the joker from *Batman.*

The analysts are at the bottom of the shit heap. They are the algae under the rim of the public toilets at the Port Authority bus station, the scum below the scum at the bottom of a beer keg. They'll spend two to three years being mentally, emotionally, and physically abused, and for that benefit they'll be well trained and extremely well compensated. No matter how bad things get, they'll never have anybody *lower* on the corporate totem pole to whom they can off-load their misery.

Following their two- to three-year stint, the vast majority of the analysts will either strike out for any of a handful of graduate business schools, depart the firm for other opportunities within Wall Street's financial community, or regain their sanity and elect to pursue other interests entirely. There's very little upward mobility from the analyst programs into the higher echelons of the investment bank. Analysts quickly learn, in no uncertain terms, that their days as analysts terminate after three years. To the uninitiated this may seem, at best, shortsighted and, at worst, akin to infanticide. Why jettison these young minds with two to three years of hardcore financial training? The answer is simple. The analysts have been tortured and abused for three years. They've reached the point of being dangerous. To keep them on would be to institutionalize sure seeds of discontent within the investment bank.

A majority of the analysts leave the job pissed off and with a deep-seated hatred of the investment banking institution. They learned a lot and enjoyed being paid more money than they ever thought they could make, but they also despised the work and the people that made them do it. However, amazingly, it seems that about 50 percent of those analysts who hated what they did go back into investment banking after two years in a graduate business school program. Somehow, absence makes the heart grow fonder. As with a bad injury, they tend to forget how terrible the pain was. They know it was horrible, but they just can't remember exactly how much it hurt. So these analysts go back into banking thinking that life as an associate will be different. Basically, they reinjure themselves. Troob was one of these injured veterans who decided to return for a second tour of duty.

The Associates

At the next rung up the investment banking ladder are the associates, that's what we were. You can generally assume that the associates are a happier lot than the analysts, since they have both the institutional backing and the ability to ease their own misery by heaping agony onto the analysts. Therein lies the beauty of the hierarchy. Since the investment banks are in the aforementioned practice of regularly paroling virtually the entire third-year analyst class, which class would have included any analysts with the potential for promotion to associate, the recruitment of associates and the replacement of these departing third-year analysts becomes a full-time process.

For the associates in an investment bank, there is no

corresponding get-out-of-jail-free program to avail one-self of at the end of a two-to-three-year stay. There is no light at the end of the proverbial tunnel. The associates are recruited under the expectation that they know what it is they're signing on to do, and that once on board, they'll dutifully climb the corporate ladder to the top of the golden pyramid. Vice president, senior vice president, managing director. The path is clear. In reality, the attrition level for associates is fairly high. They leave for competing investment banks. They leave to work for clients of the investment bank. They leave when they realize that sex with themselves is becoming the norm. Whatever the reason, between the moles brought on board to climb the ladder, and those helicoptered in to replace the departing lemmings, the flood of fresh-faced associates is constant.

The Others— Vice President to Managing Director

Above the associates are the vice presidents, the senior vice presidents (or junior managing directors, depending on the firm), and the managing directors. The associates all have the same goals. They want to make vice president in three to four years, senior vice president in five to seven years, and managing director in seven to nine years. They all hope to be making seven figures by the time they hit managing director.

Sometimes, though, from the associates' perspective, it seems like there are just three levels in the banking hierarchy: analysts, associates, and everybody else. After all, anybody senior to an associate has the institution's divine sanction to shit on the associate's head, and if you're the one getting shit upon there isn't usually much reason to further subdivide the hierarchy of those doing the shitting.

The Breeding Ground—Business Schools

The most fertile grounds for the associate recruits are the nation's graduate business schools. Due to the sheer number of recruits now requisitioned by Wall Street, the preferred hunting grounds have broadened from their original select subset of only the most arrogant Ivy League institutions of the East (i.e., Wharton, Harvard, Columbia) to include other marginally less pompous institutions. As distasteful as this decrease in the overall level of enlistees' arrogance has been for the old-line bankers, it has been driven by necessity.

The business school students, for their part, are in no way gullible victims of the evil capitalist pigs. Most have returned to business school with a sole objective: to further their career goals through exploitation of the recruiting opportunities that the business schools provide. In all fairness, it should probably be acknowledged that a small minority of the graduate business school students do in fact return to school with the accumulation of knowledge as a primary objective. Those that do, however, are swiftly enlightened and made to see the error of their ways.

The indoctrination into the money culture and the transition to job-search mode begins long before the arrival of the MBA-to-be on campus. Following the receipt of the school's acceptance letter, which goes to great lengths to assure all budding MBA candidates of their status as members of an academic aristocracy, a large packet follows in the mail.

At Wharton and Harvard, the packet was similar. It was filled with policy manuals, health care application forms, and sundry other administrative delights. The most important enclosure in the Wharton packet, however, was a pamphlet titled *The MBA Placement Survey*. The placement survey was a gold digger's delight. Every imaginable statistic on the recruiting success, or lack thereof, of the prior year's business school denizens was broken down and reported: percent taking jobs in given industries, percent taking jobs with given employers, percent taking jobs in given geographic regions, it was all in there. There was only one overriding statistic that really mattered to the budding MBA, though: average starting salary by industry.

The first time I saw these figures, my ticker skipped a beat. I was a guy who was coming out of the advertising industry making $17,500 a year and eating black beans and rice four nights a week. There were salaries in *The MBA Placement Survey* with six figures, and that wasn't counting any decimal places.

We were entering the land of the obscene here. If the starting figures were up on into six-figure range, where would the madness end?

A somewhat closer look at the heavily laminated pages should have yielded another clue as to the goals and mind-sets of our future business school classmates. The two job categories snaring the highest percentage of the graduating class, management consulting and investment banking, also happened to have some of the highest starting salaries. A coincidence? I think not. Troob and I were about to jump into a velvet-walled cage with some of the *greediest* bastards this side of Ebeneezer Scrooge. Unfortunately, at the time, we were both wrapped up in a Richie Rich fantasy of our own. We were about to start a frenzied two-year race with America's most prized business school graduates, blindly thrashing our way toward the almighty dollar.

At Wharton, the official start to this seminal marathon was the "Welcome to Wharton" seminar during orientation week. Whatever delusions I may have had prior to this cozy little gathering were quickly dispelled. Surrounded by 750 other hearty young business schoolers in a massive auditorium, all feelings of being part of something elite, something special, began to melt away. When the progression of second-year students took the podium and began describing, in lurid detail, exactly what awaited everyone on the job-search front, the essence was laid bare. We were there for a two-year mating dance with the recruiters. What the Wharton name would get us was a shot at the best of those recruiters. Given that opportunity, though, it would be up to us to distinguish ourselves from the sea of equally qualified candidates in the seats all around us. We'd have to be willing to climb over these people while wearing golf shoes with sharpened cleats to get where we wanted—no, *needed*—to be. Fuck camaraderie.

What I didn't realize at the time was that not everybody in that auditorium was reaching these same wrenching realizations that day. Something between a sizable minority and a majority of my new classmates that day already knew exactly what game was being played. There were bastards there who knew what awaited them, and had voluntarily come back to subject themselves to the process, all for the sake of professional advancement and the accoutrements that accompanied it.

The phenomenon, mind you, was in no way peculiar to Wharton. In fact, 350 miles to the north, at that most venerable of all institutions—the Harvard Business School—a like scene was being played out. And among the 750 dandy young recruits there was one of those bastards who knew the game. A stocky little former investment banking analyst whom I'd later come to love as we wallowed together in our collective misery paying our dues as investment banking associates at DLJ. Peter Troob.

Later, after we got to know each other, Troob would confirm my suspicion that things at Wharton and Harvard were just about the same.

Yeah, I was going through the same mating dance at Harvard Business School. However, I had a big advantage: I'd worked in investment banking before going back to business school. I'd been an analyst at Kidder Peabody. I knew the pain, I knew the long nights and the late dinners eaten in the office six nights a week.

The thing was that I had sworn off investment banking. The sixteen-hour days, the people who had institutional authority to kick my ass, the extra ten pounds I had put on since college, and my nonexistent social life. The investment banking life as a junior guy sucked and I knew it. It paid me well for a twenty-two-year-old snot-nosed brat from Duke, helped me get into Harvard, and taught me how to break out a company's financials with my eyes closed, but as I sat in Harvard Business School I promised myself that I wouldn't go back. No way. I promised myself that I would find a more rewarding career, one that made me feel good about myself. One that cleansed my soul instead of soiling it.

So why was I willing to jump right back in? That's a good question. I remember sitting with one of my good friends, Danny, in the steam room at the beginning of the school year discussing that very question. We had both come from a two-year boot camp at Kidder Peabody and we were both at HBS. Danny asked the question first.

"Troobie, are you gonna go back to banking?"

"No fucking way, man. Are you kidding me? Kidder sucked and my life was hell. Fuck banking. I'm gonna do something else."

"What?"

"I don't know, consulting or some shit like that."

"Consulting? Making all those two-by-two charts and matrices and being shipped to some buttfuck place like Biloxi, Mississippi, to help consult some manufacturing company for two months? No thanks."

"Yeah, maybe you're right, Danny Boy. Not consulting. I'll try to get a job in a buyout fund."

"Yeah, right, Troob. Tommy Lee is only taking two guys this year and KKR is taking one. You're good, but either your dad has got to be loaded or you've got to get the managing partner laid if you want that job."

"Well, maybe I'll look at the banking jobs again."

"What! Troob, are you fucking insane?"

"Where else am I going to make that kind of money? Anyway, it's a stepping-stone to a better job. It'll open up opportunities for me in the future. It'll help me get to the buy-side."

"Jesus, man, I don't know."

"Look, I can't discuss this anymore, Danny. I've got to get out of this steam room. My balls look like raisins."

Danny and I ended up interviewing at all the investment banking houses. We were sucked in even before the whole recruiting process began. We had fallen into the trap of money, prestige, and security. We were about to start the selling of our souls. We entered the Harvard Business School fray and away we went.

Presentations and Cocktail Parties

At Wharton, the highly scripted mating dance during which the recruiters first made contact with the recruits corresponded, by no great coincidence, with the first few weeks of classes. Rolling updates of scheduled recruiter visits were distributed to all the students on a weekly basis, and a prominent announcement heralded each day's corporate arrivals: "Coming today, Merrill Lynch in Room 1, Booz Allen in Room 2, and Johnson & Johnson in Room 3."

Subliminally, what was being said was, "Those interested in the big money will head directly to rooms 1 and 2, and anybody with a yen to learn how to market rubber nipples and non–petroleum-based sexual lubricants will kindly report to room 3." The daily routine was nothing if not consistent. The last classes of the day ended at 4:30

P.M. The first corporate presentations of the day began at 4:45 P.M. For Troob at Harvard, or for me at Wharton, it was all the same.

The recruiters' presentations were no small-time affair. More often than not, the big guns themselves came out to make the sales pitch. CEOs and presidents of America's *Fortune* 500 regularly swallowed their pride, pressed their suits, and shuffled past the rows of Formica-topped desks to go to the head of the class. Once there, they described in gushing terms how incredibly honored they were to be standing in front of America's finest business school students, and why their diamond-encrusted clubhouse was truly the only one to consider becoming a member of.

John Chalsty, then president and head of the Banking Group at DLJ, described just how fortunate he'd been to be able to spend the last twenty-five years of his career at DLJ. DLJ was the hottest firm on Wall Street. It employed a lot fewer bankers than Goldman Sachs, Morgan Stanley, or First Boston, but when it came to salaries, bonuses, and sexy deals, it was the big time. It was a swank firm full of young, aggressive bankers, many of whom were ex–Drexel Burnham Lambert employees. These were the guys who'd defined Wall Street in the eighties, and they had a flair for the adventurous. They were deal makers, and junk bonds (or, in the 1990s' cleaned-up lingo, "high-yield bonds") were their forte. DLJ was the home of the high-yield bond, and high-yield bond sales were on a rapid rise.

Chalsty, dressed like we imagined a banker would be— Hermès tie, handmade suit, Ferragamo shoes, and a monogrammed shirt—exhorted us in his regal South African accent:

"Just go out and do what makes you happy. It's so important to be happy in this life, I implore you, just go out and find what it is that makes you happy and really, truly satisfies you, and then don't stop until you've made all your dreams come true."

He spoke on, telling tales of his trip to Russia as a member of a governmental delegation sent to provide advice to the Russian economic and political chieftains on opening the markets to capitalism. He spoke of the professional opportunities that awaited us at DLJ, the camaraderie, the ability to realize our potential. By God, this man sounded like a genius! You could see the eager MBAs pleading, "Where do I sign? I'll polish shoes! I'll scrub toilets! I'll bugger a billy goat! I'll do anything, as long as it's with John Chalsty at DLJ!"

And then, in a moment of subtle biting wit so perfect for the moment that it made the whole room feel faint, Mr. Chalsty handed the podium over to Lou Charles, at that time head of the Equity Research and Trading Group: "I'd like to introduce Lou Charles, the head of our Equity Research and Trading department. Good God, Lou, where on earth did you get that tie? It looks like the tablecloth at the Mexican restaurant I dined at two evenings ago." The walls of the classroom literally shook with laughter. An unprecedented level of mirth! Amazing! Unprecedented hilarity! They're such good friends that they're making fun of each other right here in front of everybody! Everyone in the room was begging, "Tell me, HOW CAN I GET A JOB HERE?"

Lord, help the foolish. Within a two-year period we

would have heard the identical "do what makes you happy" speech, an indistinguishable rendition of the governmental delegation to Russia story, and the very same Mexican tablecloth tie introduction line for Lou Charles a total of no less than four times. But that was later. This was the present.

In general, the recruiting presentations lasted for about an hour. A question-and-answer session usually followed. The Q&A sessions were an opportunity for the sycophants of the student body to shine. It was their opportunity to show the corporate chieftains how smart and well informed they really were, and to vie for entrance to the International Pantheon of Brown-nosers.

"Sir, could you tell me whether you're planning to generate any new revenue streams through *international diversification?* Will the *emerging markets* provide an important strategic opportunity for you?"

"That was an absolutely fascinating presentation, but tell me, does your firm provide the *entrepreneurial* atmosphere which is so important to today's top MBA candidates?"

"I'm wondering, what *competitive advantage* are you able to exploit to maximize the *economic value added* with respect to both human and economic capital at your company?"

MBA-speak filled the air. *Teamwork, mission statement, top-down approach, information age, global view, downsizing,* it went on and on.

Fortunately, these sickening ass kissers represented only a minority of the entire business school population, but the antipathy that they engendered among their classmates was far-reaching. Most of the other students made no attempt to disguise their loathing for this human detritus. The reassuring element, and the one that we weren't privy to until we were on the other side of the recruiting table (sadly enough trying to cajole others into our misery as associates in banking), was that the recruiters—without exception—hated these sniveling little dogs as well.

The recruiters, after being asked one of these imbecilic questions, would generally respond with something akin to "That's an excellent, excellent question . . ." What was really going through their mind, though, as they proceeded to answer the questions, was generally more along the lines of "Come on up here, Doughboy, so I can jam this Gucci loafer so far up your ass that the tassels bounce off your tonsils."

Unfortunately for most of the recruiters, the question-and-answer session was only the second step in the entire wretched experience. A recruiter reception at which the mutual ass kissing reached even more nauseating levels generally followed the Q&A session. At these receptions, the complimentary food and booze flowed as freely as the bullshit. It was a golden opportunity to get a full stomach, a swelled head, and a skewed sense of reality all in one place. The orgy of backslapping would have made Hulk Hogan proud.

There was a widely held misconception among the student body that going to the receptions and meeting the recruiters actually increased one's chances of later being granted an interview. However, what really mattered was experience. And so it was that something of a chicken-and-egg situation existed for those people who didn't have any relevant banking experience but who wanted to try to make the transition to becoming career bankers. Without experience, you couldn't get experience. It made life difficult. There was really only one route to redemption. That was to land a banking job during the summer between the first and second year of business school. If you were lucky enough to do so, you would have the requisite experience to land all the necessary interviews for full-time positions during your second year, and you would then be in a position to ride that gravy train straight into the sunset.

So there we were. Me, clueless about what investment banking was but willing to cut off my left nut to receive a coveted summer job offer, and Troob, an ex-analyst who knew exactly what he was getting himself into but who needed something to believe in. We both needed a vision to follow, something to aspire to. We needed a dream.

The dream was to overcome untold obstacles, become wildly successful, and have fun getting there. The vision was to stand like a giant among mere mortals. We would shoot for the stars and at least land on the moon. We would walk into the Ferrari dealership and say, "I'll buy that one." The salesperson would say, "But that's over one—" and we would cut him off and say, "Whatever it is, I'll take it." We would be rich, powerful, intellectually challenged, and happy—all by the time we were thirty. We were going to live the high life. We just knew it.

With these dreams burning in our souls we both decided to interview for any and all of the investment banking jobs out there. Lehman, Goldman, Salomon, DLJ, Merrill, First Boston, Morgan, Bear—we were coming to join the investment banking parade and travel down streets paved with gold.

Interviews
and Ecstasy

Hello, sucker!
—Texas Guinan, greeting to nightclub patrons

Troob and I knew that there were some basic things that we had to get done in order to begin turning our dreams into reality. Step number one was the interview process. Troob's experience interviewing was extremely different than mine because he knew the ropes, but interviewing was stressful for the both of us. Let's just say that Troob was stressed about *different* things than I.

Before going to business school, I had worked at Kidder Peabody as an investment banking analyst. I knew what buttons to push in order to get a rise from the I-banking recruiters. However, this was now the big time. This was the interview process for the real thing—a summer associate position that any idiot in business school knew turned into the opportunity for a full-time offer and a real job. As they said in business school, "Not just a job, but the first step on your career path." The pressure was palpable.

At HBS the entire interview process lasted one weekend, three days. It was amazing. We went through this months-long process of presentations, cocktail parties, and question-and-answer sessions to get to know all the different companies, but then the part that really mattered, the interviews, got squeezed into one long weekend. For a prime recruit, that meant that you were gunning for five, six, even seven different jobs in a single weekend. Here's how the weekend usually played out.

Friday was initial screening day. You either squirmed by and got to round two, which was on Saturday, or else you got dinged. The interviews on Saturday were usually two-on-one interviews. These sucked. Two people instead of just one made you feel insecure for half an hour. If you passed this stage you got to interview on the big day— Sunday. On Sunday, you could potentially have three interviews with the same firm. Many of these interviews were three-on-ones and four-on-ones. Questions got shot at you like darts and you either had to catch the dart head-on and answer the question or you had to scramble like a scared rabbit to avoid the question because you didn't know what the hell the interviewer was getting at.

Finally, Sunday night arrived and if you were lucky enough to have had an interview during the day it was possible that you would get called and asked to join the firm for the summer. Sometimes, if enough people decided to reject offers from a particular firm, the firm would call people that they had interviewed on Saturday but had dismissed and would then offer them jobs. Yes, these reusable Saturday interviewees knew that they were the second choice, but because they needed a coveted investment banking summer job they took what they could get. It wasn't the means that was important, it was the end that counted.

I gave the same shameless pitch to each and every bank. The pitch went something like this:

"I was an analyst at Kidder and I know that I'll have to work long hours, but I'm ready, willing, and able. I'll be able to hit the ground running and your firm is the one that I really want to work for. You guys have a great reputation and I would be honored to be part of your team. I'm eager, able, and ready to work for you. I know the reputations of the firms because I worked on Wall Street before and I know that your firm is a good fit for me. I liked what I did as an analyst and I really want to go back into investment banking as an associate for a premier firm like yours."

I had to bite my tongue at times. However, this was the epitome of one bullshitter bullshitting another bullshitter, and usually it worked.

The first interviews were on campus in these little interview rooms. I was able to get through the first round of interviews unscathed. I moved on to the second round with all of the investment banks. Now the fun began and the pressure mounted. The bullshit wouldn't work as well in the second round. In this round I needed to look and act sincere, and tell them what they wanted to hear. I was nervous.

The second and third rounds of interviews were held off campus in hotel rooms. When I entered the room for my interview with Bear, Stearns, there were two bankers sitting there facing me. To their right was a king-size bed. In front of them was a chair for the interviewee to sit in. There was a sealed window behind them that overlooked a courtyard, and a bathroom behind them off to the right. It was a pretty standard hotel room. The air-conditioning was humming and the room was kind of chilly. One of the interviewers stood up and said, "Hi, I'm Mike and I'm a managing director in the Utilities Group. This is my colleague Joanne, a vice president in the Real Estate Group. Peter, please sit down."

I sat down, and Mike continued. "When you worked at Kidder Peabody, did you like it?"

A layup question to start the interview. No problem. Any well-trained baboon could answer it. I should have leaned over and given Mike a big kiss. "Yes, I liked my time at Kidder Peabody," I began confidently. "I learned a lot and I want to continue in the investment banking business."

"Well," Mike said, "why do you want to continue in the investment banking business? Is it the money or the challenge?"

Ahh, shit. This was one of those questions where no matter what I said I'd be wrong. If I said the money, then I'd look like a greedy little bastard. If I said the challenge, then they'd know that I was full of crap. I was already treading water on the full-of-shit category due to my answer to the first question. They had to know that there was no way anybody could have ever enjoyed being an analyst. The clock was ticking. The extended pause conveyed my indecision.

I could see my chances at Bear slipping away, and my nervousness had sunk down into my stomach. I felt a sharp pang in my gut. I said, "May I use your bathroom, please?"

"Certainly."

My stomach was growling. I was so nervous. This was my first second-round interview. I walked past Mike and Joanne into the bathroom. The question still hung in the air. The pain in my side was excruciating. As quick as Flash Gordon, I had my pants around my ankles. I experienced a moment of anticipation, a flood of relief, then complete bliss. However, the breaking winds were a little loud. I knew that it would stink up the whole room within minutes and that there was no window to open. It was not easy keeping a straight face when I came out of that bathroom. I walked past Mike and Joanne again and sat down in the interviewee chair. I lamely answered their question and said, "Both the challenge and the money." Then I proceeded to finish answering all of their remaining questions. We all pretended not to notice the rotten egg smell surrounding us. I knew that I had no chance to get asked to the next round.

The worst part of this interview was that I knew that they knew that I did it. It wasn't like when three strangers are in an elevator and one farts and no one except the culprit knows who farted. This was clear. I went to the bathroom and stunk up the joint. However, the next interviewee would probably think that one of the interviewers from Bear, Stearns took the crap. That made me feel good.

My second-round interview with Goldman Sachs was held in the same hotel. The Goldman interviewers sat me at a long table. They must have made a special request to have this table put into the room because no hotel operator in their right mind would have put a table of this size into this particular hotel room. The two interviewers sat on either end and I sat in the middle. I couldn't see both of them at the same time so I had to keep turning my head back and forth like I was at a tennis match. This was a real pain in the ass, and I knew that they had set the room up that way on purpose.

In that interview I screwed it up when they asked me if I thought I had been a good analyst or an excellent analyst. I first thought, damn, another one of these catch-22 questions. If I say "excellent," then I'm a pompous jerk. If I say "good," then they'll ask me what my shortcomings are. I sheepishly said, "Excellent?" Both of the interviewers paused and a hush filled the room. They were looking for the "I was good, a team player, and always looking to improve myself" answer. Actually, I knew that they were looking for the "good and team player" answer. The "excellent" answer made me look pompous, and Goldman didn't want that. I felt like a schmuck for screwing up the question when I knew what they wanted to hear.

Well, I knew that was the end of my chances at Goldman. It was that quick. One screw up and I was out. The interview process is a pressure game, and in order to succeed you have to be a pressure player. Goldman wanted "good and improving" and I gave them "excellent." That was it. I was dinged. At least I didn't shit in their bathroom. Maybe I should have.

I interviewed Friday, Saturday, and then again Sunday with DLJ. The interviews went well. The most entertaining interview with them came on Sunday, when I met with Blake Randolph, Greg Weinstein, and Frank Alario.

Blake Randolph's nickname was Face Man. That was

because he was tall, good looking, and a smooth talker. Blake looked like a *GQ* model, and he was always the guy out on the front lines pitching the business. He was damned good at it.

Greg Weinstein was a jack-of-all-trades at DLJ. Weinstein didn't think his shit stank. Many people in the firm wanted to whack Greg upside the head. I would soon learn that his nickname was the Widow, as in the black widow spider, because a black widow spider kills her lover immediately after fucking it.

Frank Alario was Mr. Nice Guy. We called him Sweetcheeks. All the junior bankers loved Sweetcheeks because he was really, truly nice. That made him a prized commodity. However, Sweetcheeks had to compete with guys whose cheeks weren't as sweet as his, and this sometimes posed an interesting dilemma for him.

I sat down and Blake said, "How about those Knicks?"

I knew a lot about the Knicks and we hit it off. We talked about Charles Oakley and whether the Knicks should trade him. We talked about Ewing and whether it would be his last chance at a championship. The conversation went on. An hour went by and we were still talking about the Knicks. Finally, Weinstein said, "We've only got five more minutes. So, do you think that you were a good analyst or an excellent analyst?"

It was the same question that Goldman had asked me. But this time Greg Weinstein was asking the question. I could already tell that he was a pompous ass. I was ready. The answer was obvious.

"I was excellent," I said. For the Widow that was the right answer. I knew that I had a good chance of getting an offer.

MONKEY BUSINESS

On late Sunday night, I got the call from DLJ.

"Hey, Pete, it's Blake Randolph. You're the man. You're a great guy and we want to talk to you. Before we discuss what we have to ask you, though, do you have any other offers from any other investment banks?"

They wanted to know if I had any other offers to corroborate their belief that I was a suitable candidate to work at their firm. If I had no other offers, then I was a dud and they, too, should think of me as a loser and not worthy of working for them. It was a weird, insecure game the investment banks played.

"Yes, two others," I said. I actually only had one other offer and one pending, but I wanted them to think that I was a desirable candidate. They took the bait and the heavy ammunition came out. The mating dance was stepped up a notch. And now they didn't just want to mate, they wanted to make passionate love.

"Well, we want you to work for DLJ. You'll get paid the best here and you'll be treated well. Come on, jump aboard. You're our favorite guy. We can see you really excelling at DLJ. You remind me of Les Newton [a very young and very successful banker]. Yes, you could move ahead quickly. We're also thinking of paying more this summer. Maybe a stipend or a bonus at the end of the year."

More money. That was good, especially because I was paying for business school and I needed the cash. DLJ was an up-and-coming investment bank known for its aggressive style and above-market compensation. The top brass were young, and I figured that rapid acceleration through the ranks at DLJ was achievable. Unlike some of the larger firms such as Salomon, Lehman, and Merrill,

DLJ was a lean, mean, overpaying hotshot machine. I thought that I would fit right in. "OK," I said. I was in.

That was it. It all happened so fast. It sounds sort of anticlimactic, but it's the truth. I truly had no idea what I was in for even though I'd been an analyst before. With this one-minute conversation, I had sealed my fate for a summer job as well as for permanent employment after business school. I had made a career choice. I thought that I was on my way to heaven.

Troob knew the game, that was his advantage. I didn't, which meant that the path I took in order to catch the brass ring was a little bit more circuitous. While the usual suspects like Troob were getting slotted for interviews with every imaginable bank, the career-changers like me were fighting for the remaining scraps. We had to become banking whores—sending our résumés to absolutely every bank with the hope of landing that elusive summer associate employment opportunity. As for me, the distribution of over forty résumés and cover letters had landed me exactly three interviews: one with a money management firm and two with investment banks—First Boston and DLJ. The grand plan of heading back to business school, landing a great summer job, and then moving on to greater glories after graduation had begun to crumble before my eyes.

By the time I rolled into my interview with DLJ, the crumbling of the dream was one step closer to being complete. I'd already punted on my first two interviews. The First Boston interview had taken a turn for the worse when it became clear to the interviewers that I had no idea what an investment banker actually did. I was promptly dismissed from their hiring roster. I'd always assumed that I could figure out that piece of the puzzle later on, but they saw it differently. Following that debacle, I concluded that my only shot at redemption would be to play it straight—admit that I was ignorant to the ways of Wall Street but was willing and able to learn quickly. I could tell them that I had the tools but not the instructions. I thought that I might be able to pitch naïveté as an advantage, a fresh perspective in a jaded investment banking world.

It worked. At least for a while.

I walked into my first-round interview with DLJ and, by a stroke of good fortune, happened to be face-to-face with two of the firm's more deviant personalities. The first was Yves DesChamps, whom I'd later come to learn was known within DLJ as the Antibanker. The second was Rod Ferramo, an associate. Now at the time, there was no way I could have known who was facing me, but later it would all become clear.

Yves was fifty-five. He was a former disc jockey, and most people within DLJ thought that he had made his way into the investment banking world through a completely random series of events. I'd later learn that nothing he ever did was random. Yves was thinning out up top but had grown out the hair on the sides and back of his head just long enough to put it into a ponytail. Yves was a flashy dresser. The day I met him, he was wearing an Armani suit and a bright red Sulka tie. He looked like Steven Seagal meets Wall Street and I couldn't tell if he wouldn't just as soon kick my ass as interview me.

I'd later learn that Yves was known as a connoisseur of

"dance clubs," those establishments whose primary goal is the satisfaction of the fundamental male needs, and whose employees' primary goal is the extraction from the patrons of as much money as possible in the shortest feasible amount of time. To most, they may be known as strip joints or titty bars, but to Yves they were always the "dance clubs." It lent, I suppose, just the right panache for a banker who wanted to take part in their goings-on. I was later told that Yves's infatuation with dance clubs went so far as to entail his having a custom-designed computer database containing the names, addresses, and qualitative attributes of dance clubs worldwide, all indexed by city. The database allowed him to begin planning his evenings before ever arriving in a city, and ensured that he would never be far from a nicely siliconed young lady.

As I walked into the interview room, Yves and Rod were sitting back with their feet up on the interview table, plowing their way through a large plate of fruit.

"Hi, I'm John Rolfe. Nice to meet you."

"Hi, John, I'm Yves DesChamps. This is Rod Ferramo. I hope you don't mind if we eat while you're talking."

"No, of course not."

"Why don't you tell us a little bit about why you want to go into banking."

"I'm a masochist."

Rod started to laugh. "What do you mean by that?"

"I'm a masochist. Not an S&M kind of masochist, although I'm willing to learn. I mean I like to work hard. I want to work a lot of hours. The way I see it, that's about the quickest way to learn, and that's what I want to do— learn this business. I don't know much about it right now but I think I'd be good at it. I've done a lot of other shit, just never anything like this. I'll be honest with you guys, I'm not gonna waste anybody's time here by trying to weave a tapestry of bullshit, I'm just going to tell it like it is. . . ."

Against the odds, the approach worked. I was sitting at home that night when the phone rang.

"Hello, can I speak with John Rolfe?"

"You've got him."

"Hi, John, it's Rod Ferramo from DLJ. Good news. You've made it through to the second round of interviews. We're going to be holding them over at the Four Seasons tomorrow morning. We've got you slotted in for a nine A.M. session. Good luck."

Holy shit. I'd actually cleared the first hurdle. Un-fucking-believable.

The second-round interviews wouldn't be so easy.

For the second round I interviewed with a senior vice president named Jack Gatorski, who I'd soon learn was nicknamed Gator. His sidekick was a vice president, Mack Reeling.

Gator sat down and threw the first punch. "Why don't you start things out by telling me why you want to go into investment banking."

I launched into my speech, the one about being a masochist and being ignorant of what bankers did but wanting to learn. This time, though, it fell on deaf ears. There were no chuckles, no smiles, no conspiratorial nods of understanding. I'd hit my iceberg and was too far from shore for anybody to hear my calls for help.

That evening, I sat at home once again holding on to only the slimmest sliver of hope. In the face of all evidence to the contrary, I continued to maintain faith that by some act of God I'd somehow manage to garner an offer to be a summer associate with DLJ. The phone rang. "Hi, John? It's Mack Reeling from DLJ. I'm sorry, but we're not going to be able to make you an offer for the summer associate class. You just didn't end up having the support you needed from the people you interviewed with."

And so it would be. All was blackness and death.

I'd be the only first-year Wharton MBA student who hadn't been able to land a summer job. Years later the legend would have perpetuated itself, they'd remember me as the Loser of the Class. I began to resign myself to my destiny.

Little did I know, however, that much more powerful forces were at work. The forces of sex and desire. Yves DesChamps, the managing director who had conducted my first-round interview the previous day, had an unstoppable libido. That libido was busy working overtime in my favor.

Flash back twelve hours.

Following the previous day's first round of interviewing, the entire DLJ recruiting team had made their way down to a local Philadelphia brew pub, the Dock Street Brewery, to moderate their boredom through overindulgence. Now as it turned out, a close friend and classmate of mine, Veronica, also happened to be spending her Friday evening at the Dock Street Brewery with a couple of our other Wharton *compadres.* As Veronica was sitting at the bar enjoying a drink, our good friend Yves DesChamps took a seat next to her. Yves's appearance next to Veronica was no coincidence. In the presence of

any shapely blonde he became a slave to his carnal desires and was driven by an uncontrollable force to attempt to effect an eventual union of the flesh. One flick
of her hair later, Veronica's blond locks had found their
way into Yves's tumbler of overpriced scotch, thereby
providing an ideal opening for conversation.

Soon thereafter, following an opening volley of light
banter between the two, it dawned on Veronica that Yves
was not only with DLJ but was in town for the weekend
interviewing at Wharton for summer associate candidates. And it wasn't long after *that* before Veronica did a
further bit of digging to discover that Yves had actually
been the one to lead the first-round interview with me.
At this point Veronica, well aware of the distinct possibility that DLJ represented my last shot at a summer job in
investment banking, began hatching a most devious plan
of assistance. Her devices: feminine wiles, an overpaid
banker with a weakness for women, and a set of bosoms
that horny old dog couldn't keep his eyes off of.

It wasn't long before Yves was feeding Veronica drinks,
buying her dinner, and pumping quarters into the side
of the pool table to keep her occupied. Once she had
him fully enraptured, Veronica launched her subtle plan
of attack.

Veronica blithely turned the conversation toward the
events of the day, namely Yves's recruiting activities. This
turn of conversation led, most naturally, to further dis-
cussions of her association with me and her intimate
knowledge of me as a person. Her breasts hypnotically
swaying against the pool table's felt surface, Veronica
began to paint a vivid picture for Yves. It was a picture of
me as God's greatest gift to DLJ, the savior of the bank-

ing world. She detailed for Yves how I was the *smartest, hardest-working,* most *capable* person she'd ever met. Moreover, she assured him, I already had numerous job offers on the table, and if DLJ wasn't prepared to act quickly to make me an offer there was a high probability that they'd lose me. That was the clincher. There was no way that DLJ could pass up on a potential candidate who was wildly attractive to a bunch of other banks. If the other guys liked me that much I must be good. *Really* good.

Veronica's carefully crafted dialogue, coupled with just the right number of touches, caresses, and beguiling glances, was more powerful than the most potent magic spell. Whether Yves truly took to heart all the lies that Veronica had crafted about me, or whether he saw through them but believed that by becoming my proponent he would be given the golden key to Veronica's chastity belt, I'll never know. All that mattered was that less than twenty-four hours after I'd received the telephone call from Mack Reeling informing me that I wasn't going to be given a summer job offer from DLJ, he gave me a call back.

"Hi, John, it's Mack Reeling from DLJ calling back. Do you have a minute?"

"For you, Mack, anything."

"I've got some good news. It seems that when word got higher up in the organization that you hadn't been made a summer offer somebody went to bat for you. They've decided to increase the size of the summer associate class by one. That extra spot's for you if you want it."

I knew immediately that I was going to accept the job,

but I also knew that I had to be coy to save face. "Let me think about it. When do you guys need to know whether I want to accept the offer or not?"

"We'd appreciate it if you could let us know within a week."

I was in. In a time frame of under seventy-two hours I'd been interviewed, dinged, resurrected, offered a position, and made a decision based on next to no information to accept a job that would dictate the better part of the next three years of my life.

The fox was in the henhouse.

Summer
Boot Camp

*For the right amount of money, you're willing
to eat Alpo.*

—Reggie Jackson

Our summer at DLJ began with a whimper in late May.
On day one of orientation, a week after spring semester
classes had ended at our respective business schools, we
sat around an Early American antique oak table in a conference room deep within the confines of DLJ's Manhattan citadel. It was the first time I had ever met Rolfe. I
remember that Rolfe was sweating a lot. He looked pretty
nervous. There were nine of us all told; eight men and
one woman—three from Harvard, three from Columbia,
and three from Wharton.

Our orientation was brief, lasting only about two
hours. A contingent of full-time associates, as well as a
handful of more senior bankers, came through to greet
us. They made sure that we understood just what it meant
to have been selected to be a member of DLJ's summer

associate class. We were the best of the best, the elite of Wall Street's financial mavens. And we weren't going to be pussyfooting around that summer, oh no. We were going to be treated like real, *full-time* associates. We were going to have to hit the ground running because we were going to do deals. Some other banks might spend the entire summer wining and dining their summer associates to sucker them into signing on full-time after the summer was over, but not DLJ. By the end of the summer we would know, they assured us, what it was like to be a full-time associate at DLJ. If we *really* worked our asses off, and were lucky enough to get one of the coveted full-time offers in the fall, we'd be in a position to make an informed decision as to whether we wanted to sign on full-time because we'd know exactly what we had to look forward to. Of course, we all understood what was implied but unspoken—that anybody who eventually received an offer for full-time employment and didn't accept it would be a fool. It would be something akin to the parish priest in Sioux City, Iowa, being chosen to become the Pope and turning it down. It just didn't happen.

The desire to garner a full-time offer would be the motivating force behind nearly every aspect of our behavior that summer. There was nothing that any of us wanted more than a phone call in the fall offering us a full-time position at DLJ following graduation. The all-night work sessions, the subsuming of any semblance of pride, the absolute devotion to the job—all would arise as a result of that single-minded desire.

We all knew how the summer job was supposed to be played. It was a game of survival. There were nine summer associates, and six would probably get offers. We all knew that we had to work for *vocal* managing directors who would go to bat for us when offer time came around. If we could kiss a lot of rump and get those managing directors on our side then we'd be shoe-ins for full-time offers. We'd loathe ourselves for being sniveling little ass-kissing summer bankers, but if we wanted to get the full-time offer, then we had to play the game.

So, our summer was full of carrying pitch books, running models, faking smiles, late nights, and self-degrading ass kissing. We were the butt boys and indentured servants for a generation of senior bankers. We had to bust our humps and avoid all conflict or rebellion. If we rebelled, the managing directors would go off and find a more willing servant and we'd end up with no full-time offer. All bets would be off. We'd be fucked.

With an offer for full-time employment, on the other hand, we could expect peace of mind, leverage over other potential employers, and the option to coast through the entire second year of business school with a great, big "FUCK YOU" tattooed on our foreheads. The problem was that our desire was no secret, and every banker in the joint was prepared to fully exploit it. The best of them would dangle that golden carrot out in front as they cracked the whip behind, exhorting us to push just a little harder.

The race for full-time offers would throw a perverse internal dynamic into the midst of the summer class as well. As members of a summer associate class, we were supposed to be there to support each other. We were all in it together, after all. But at the end of every day, none of us knew exactly how many full-time offers would be made that coming fall. If only six full-time positions were going to be set aside for the nine members of our summer associate class, then why the hell would we want to help each other out in a bind? Some other associate's offer could well be the one that we didn't get.

Taken to an extreme there was, in fact, some level of motivation to sabotage each other's work in order to further our individual selfish motivations. So as we sat around the table at orientation that morning, eyeing each other warily, just the slightest hint of distrust hung in the air.

All the critical information was conveyed to us during that two-hour orientation: the account number for the limousine service that handled the DLJ account, the procedures for expensing our nightly dinners to the firm, the rules governing when we could and couldn't fly first class when traveling on business. By the end of the orientation the secrets regarding how to live the good life at the firm's expense had been laid bare. We were on our way to becoming real investment bankers.

The Bullpen

Following our breakfast meeting we were led to our new offices. The summer associate offices were in an internal area of the bank known only as the Bullpen. Every summer for as long as anybody could remember the Bullpen had been occupied by the summer associate class. Every August, when the summer associate class departed, the incoming full-time first-year associate class took up residence there. The second-year associates, who had spent the previous year together in the Bullpen, were shuffled and scattered into other offices all over the firm. And so it was that the Bullpen perpetually housed the lowest common denominator among the entire pool of associates and, ignoring the analysts, the lowest common denominator among the entire cadre of DLJ bankers. Naturally, the greener the banker the harder he worked, which meant that the Bullpen hummed around the clock 365 days a year.

The Bullpen was a fortress. Like the hold of a slave ship, it was in the middle of the building tucked away in an area where visitors to the DLJ offices would never see it. It housed eleven offices, five singles and six doubles, which surrounded a sizable common area. The carpeting was dingy, the walls filthy. Somebody at one point had tried to add a personal touch with the addition of a couple of plants to the central common area, but these had long ago lost most of their leaves and stood there like decaying carcasses. Whoever it was should have known better. There were no windows in the Bullpen, and the fluorescent lights were in no way conducive to the healthy development of any living creature, plant or animal.

Each associate, in his or her windowless office, had a standard-issue steel desk, filing cabinet, and adjustable chair. The desks and filing cabinets looked like they'd been carted off a NATO base. The chairs were slightly more up-to-date, a necessity given that we'd be spending the majority of both our waking and sleeping hours in them over the coming months. All this furniture sat on a worn carpet. The walls were scuffed with numerous heel marks, and the fluorescent lights hummed constantly like a set of high-voltage electric wires. By the time we moved in, most vestiges of the previous tenants' existence had been removed, but within weeks each office would look once again just as it always had—a tangled mass of pitch books, financial filings, and research reports. No personal effects. No pictures of loved ones. DLJ was our family now, and there could be no competing loyalties.

The Bullpen stood in stark contrast to the majority of the DLJ office space. DLJ prided itself on its collection of Early American art, historical documents, and antiques—all of which graced the halls, waiting areas, and managing directors' offices. Not the Bullpen, though. The Bullpen was all about business, which was befitting for a place where most of the real work got done. The Bullpen's residents took a perverse pride in their squalor, and the Bullpen itself served as a grim dose of reality for those whose imaginations had carried them too far down the path of believing that their chosen profession was actually a glamorous one.

While the Bullpen's general atmosphere was in large part set by the wretched physical conditions therein, of equal importance in determining the ambience was the general stress level of its young bankers. The combination of the demands that were placed on them and their eagerness not to fuck up produced an atmosphere second only in intensity to that of a Duke-UNC basketball game. At any given moment, staccato expletives could be heard erupting from multiple Bullpen offices: "fucko," "shit," "asshole," "dick," "douchebag." Generally, these were in response to phone calls from DLJ senior bankers who were making unreasonable and sometimes unnecessary demands on already-overtaxed associates. The level of animosity toward many senior bankers that generally permeated the Bullpen had caused these senior bankers to develop a healthy respect for its real estate, and only the bravest of them ever dared to penetrate its dark recesses. Even those senior bankers whose offices were in the Bullpen's environs tended toward communications with its populace only by telephone. Concerns over their personal safety outweighed whatever desire they may have had to experience the Bullpen firsthand.

On our first day as summer associates, though, we didn't know any of this. We were eager, we were ignorant, and we had stars in our eyes. Moreover, upon our initial entry into the Bullpen, its squalid nature was temporarily displaced from our mind's eye by the presence of four young women as supple as any four we'd ever seen assembled at the same place and time. At first blush, they all appeared to be products of a gene pool from the Valley of the Dolls. As one of our classmates, Enrico de la Hernandez Franca—a Peruvian by birth—would later put it: "Jewels, each of them in their own way. It's imperative that I have a taste."

They were our banking assistants, "BAs" for short, and they were there to help and guide us. They answered phones, did graphics work, prepared documents, made travel arrangements, and did database work. At that moment, the four who were assigned to the Bullpen knew far more in aggregate about banking than did our summer associate class. They were equal parts smart, beautiful, and tolerant, but as we stood and ogled that day it was their beauty that was foremost in our minds.

The four introduced themselves to us: Heather, Hillary, Hope, and Tiffany. A second-year associate would later inform us of a long-standing DLJ tradition whereby at least one member of the summer associate class would be encouraged to put the wood to at least one of the BAs over the course of the summer. There were eight volunteers ready to step forward that day, and had the one female member of our class had any lesbian tendencies whatsoever, our voice would have been unanimous.

We congregated around the center of the Bullpen, making small talk and wondering when we were going to start doing deals. Never mind that most of us had no idea what doing a deal entailed. We knew that we were there to do deals, that we weren't doing them presently, and that we had better start doing them because we only had ten weeks to prove ourselves.

Two full-time associates, Reid Wexler (or "Wex") and Mark Brown, had been assigned to run the summer associate program. Their tasks were to ensure that we all had good summer experiences and to shepherd us through the political maze that was DLJ. They would be responsible for fielding calls from senior bankers in search of vigorous workhorses, and parceling out those requests in some sort of equitable fashion to the summer class. For the duration of the summer, their offices would be in the Bullpen with ours. They'd be there to share in our triumphs and commiserate with our defeats.

That day, they gave us some sage advice: "Don't worry, the work will come. Don't ever wish for more, because that nightmare will inevitably come true. If it's seven P.M. and you don't have anything to do, then leave. Go the fuck home." Of course, none of us would listen to their wise words. We'd look around, see our classmates working, and convince ourselves that we, too, needed to be there doing something. None of us planned on losing out on that full-time offer by virtue of not working hard enough.

For one of us, a deal would come quickly. After several hours of aimless lounging in the Bullpen, Wex's phone rang. Thirty seconds later we heard him shout from his office.

"OK, who wants a deal?"

Well, of course, we all did but decorum dictated that nobody appear to be too eager. There were a couple of moments of silence.

"I said, which one of you slick bastards wants a deal? Perentazzi, you out there? You have some high-yield experience, don't you? Get in here so that I can get you up to speed. I need you to be on a plane to Cleveland within the next two hours. You've got to start drafting for a high-yield deal."

Drafting? High yield? It all sounded so exciting. Our classmate Perentazzi, now known as "Slick," was getting on a plane on our first day on the job, and if he'd been listening as closely as we had that morning during orientation he was going to know how to fly first class. That was living, man, really living. We could see it, Slick had been staffed on a deal within the first couple of hours; it couldn't be much longer before the rest of us got staffed. Hell, by the end of the first week we'd all be doing deals just like old-timers. We could hardly wait.

Eagerness and Fear

Rolfe and I knew that desire alone, unfortunately, didn't get anybody staffed on deals. So we had to wait . . . and wait . . . and wait. It wasn't until four days later, on Thursday afternoon, that I'd finally get the call I'd been waiting for. As for Rolfe, he had to wait another entire week before the call came through. That bothered him. He began to worry that he was an untouchable.

I saw Troob and the others all getting staffed those first couple of weeks, and I couldn't figure out why nobody wanted to work with me. I didn't understand how random the whole staffing process was. For those first two weeks I sat in my office alternately staring at my watch and playing games of Minesweeper on the computer. I was a Minesweeping machine, but I wasn't learning a thing about banking. With each passing day, as my summer classmates gradually got staffed on deals and I didn't, my paranoia increased. I saw the summer passing before my eyes with nothing to show for it. When I finally got staffed, though, my demeanor would quickly change from concern that I'd never get a chance to prove myself to realization that I was incapable of proving anything. If ignorance was bliss, my beatific aura should have rivaled that of a magic bus full of Moonies. Unfortunately, ignorance in this case felt more like sure professional suicide.

The call, when it came, was from Wex.

"Rolfe, I've got a deal for you. One of the financial sponsors we do work for is contemplating a buyout of a medical supply company. They may want us to provide some high-yield financing for the transaction. We're gonna need a model, comps, the whole nine yards. I've got some information in my office here that should get you up to speed. Why don't you come grab it and take a look at it."

This was great. A junk bond financing for a hostile takeover, I couldn't have asked for anything better for my first deal. I made my way into Wex's office, where he gestured to a five-hundred-page stack of documents; the company's public financial filings, financial filings of competitors, research reports on the company, and research reports on the industry. I took it back into my office and began to plow through it, line by line. I knew nothing about the medical supply industry and had so much to learn . . . or so I thought.

Wex hadn't been so kind as to brief me on one of the key precepts for the investment banking associate, "Thou shalt hand over all documents and be exonerated." Just because I was being given five hundred pages of documents in absolutely no way implied that I was supposed to read five hundred pages' worth of documents. Wex had merely supplied me with five hundred pages of documents so that nobody would accuse *him* of not having given me all the relevant material. He was covering his ass and it was up to me to determine what really mattered and what didn't. I'd made my way through about a hundred pages of the stack when Wex called back two hours later.

"Rolfe, you done looking through that shit yet?"

"No, Wex, I've only gotten through about a quarter of it."

"You're gonna have to do better than that. We need a leveraged buyout model by late this afternoon. We've got a meeting with Greg Weinstein at six o'clock. They don't call him the Widow for nothing, man. You better get it together. This guy eats summer associates for breakfast."

I started to panic. Who was this guy they were calling the Widow? I'd built financial spreadsheets before in business school, but I'd spent days, not hours, on them. I thought briefly about buying a van, dropping a tab of acid, and heading out for Santa Cruz. "Wex, I don't know if I can get it done that quick. You've got to remember that this is my first time trying this."

"All right, Rolfe, look here. You summer guys aren't supposed to work together, especially since you have to get up the learning curve, but in this case I'm gonna make an exception because we've got some time pressure. I'll get Troob. He's an ex-analyst. He'll know how to build a model. In the meantime, you just focus on figuring out some simple transaction multiples ahead of time."

Relief flooded over me. I didn't have to build the model. I'd been able to forestall inevitable failure. I sat back in my chair and breathed a sigh of relief. Now I could spend the next few hours working out the transaction multiples. Problem was, it slowly dawned on me, I didn't know what a transaction multiple was. Fuck. There wasn't going to be any easy way out of this one, I'd have to suck it up and confess my ignorance. I called Wex back.

"Wex, it's Rolfe. There's a little bit of a problem here. I'm not sure that I know what a transaction multiple is. Can you give me some help?" This was it—utter, abject humiliation. "I'm sorry, man, I feel like an idiot."

Wex was silent momentarily, then he spoke. "Oh, Christ, what rock did they pull you out from under? I don't have time for this shit. Call Troob and ask him to explain it to you, all right? Don't forget, we have to meet on this at six tonight so you'd better get it together and figure this out."

I called Troob and told him that he needed to explain to me what it was that I needed to do. There was silence on the other end of the phone. This was a new one for him. He was also trying to secure a full-time offer, so why should he save my ass? He came to my office and shook his head. He'd never seen a nincompoop of my magnitude. Perhaps, in his mind, I was testing him, or more likely he worried that in some perverse way I could turn my idiocy against him like a weapon. Ignorance, after all, could be the most dangerous weapon of all.

Troob knew the investment banking lingo. He tutored me like a third grader with flash cards, imparting his knowledge. I had learned about finance theory in business school, but Troob stripped all the crap away and let me in on the stuff that really mattered. "This is what you need to do. This is how you do it," he instructed.

"Don't be scared of the Widow," Troob said as he schooled me. "I was told that he's a little asshole with a big attitude, but I interviewed with him and he's not that bad. I'll build you a good model. You just keep your mouth shut. Everything'll be OK. This deal's never gonna get off the ground, anyway. You can take a quick look at the numbers and see that."

My meeting at six that evening was a big success. I followed Troob's advice. I sat quietly and nodded intelligently every time the Widow spoke. I threw in a few random comments, ones that I hoped wouldn't further betray my lack of investment banking knowledge.

"Ahhh, yes."

"Of course."

"How interesting!"

"Certainly."

As events would turn, within twenty minutes the deal had died. Troob had been right. The model he'd built and the transaction multiples whose computation I'd had to be instructed upon had both indicated that the investment returns to the financial sponsor were insufficient to warrant their ongoing consideration of the deal. There was a consolation, though. I'd found a new friend in Troob. He'd saved me from the Widow's fatal clutches, and for that I owed him my life.

Rolfe and I became fast friends when we worked together on his first foray into the world of I-banking. He owed me one after that. He was green, really green, but he was smart and he didn't have an attitude. Those were two big positives. I figured that if I taught him a few things, he'd be a guy I could rely on. I knew I'd need that.

The Social Scene: First Night Out

The summer at DLJ wasn't all about hard work and subservience. DLJ had a plan, and that plan centered around showing us *just enough* of the good life during our summer sojourn to leave us wanting more. Their plan was a microcosm of what they would try to do to us once we'd signed on full-time. At that point, they'd pepper us with a parade of high-profile events—black-tie dances, expensive dinners, and private parties at the Greenwich estates of our managing directors—in order to convince us that through unwavering devotion to our jobs we, too, could one day hope to live the good life. During the summer, though, the focus was more on showing us what a bunch of laid-back, easygoing guys investment bankers were despite their tight-ass reputations.

The summer associate experience at DLJ centered around a calendar of social events: dinners, booze cruises, baseball games, dance clubs, at least one event each week. We were trained through repetition to understand that our attendance at these social events was more than just hoped for, it was mandatory. From our first day as summer-DLJers, we were made to understand that when it came to getting a full-time offer, our attendance at the summer social functions was equal in importance to our on-the-job performance. Of course, this advice had predictably fallen by the wayside by our third week on the job, at which point the majority of the summer class was regularly putting in work hours that extended well past midnight.

Our first social event of the summer season fell on Thursday of our first week at DLJ and, as it was still the first week, was well attended by our summer class. Wexler and Brown, the two full-time associates running the summer program, had decided to break us in easy on our first night out and had planned dinner for us at a local barbecue dive followed by some dancing at a Midtown club—Le Bar Bat. In addition to the summer associates, these nights out generally included as many full-time associates as our mentors were able to round up and, in addition, our four BAs. The BAs' presence not only ensured that such a large group of vain, predominantly male bankers wouldn't be mistaken for a group of West Village fairies but also provided an opportunity for our summer associate class to initiate our attempts at sexual conquest of the BA pool.

Upon our arrival at the restaurant, and prior to our being seated, the liquor started to flow freely. The liquor barrage was a result of the efforts of one Rod Ferramo, the associate who had originally interviewed Rolfe down at Wharton. Ferramo was an old-school vulgarian, born and bred in Greenwich, Connecticut. He was heralded inside DLJ as a young banker known for his ability to spend egregious amount of money in the pursuit of carnal pleasures. Rumor had it that on a business trip to Mexico for DLJ, he'd once spent three thousand dollars for two local whores to service him in his hotel room. Given that a moderately priced south-of-the-border whore was going for less than fifty bucks at the time, Ferramo's weakness for upper-end pleasures was evident.

That night, though, it wasn't Ferramo's lust for flesh that would dictate our demise but his penchant for drunkenness. Ferramo immediately began ordering up rounds of shots for everybody, whether they wanted them or not. This presented the class with something of a dilemma. We wanted to be professional, but enough booze would undoubtedly loosen us up to the point of being dangerous. There we were with rounds of shots being passed around. It was clear that we were being set up for an evening of drunken excess. We had to be team players. Our success in investment banking would depend upon our willingness to subjugate all personal goals to the greater good.

Ferramo ended everyone's initial hesitation with a loud question: "Why the fuck isn't everyone drinking?"

We all took our shots of Jaegermeister.

Our first dinner as a group was in true DLJ style—marked by excess. After we'd been seated, the waitress came over to take the appetizer orders. Ferramo took it upon himself to order for all of us. "We'll take three of everything, and keep the drinks coming. I don't want to see anybody's glass empty." We gorged ourselves as wave after wave of food arrived. Before long, not only were we corralling every passing waitress to bring additional food, but the busboys as well.

By the time we had departed from the restaurant and pointed ourselves in the direction of Le Bar Bat, the aggregate level of drunkenness in our merry band had increased considerably. Our merriness increased as the hours in Le Bar Bat slipped by and we continued our rum-fueled binge. Then came the debaucherous display of Rod Ferramo.

One of the BAs, Hope, had been downing shots with increasing rapidity over the course of the evening. The combination of the shots, the heat, and the level of the music at Le Bar Bat had pushed her beyond her limits. As she stood at the bar waiting for her next drink to arrive, an uncontrollable urge to vomit overcame her. She ducked her head underneath the bar, and began spewing forth a fragrant mixture of barbecue chicken and Captain Morgan spiced rum. Ferramo, who at the time of the opening projectile was on the dance floor immediately adjacent to the bar, witnessed these initial throes of expulsion and interpreted Hope's temporary incapacity as an opportunity to initiate an impressive public display of vulgarity. He quickly positioned himself behind her, whipped out his hogan, and as she continued her litany of expurgation he straddled her backside, grabbed her hips, and began to grind her from behind in a simulation that would have made a dog in heat blush.

As we viewed this display from across the dance floor we were thoroughly befuddled. Was this guy really so desperate and so sexually depraved? What the hell was going on? Some of the people whom we knew in investment banking were good guys. Did the pressure just cause some of the others to snap? We didn't know. Maybe it was the sleepless nights. Maybe it was the lack of a social life. Maybe it was the opportunity to finally not be the one getting shit upon but to be the one doing the shitting.

Either way, we didn't realize that in the not-too-distant future we, too, would be full-time associates doing things we never thought we would stoop so low to do. It was uncanny what a twenty-four-hour, seven-day-a-week nonstop-stress career choice would do to our judgment.

The Social Scene II: Dinner with the Chairman

Not all activities on the summer associates' social calendar lived up to the standard set by our initial outing at Le Bar Bat. Many of the dinners, baseball games, and nights drinking and dancing were uneventful. Others were, however, notable in their own right. One of the most anticipated evenings out was a summer associate dinner at the Links Club with Dick Jenrette, one of the founders of our firm. Jenrette was a legend on Wall Street. He was chairman of The Equitable, a company that was both DLJ's corporate parent and one of the country's largest insurance companies. Jenrette was famous not only as one of the founders of DLJ but also for his instrumental role in having brought The Equitable back from the brink of insolvency in the early 1990s. For our summer associate class a chance to meet the man was a real honor.

Basically, the reason for us to meet Jenrette was summed up by an older associate. He said, "It's a yearly tradition. The old man sucks it up for a night and presses the flesh with all the summer idiots. I think they figure that trotting Jenrette out gets people to sign on full-time when the offers come out in the fall."

That evening's dinner at the Links Club, hosted by dear Dick Jenrette, was well done. The Links Club was an all-male institution whose membership roster was among the most exclusive in New York City. Special permission had been sought, and granted, to allow for the presence of our one female summer associate classmate, Diane. Even then, Diane's permission slip only gave her access to a limited number of the Links Club's rooms.

The dinner was preceded by a cocktail hour during which gloved waiters made the rounds taking drink orders and delivering trays of mushroom caps and raw oysters. Jenrette made his own rounds to each of us and, in the most gracious manner possible, listened intently as we stammered out how honored we were to meet him and how we were so incredibly thankful to have been given the opportunity to spend our summer at DLJ.

The dinner came and went with no significant occurrences. Seating positions at the table had been apportioned on a musical-chairs basis, with most of us attempting to arrange our seating positions so as to avoid being too close to Jenrette. Although the man was unusually friendly, most of us felt that it might be somewhat awkward to have to carry on a conversation with somebody whose station in life was so far removed from our own that he couldn't possibly give a shit about what we had to say. With our business school debts, most of us were worth about fifty dollars. Jenrette was worth hundreds of millions. We were young. He was old. We just had nothing in common. The fact that we knew he would feign interest in our miserable lives made the specter of conversation that much more unappealing.

Afterward, during dessert and coffee, the informal conversation that had dominated the dinner was replaced by a question-and-answer session. We'd been warned to expect this ahead of time, and it had been strongly suggested that we prepare at least one intelligent question each to ask Jenrette. The usual garbage spilled forth from our mouths as we drew upon our business school skills to formulate meaningless, inane questions about the future of DLJ. Only one of our classmates distinguished himself during this session, Mike Stevens.

Stevens was one of the Harvard boys. Although he was attending business school at Harvard, he had spent his undergraduate days at another Ivy League powerhouse— Penn. Stevens was a big man, he'd played football for Penn as an undergraduate. Between his size and his classic bowl haircut, he bore an uncanny resemblance to Lurch, the butler from *The Munsters*.

Over the course of the summer, most of us had come to the conclusion that Stevens was a manic-depressive.

When Stevens was on a high nobody could touch him. A common fixture in all the summer associates' offices were foam footballs that were gifts from a foam processing company whose initial public offering DLJ had recently underwritten. Stevens could frequently be seen in any number of offices in the Bullpen clasping one of the foam footballs to his abdomen and rolling around on the floor, proclaiming all the while that he was going to impart his football knowledge to the masses by offering each of our BAs free fumble-recovery lessons there on the office floor.

Prior to returning to business school, Stevens had been an investment banking analyst with me at Kidder Peabody. Stevens was one of the most focused, motivated, intelligent individuals I'd ever met. During our time at Kidder, I'd once seen Stevens spend an entire weekend balling up enough wastepaper to fill a colleague's entire cubicle waist-high. The colleague had been furious upon returning to his office the following Monday morning, but even he had to admire Stevens's determination.

Stevens's focus and determination could just as easily manifest themselves through his dark side, however. His temper was legendary. Stevens regularly held wicked battles over the phone with his fiancée, with the decibel level generally rising to a point where it was impossible for anybody in the Bullpen to escape exposure to his invective. In addition, we think that the facilities personnel at DLJ had taken to stocking an inventory of spare telephone handsets following Stevens's arrival for the summer, as Stevens had a habit of regularly smashing his handset to pieces against his desktop after receiving phone calls from DLJ managing directors whose requests he didn't appreciate.

MONKEY BUSINESS

Stevens's capacity for work far surpassed that of the rest of us. He was concentrating most of his efforts during the summer on work for DLJ's insurance banking effort, an industry with which he had considerable expertise. While the rest of us typically had our hands full with one or two concurrent projects at any given time, Stevens was doing yeoman's work by managing up to three live deals and multiple pitches at the same time. For the seventy-two hours prior to our dinner with Jenrette, in fact, Stevens had been assembling five pitches at the same time, an incredible feat for anybody, let alone a summer associate. Stevens's physical and mental capabilities were being pushed to the limit, as he had done back-to-back all-nighters, but the reigning powers at DLJ had indicated that the Jenrette dinner was absolutely a mandatory event.

So there was Stevens, with no sleep for the preceding seventy-two hours and with a full meal under his belt, fighting to stay awake during our after-dinner question-and-answer session. Rolfe and I were seated directly across from him, and had watched him come close to nodding off several times during dinner. Each time he'd been able to fight off the urge and stay conscious, but the effort this required was clearly increasing with each occurrence. At times his eyes came within a hair's breadth of being closed, so that he looked like a Korean fighter pilot after two quarts of rice wine. When a short lull in the question-and-answer session arose Stevens elected to fire off a question of his own, more to keep himself awake than for any real desire to hear the answer.

"Mr. Jenrette, can you please talk a little bit about which product or industry areas DLJ intends to focus on over the next few years as potential growth areas?"

"Certainly, Mike," Jenrette replied, having already committed each of our names to memory.

As Jenrette launched into a discourse on potential areas ripe for expansion in the investment banking world, a struggle of epic proportions began to unfold directly across the table from us. With each word that came out of Jenrette's mouth, Stevens's eyelids grew heavier. Several times, his head began to sink backward as his body's desire for slumber began taking over, and it was only at the last minute that his head would snap back to vertical. Finally, there was nothing left that Stevens could do. His head fell backward, his mouth fell wide open, and there he lay in deep slumber while the chairman of the board answered the question Stevens had asked just moments before.

Fortunately for Stevens, Jenrette was too good of a man to draw attention to his condition. While a more devious soul might have chosen the moment to either humiliate Stevens verbally or, at the very least, pour a shot of tequila past his open lips and directly into his gullet, Jenrette chose instead to wrap up the question quickly and move on to the next one. In the investment banking land of wall-to-wall hard-asses, the man was a true gentleman.

Kinetic II

With the exception, perhaps, of Stevens and Slick, not many of us had particularly enviable live deal experience over the course of the summer. For the most part, the summer consisted of a whole lot of pitches and just a few scattered deals. Ten weeks was barely enough time to see a deal from beginning to end, but it was more than enough time to do multiple pitches for potential clients. When it came to these pitches, one managing director took the blue ribbon. His name was William DeBenedetti; his fellow managing directors called him Billy, but we knew him as "Bubbles."

Bubbles was as much fun as a bottle of lukewarm castor oil. He'd only been at DLJ for two short months and he'd already garnered a reputation as one of the most fearsome pitch book generators in DLJ history. He'd come to DLJ from Lehman Brothers, receiving a bump from senior vice president to managing director in the process. Legend had it that among the junior bankers at Lehman he'd been the most reviled man on staff, and upon his departure the entire analyst class had thrown a party where the collective level of joy approached that at Christ's resurrection. Bubbles was as short as they came—somewhere between a dwarf and a midget, and collective conjecture was that his tyrannical behavior was as much a result of a Napoleon complex as anything else. He'd been hired into DLJ's mergers and acquisitions (M&A) group as part of an initiative to increase the bank's presence in the advisory business.

There's an important tenet of investment banking: It's not the work you have to do but who you have to do it for. Pitch books aren't always all-night affairs, but working for Bubbles was virtually guaranteed to be a twenty-four-hour-a-day, seven-day-a-week job. The job included lots of humiliation, and a willingness to take it up the rear without Vaseline.

Bubbles's focus was on the universe of financial buyers, those groups whose charge was to use borrowed money to buy businesses from their existing owners, make subsequent operational and strategic changes, and then sell the businesses several years later at a healthy profit. As a group, the financial buyers had enjoyed several years of enormous historical returns on their invested capital and, as a result, had received a large influx of money from other investors looking to join the party. All this money was out looking for new companies to buy, and Bubbles had made it his mission to bring as many acquisition ideas to the financial buyers as he could churn out. In concept, the idea was a simple one. In reality, it was another matter entirely.

Bubbles's pitch books could contain anywhere from five to twenty potential acquisition candidates for the lucky recipient. For each potential candidate, the pitch book contained a summary of the company's product lines, a listing of current news events on the company, detail on the company's historical financial performance, a build-up of the company's current capital structure, current valuation parameters, a listing of the current ownership profile, and short biographies on each of the company's senior management and board of directors. It was a lot of information. It filled up a lot of pages. That made the pitch books heavy, which was what Bubbles liked. Given the high degree of likelihood that none of the material would ever be given more than the briefest consideration by the recipients, the compilation of the necessary components should have been a relatively mechanized event for the associates and analysts involved. The associates and analysts, though, had been trained through negative reinforcement to develop an attention to detail that turned the compilation process into an event of major import. Creation of a pitch book for Bubbles was approached by analysts and associates alike as an activity akin to the illumination of a holy manuscript by medieval monks.

As Bubbles became aware of the wealth of productive pitch-making capacity that the summer associate pool provided, he began directly staffing summer associates on his weighty pitches. He bypassed the usual staffing channels, preferring to corral the fresh meat himself. As the weeks passed, moreover, his ambitions grew grander and grander. As his ambitions increased so, too, did the number of companies included in each pitch. Bubbles's pitches, in fact, began to expand to such generous proportions that they became living, breathing creatures that were incapable of being tamed by a single associate. Development of the pitches began to require the input of multiple associates.

The granddaddy of all of Bubbles's pitches was code-named Kinetic II. All of Bubbles's new business hunts had code names because in his eyes it heightened the air of mystery and secrecy surrounding the projects. He believed that everybody was trying to steal his ideas, and this drove him to swear all junior bankers with whom he worked to total secrecy. In Bubbles's mind, competitors were even trying to tap into his cellular phone conversations to get a leg up on his professional endeavors. Any conversation with Bubbles that he was conducting from his cellular phone or from an airplane took place only under the strictest of rules. Company names could never be used; code names were used instead. This led to frequent conversations that, taken out of context, sounded positively ludicrous. For instance:

"Hi, it's Bill. I've been thinking, why don't we look at a scenario where Big Bear acquires Pumpernickel Dough's Butterbean division?"

"Okay, Bill, but what should I assume happens with Pumpernickel Dough's Tinkerbell division?"

"Assume it gets rolled up into Big Bear's Claw division."

"You got it, Bill."

It was like listening to Warren Buffet on acid.

Kinetic II was, not surprisingly, the descendant of Kinetic I, a pitch that Slick had initially spearheaded with the help of both a full-time associate, Brian Goldfarb, and an analyst, Adam Davis. Both Kinetic I and Kinetic II were designed as generic pitches that could be made to any of the big financial buyers. Like a two-dollar whore, Kinetic I had made the financial buyer rounds on Wall Street. Bubbles had pitched Kinetic I to the likes of Forstman Little, Oaktree, KKR, and Kelso & Co., all of whom were significant players in the leveraged buyout business. Although none of them had been tempted by the bait, Bubbles had been emboldened by his first trip round the Street to take another shot at the stars. And so, the beast that would become Kinetic II was born.

Kinetic II, as conceived by Bubbles, was considerably more ambitious than Kinetic I. Whereas Kinetic I had included profiles of just ten companies, this number would be doubled to an even twenty for Kinetic II. And with a doubling of the pitch's inherent size, additional staffing resources would be needed to bring the behemoth in on schedule.

Rolfe had established his reputation early on in the summer as master of the pitches. The luck of the draw had ensured that he got no live deal experience but instead a wealth of seasoning in new business initiatives. In an attempt to turn this apparent sow's ear into a silk purse, Rolfe had decided that if he were to be relegated solely to producing pitches, then he'd bring his entire arsenal of capabilities to bear on development of the most awesome set of pitch-making abilities that any DLJ summer associate had ever commanded. It was no surprise, therefore, that he was the one chosen to augment the original Kinetic I pitch team for the genesis of Kinetic II. With his addition, the team stood at five: Bubbles, Goldfarb, Slick, Rolfe, and Adam. When Bubbles called the shots, they all jumped. The problem was that with a full-time associate, two summer associates, and a senior analyst all on the same team there were effectively four junior bankers who were all fairly close to each other in the DLJ hierarchy. This circumstance, coupled with the general loathing and disrespect that they all had incubated for Bubbles, led to a dynamic whereby none of them wanted to take ownership of the project and drive the process toward completion.

Goldfarb was busy on a real deal and Adam was as elusive as a fox, so as luck would have it, Rolfe and Slick became the Kinetic II go-to guys. Kinetic II went through so many rewrites and drafts that the latest version was rarely ever more than two hours old.

As the day approached for the first presentation of the Kinetic II pitch book to one of the financial buyers, the level of frenzy surrounding the project increased. Bubbles was about to burst, calling down to either Rolfe or Slick with demands for changes to the book at least twice an hour. On the day prior to the book's initial rollout,

Bubbles had planned to travel to Chicago to work on another engagement. Rolfe and Slick were looking forward to his departure because, although they knew that he was never more than a phone call away, they believed that the logistics of his calling to demand more changes to the book would at least slow down the rate of calls they had, to that point, been receiving. At the very least, they figured that they would be spared the annoyance of his calls while he was in the air. What they didn't know was that Bubbles was about to both cement his reputation as a dickweed and teach them the futility of ever believing that they could escape their masters' clutches, all with one phone call. Rolfe was the lucky recipient of Bubbles's initial affections.

Slick and I had been going nuts for the entire week trying to get Kinetic II into shape. We were down to the short strokes. Bubbles had departed New York on a 3:30 P.M. flight headed for Chicago. I was sitting at my desk fifteen minutes later, at 3:45, when the phone rang. Heather, one of our BAs, picked it up.

"Rolfe, you've got Bill DeBenedetti on the phone. He says it's urgent."

My peace was shattered.

I yelled to Slick, "Slick, get in here, Bubbles is on the phone."

Slick came running in from his office. I picked up the phone.

"Bill, hi, it's John. I've got Perentazzi in here. I'm gonna put you on the box." I flipped the speakerphone on. "OK, Bill, you're on the box. What's up?"

"Hi, guys, sorry if the connection's bad. I'm calling from the plane. Look, I've got lots of changes to the book. You two are gonna have to get these processed as quickly as possible. We've got to get these books into production. Our meeting's at nine tomorrow morning."

"OK, Bill, go ahead. We've got a draft of the book here. Why don't you start going through the changes one by one."

"All right. Most of the changes are to section two. I want to change the structure of this section around. Page forty-six should now become the new page forty-three . . . the old page forty-three should now become the new page forty-one . . . you need to change the heading on the old page forty-one to read 'Strong Operating Leverage Will Contribute to Outstanding Investment Returns,' then bold it and double underline it and then make that page the new page forty-four. Box page fifty in a bold box and shade the right column that says 'Returns.' Oh, yeah, back on page thirty-eight, double underline the IRR percentage and make the chart blue and green, not blue and red. Change the chart on page forty to a more neutral color like yellow. You guys should know better than to put a chart in red. Red means losses—c'mon guys, get with the program. And . . ." Bubbles continued to rail off changes during a two-minute rapid-fire monologue.

I scribbled down the desired changes furiously while Slick reordered pages in a whirlwind of paper. Bubbles finished his directives and the phone went silent momentarily.

"You got all that?" he asked.

"Bill, maybe you could run through those one more

time to make sure that we've got everything right. We don't want to fuck this up."

"Goddamn it, I don't have time for this. I'll do it once more, but you'd better listen carefully. I've got other things that I need to be doing."

Bubbles ran through the changes again. I checked his second run-through against my notes and everything was checking out fine. My anxiety moderated slightly. I muted the speakerphone and turned to Slick.

"I think we're OK. Everything he just read back matches what I've got written down here."

Slick looked at me blankly. "What the fuck are you talking about, Rolfe? I've been rearranging pages here and nothing that he just said makes any sense. He just re-ordered everything to look like complete bullshit. He's got us writing text headers on section title pages, and has us pulling out pages that cover all the key financial data. This doesn't make any fucking sense."

"Hello, hello, are you guys there?" Bubbles was getting impatient.

I took the phone off mute. "Hold on just a second, Bill. We're trying to get everything straight here."

I turned back to Slick. "What do you mean, nothing matches? He just read us off the page numbers, how could nothing match?"

"I don't fucking know."

"Hello? Are you guys there? I don't have time for this shit." Bubbles's voice was getting louder. Heather, our BA, and a couple of our summer associate classmates had heard the commotion on the speakerphone and had now stuck their heads through my office door to listen. I took the speakerphone off mute once again.

"Look, Bill, I apologize, but we don't seem to have all the page numbers down just right. Could you read them off one more time."

"Jesus Christ, I don't have time for this shit. I may be working from an older draft version than you, but don't worry about the fucking page numbers. Just listen to what you have to do and then do it. Think, you stupid assholes." Bill's voice was getting louder. He wasn't a happy man. He began to read through the list of changes again, twice as fast and twice as loud. I muted the phone and looked at Slick. He looked back at me as Bubbles continued to read.

"This still isn't making any sense," Slick said. "Bubbles is working off an old version of the draft. Man, I hate this guy." Without thinking, I took the speakerphone off mute and interrupted Bubbles for the final time. "Bill, we need to go through this without talking about page numbers. They're confusing us." The phone went silent. Then the eruption occurred.

"WHAT? WHAT? I DON'T GIVE A FUCK ABOUT THE GODDAMNED PAGE NUMBERS. READ THE FUCKING HEADERS ON THE PAGE . . ."

The level of abuse coming through the speakerphone, and the volume at which it was occurring, was amazing.

"WHAT ARE YOU GUYS? FUCKING ASSHOLES? YOU THINK I HAVE TIME TO WASTE ON THIS FUCKING SHIT?"

I put the speakerphone on mute and looked at Slick. As Bubbles's diatribe continued Slick and I started to laugh. There was Bubbles, 35,000 feet up in the air in an apoplectic rage. He was yelling so loud that not only were the other first-class passengers undoubtedly privy to his thoughts but so was everyone in coach class, including those who were locked up in the bathrooms all the way in the back of the plane. We, meanwhile, were on the ground in New York and there was absolutely nothing that we could do, other than let his fury run its course.

Eventually, after determining that he had debased us sufficiently, Bubbles gave both us and his fellow passengers a break. He hung up the phone and Slick and I got to work trying to untangle the wicked web of changes Bubbles had delivered. Seventeen hours later, I would deliver the books to the offices of D. L. Thompson & Co. for the first public airing of Kinetic II.

By this point in the summer, my exposure to the dysfunctionality that defined the investment bankers' world should have been sufficient to allow me to make a reasoned decision to pursue other career paths. If it hadn't, the visit to D. L. Thompson & Co. should certainly have driven the point home.

The D. L. Thompson partner who greeted us was straight out of a Charles Dickens novel. He had stuffed his generous ass into a tight pair of seersucker trousers. On top, he wore a bright red sweater vest that looked as if it had recently been pulled from the garbage receptacle behind the office tower that was home to D. L. Thompson & Co.'s offices. The D. L. Thompson partner's defining feature, however, was a set of sideburns that were half the width of his entire cheekbone and which ran all the way from his ears down to the corner of his mouth. Stuffed into that mouth was an unlit cigar that had been chewed down to a raggedy, soggy pulp, and which was leaving tobacco shards all over his teeth, lips, and sideburns. The guy was a freak, a bad Halloween rendition of an innkeeper out of the *Canterbury Tales,* and we were there to kiss his ass. His name was Chester Goodman III.

Bubbles started out the meeting in his customary style with an effusive show of gratitude for having been granted the meeting. He then proceeded to launch into a needless round of name-dropping, during which Chester cut him short.

"Billy, what do you have for me today?"

"Oh, we've got some good ones today, Chester. If you open your book to page four, the table of contents, you can see what we've got lined up."

Chester opened to page four, scanned the table of contents, then looked up at Bubbles.

"Billy, how many times have I told you that I don't want to look at any baking businesses. You know I hate bakeries. You've got four baking companies listed in here. This is a waste of my time."

"But, Chester, these are really *good* bakeries. I think that you might want to consider these."

"No bakeries."

Poof—just like that, four of the twenty companies in our pitch book had gone up in smoke. And Bubbles, the little bastard, had known ahead of time that this guy with the sideburns didn't like bakeries. Chester was just beginning.

"Furthermore, Billy, your friends from Bear, Stearns have already been here to show us Colemack Company, Circular Toys, and Fountain Healthcare. And you can forget about Extruded Synthetics and Condor Can, Inc.

They're too goddamned expensive. We won't pay a premium for businesses trading at those kinds of multiples."

We'd been in the meeting for under two minutes, and Chester Goodman III had already eliminated nine out of our twenty companies without ever making it past the table of contents. Hours upon hours of work, our beautiful charts, graphs, and plagiarized prose would never see the light of day.

"Now this one could be interesting. Finale Industries—a consolidation play in the death care industry. I tell you what, the demographics should really drive this one. Gonna be lots of dead people over the next few years. I wouldn't mind owning a piece of the market that sucks their money up before their corpses get dropped down into the dirt."

Bubbles had been given an opening. One of our ideas had sparked a flicker of interest from Chester. Bubbles seized the opportunity and proceeded to wheedle, cajole, and beg for Chester's continued attention. Chester, however, was like a fat pussycat whose attention was drawn by a passing cockroach. He batted the cockroach a few times, found temporary amusement in its confused stumblings, and then settled back to continue his slumber. There would be no deal for Bubbles and DLJ that day. There would be no deal for the young summer associate. Kinetic II's first foray out of the box had been a resounding failure. It was a harbinger of what was to come.

As I sat in Chester's office that day, I should perhaps have looked at things differently. Instead of looking upon Chester as an aberration in the human gene pool, I should have realized that it was Bubbles and I who were the human detritus. As I watched Bubbles do everything but chug down Chester's cock with the goal of securing a piece of business, I should have been ashamed. I should have immediately cast off my leather shoes and woolen suit and gone streaking naked from the room in search of redemption. I should have, at the very least, realized that the Chesters of the world were the ones with the purse strings, and the guys with the purse strings were the ones in control. I should have thought about the number of nights that I'd been at the office until 3 A.M. and assessed whether anything was worth that sort of commitment.

I didn't do any of that, though. And for that oversight, I would pay.

And so it was that the summer dragged on for Rolfe and me. Pitches, deals, dinners, nights on the town, it was one long continuous bank-a-thon. Lots of learning, little sleep, and a healthy serving of humble pie. Eventually it came to an end. The summer had been painful, but it was over. We had survived and we were ready to use the summer experience as a springboard to bigger and better things. Rolfe and I swore we would never go back. We promised ourselves that we would try to get an offer from DLJ and then use it to find other, more rewarding jobs. Once again, we were believing our own bullshit.

What we didn't know was that DLJ was beefing up and we were the beef. DLJ needed bodies, lots of bodies, and they needed them fast. Because of that, just about all the summer associates would get offers. In fact, the only person in the summer associate class with a serious chance of not receiving the coveted full-time offer was Rolfe. It wasn't because he hadn't worked hard. It was a much more serious offense. During the Summer Associate Golf Outing, Rolfe had managed to hit the managing director in charge of associate recruiting, Doug Franken, in the leg on the fifth hole. Rolfe didn't just bean him in the leg, he had done it at Franken's own country club and with one of the Titleist golf balls that Franken had lent to Rolfe. During another summer, Rolfe's transgressions might have gotten him dinged.

Fortunately for Rolfe, DLJ needed associates.

The Courtship

The summer was over and Troob and I felt pretty crappy. We hadn't exercised that much, we'd worked long hours, and we were tired. A summer that we had thought was going to be filled with social engagements, weekends in the Hamptons, and dating turned out to be a summer filled with work. However, we were paid well— about $12,000 for ten weeks of work, the first two weeks of which we did nothing. They told us that if we came back full-time we would be handsomely rewarded. We were told at the end of the summer that if we joined full-time we'd receive an advance of $18,000 and receive a signing bonus of another $5,000 that would cover our moving expenses at the end of the school year.

We went back to our second year of business school, me to Wharton and Troob to Harvard. Within two months the recruiting push for full-time employment came. The DLJ bird catchers came hunting for Troob first. He was a pigeon, and I could hear him squawking all the way down at Wharton:

Over the summer I had made some good friends like Rolfe, but I was standing on my moral high ground and saying to myself that I wouldn't get lured in by the mystique of investment banking and would only take a job that I really liked. Well, my moral high ground was about as sturdy as a drunk cowboy's shooting hand. I was weak. I called Rolfe and asked him what he was going to do and he told me that he was going to hold out. So I said I would hold out also. Then in October some senior DLJ bankers came up to Boston to take me out to dinner.

Ed Star and Les Newton came to town. I'd worked with both of these guys during the summer. They were up in Boston to seal the deal, to close the transaction, to lock me in. I was a project to them, just another deal that they needed to close. I was a steer and these were two cattle ranchers rounding me up. They wanted to brand my ass with a hot iron. Looking back, I had no chance.

Star was the head of the Merchant Bank, the most orgasmic place to work on Wall Street. In the Merchant Bank even the junior bankers were allowed to participate in the deals. Just hanging out with Star got me excited. He smelled like money. They didn't have to corral me and lead me to slaughter, I was ready and willing to walk into the DLJ slaughterhouse all by myself. I was as lubed as the women at Peepland, and ready to sign up.

I wanted to be like Star. He was married to a woman who looked like she was a dancer or a model. People said that he had bought a house in the Hamptons for around $5 million and an apartment in NYC for the same amount. He said that he played golf all the time, and did deals, in between holes, that made him rich. He seemed to be having fun. He had the life, or so I thought. What I didn't realize was that I would be entering the bank at a level so many rungs below where Star resided that our lives would have about as much resemblance as Cindy Crawford has to the bearded lady at Coney Island. There were dues to pay, pain to experience, and a long journey from associate to managing director. He may have been my role model, but I was fooling myself to think that it came easy.

Les Newton was the golden child. He was young, successful, and rapidly moving up the hierarchy. He had it all. He had investments in deals, lots of disposable income, and what seemed to be a dream job. He looked rested and relaxed. He'd figured out one of the investment banker's greatest secrets—how to stay up all night working and still look fresh the next day. He was made of rubber, and he was what all MBAs hoped they could be. He had also probably kissed more ass than a toilet seat sees in a year.

I also wanted to be like Les. Les was a good guy. Les played his cards right, played the game well, and he was rewarded for it.

They took me to a strip bar and we spent tons of dough, and then we went to a steak place, ate great steaks, and drank expensive bottles of red wine. We finished the evening off with glasses of port, cheesecake, cigars, and a discussion. They really poured it on and I was loose as a goose and eating it all up. This was what I had imagined banking was all about. Steaks, wine, cigars, naked women, and rich guys. Like the Tom Hanks movie *Bachelor Party,* except with guys who were loaded down with dough.

"Pete, we want you to join DLJ. You're our favorite candidate. We really want you, we really need you. Say yes now and I'll make sure you get your signing bonus money in a couple of weeks. I think you're the type of person who would excel at DLJ and could move up the ladder quickly. When you get to DLJ we want you to work for us. You're our guy."

At Harvard the recruiters weren't allowed to give "exploding" offers. An exploding offer was an offer that automatically got rescinded at a certain date if it hadn't been accepted. The business schools had outlawed the exploding offers because they wanted all the students to be able to fully assess all their options. This gave the savvy students the ability to shop their offers around. The really smart students would interview with all the banks, all of whom came onto campus early in the recruiting season, and build a book of banking offers. They would then use those offers as backup while they tried to get the much more difficult leveraged buyout shop and hedge fund offers.

The investment banking recruiting machine was not naive to this strategy, though. So the investment banks would not give official offers at all but would wait until the candidate gave them the assurance that he would say yes if offered a job. This was the pinnacle of the mating dance. The proverbial cat-and-mouse game. On the one hand, the banks wanted to give exploding offers so that the business school students wouldn't use the offers to find better jobs. On the other hand, the school wouldn't permit exploding offers. Well, the business schools were no match for the investment banking recruiting machines.

Les said, "We're not giving you an offer, but *if* we did offer you a job—remember we are saying *if*—would you accept it within three weeks? If you can't accept it by the end of October, then we can't offer you a job."

"So," Star chimed in, "we'd like you to climb aboard. So will you? We're not giving you an offer, but if we did you would have to get back to us by the end of October, because if we didn't have an indication that you would accept the offer, which we're not officially making, then we'd have to look for other people and extend them offers instead. So, if you can give us a *strong* indication that you want to work for DLJ and that you would accept an offer if one was given to you, then we could probably extend you an offer."

I'm still not sure what a "strong indication" should have been. Should I have jumped up on the table and screamed, "Yes, I want to work at DLJ!" Maybe if I had run outside and peed the letters "DLJ" in the snow, this would have given them a strong indication. The game was ridiculous and I played right into it.

"You have the right stuff," Star went on. "You're our kind of guy. You're the man. You'll work in Merchant Banking, and do deals, and get levered and make money. We'll protect you."

That saying—"We'll protect you"—is akin to a nineteen-year-old horny high schooler sitting in the backseat of his dad's car with his eighteen-year-old date and saying, "Trust me." Somebody's about to get screwed.

I was so high by this point. These guys had pumped me so full of hot air that I was almost floating away. My head must have been the size of a pumpkin. Right then and there I accepted. I had promised to talk to Rolfe before I accepted, but I couldn't wait. I sold my soul.

Well, maybe I really didn't accept anything because they had never officially offered me anything. I went back to my apartment and called Rolfe to tell him what I'd done, but on my answering machine there was Rolfe.

"Hey, Troob, the guys brought me out and I think that this banking thing will be a good move so I went ahead and accepted their offer."

I spoke to Rolfe and we assured each other that we had made the right decision. Explanations like "This is a great stepping-stone and the hours won't really be that bad because we'll be more senior" pervaded our conversation. We had a favorite explanation: "We'll only work for the good people. They'll protect us."

Within a week, I'd received all of the checks that I was now entitled to and had also received a bottle of Dom Perignon with a note attached: "Welcome to the DLJ family." I thought that this showed class.

A couple of weeks later they flew me to New York to say hello to other bankers and just revel in the bliss of being part of the DLJ team. They sent me plane tickets and had a car pick me up at the airport. I stayed at the Four Seasons and was told to order as much room service as I wanted. The DLJ Hoover machine was sucking me in like a piece of dust on a carpet. I liked the plane flights, the cars, the nice hotels, the feeling of being rich, the lifestyle. I was a junior banker and no one could stop me. God help me.

However, from November through June I didn't hear from Ed Star, Les Newton, or any of my so-called comrades-in-arms again. At this point, I called Rolfe and found out

that he'd had the same experience. This was our first indication that we were just cogs in the Big Machine. Star
and Newton had come to Boston and had done what
they were contracted by the firm to do. Make me accept
a job that they never really offered to me. They had
closed the transaction and moved on. Other bankers
closed on the Rolfe transaction. We were two excited and
eager suckers.

The first contact we had with DLJ after officially ac-
cepting our non-official offers came in June when an administrative assistant called to tell us that we had to take
a drug test before starting work. Well, this scuttled a
whole load of fun plans we'd had for the summer, but we
were willing to do whatever it took to be able to be part
of the elite DLJ club.

With the start of our new careers edging ever closer,
we were beginning to feel good about our choice. We
had a conversation in July and talked about doing IPOs
and doing deals in the Merchant Bank. We talked about
the big money and the time we'd have to spend it. We
discussed our grand plans of taking the New York social
scene by storm. The parties, the big life. We talked about
being hotshot investment bankers at the hottest firm on
Wall Street. We were stroking each other and it felt good.
We thought we were entering nirvana, and that we would
soar like eagles over the heads of the common folk.

Actually, we weren't eagles. We were pigeons, following a trail of bread crumbs.

Training Wheels

Never try to teach a pig to sing; it wastes your time and it annoys the pig.

—Paul Dickson

Both Rolfe and I graduated from B-school in May. DLJ training didn't start until mid-August, so we had over two months of pure, unadulterated freedom on our hands. We were both thoroughly relaxed by the time DLJ training began. We entered training bright-eyed and bushy-tailed, and believing that training was the first step on the road to the pot of gold at the end of the rainbow.

Investment banking training can be summed up pretty succinctly. It's a huge waste of time and money but a necessary step for the investment banking machine to teach you your role as an associate and lure you into a high standard of living. Once you've started living with limousines and expense accounts, it's hard to go back.

On the first day of training we did nothing. We said hello to our fellow associates and found out that they, too, had been wined and dined and told that they were the best candidates that the investment bank had seen in years. We found out that all members of the associate class had been told that they were going to be the next "golden child" and that they were going to work in the Merchant Bank and make all the dough. They, too, were told not to worry and that they would be "protected." We started to realize that we had all been duped.

However, the human brain has a peculiar way of rationalizing everything and filtering out the unpleasant realities that it knows to be true. Each of us sat there and said to ourselves, "All these other associates were told this nonsense to cajole them into taking the job, but what they told me was the truth." Somehow this warped rationale made everybody feel a whole lot better.

My father taught me many years ago not to believe my own bullshit. Well, we didn't heed this sage advice, and we were so deep in our own garbage that we were suffocating underneath its weight. All of us, as associates, made ourselves believe that we were different and special. We would soon learn the real truth. But until then, we felt great about ourselves and our choice of careers.

At the end of the first day of training, the investment banking machine handed out corporate limousine account cards, beepers, and cellular phones. It made us feel like investment bankers should feel. Like superstars. We imagined ourselves taking a corporate car to the airport while negotiating a big deal on our cellular phone. Then, we imagined going out to a restaurant with our clients and throwing down the platinum credit card to cover the thousand-dollar bill that included a four-pound lobster, porterhouse steak, and two bottles of Château Lafite Rothschild red wine, all of which would be reimbursed by the firm.

We were ready for anything because we were the superbankers, able to force huge mergers to happen in a matter of minutes and bring in monstrous fees to the bank. We were able to have our party house in the Hamptons and our memberships at Maidstone, National, and Shinnecock. We were able to crap lightning and shit thunder.

Training lasted approximately three weeks. We met every day, including weekends, in a conference room from 8 A.M. to 6 P.M. A potpourri of officers of the firm were paraded before us, and each explained a different product or service the bank offered.

Basically, training taught us our role in the process and how we could get the process done as quickly as possible. We learned that companies followed our advice for a fee and that was good. We learned that "a busy associate is a good associate." We weren't being trained to be thinkers. In training we learned what we were going to be doing for at least the next four years of our lives—processing lots of junk for fees and making things look pretty so that the Fidelitys, Putnams, and unsuspecting individual investors of the world would buy them without asking too many difficult questions.

While some evenings during training were designated as social nights out, other evenings were reserved for projects to be done the following day. Either way, every evening was accounted for. We needed to learn what we would be doing, for whom we would do it, and how to get it done.

A second-year associate came to class at the end of the first week of training and explained to us what role we were being paid to play. He didn't seem quite as excited about the whole investment banking shindig as we thought he should have been. He said . . .

"As associates, the standard stuff you'll do is to help managing directors get business. The managing directors sit in their offices and think of ways to make money for the firm, and to make money for themselves. This sets the ball in motion. We create pitch books for the managing directors so that they have something to give to the potential clients. The managing director wants the potential client to know that we worked very hard and spent lots of hours preparing for the meeting. This shows the company that we're serious about the business and will give the company our full attention.

"You'll have to do some valuation analysis so that you can prove that DLJ will be able to obtain the most money for the company being pitched. You're going to spend a lot of time while you're putting the pitch together working with the word-processing department and the copy center.

"After you stay up all night doing the pitch you make flight arrangements for you and your team, and then you go to the pitch and carry the books. If you have an analyst, then you have him carry the books. This is the advantage of being an associate.

"If you go to the pitch, and if you are able to stay awake, then you can watch how a managing director grovels for business. If you get the deal, then you and your team have lots of work to do. You may as well cancel all of your plans for the next six weeks because you're in for some long nights and hectic days.

"All in all, it's hard work. But, you know, you get paid

pretty well to do it and you're learning important banking stuff. That's really it.

"More important, tonight the firm is letting all of you live the high life on the DLJ nickel. Don't waste time dilly-dallying around here. According to my watch it's five P.M. and if I were you I'd start whooping it up. I'd love to join you, but I've got loads of work to do. Have fun, because once training's over you guys won't see the light of day again."

Rolfe turned to me with his brow furrowed. "He seems a bit bitter. Maybe he had a tough night. Maybe he's not working for the right people. He probably likes his job and is pretty happy, right?" Rolfe was looking for assurance that we had made the right choice, but I wasn't able to give it to him.

Instead of further exploring this revelation, we ignored it and jumped into one of the black chauffeured cars that were waiting for us in front of the offices, compliments of the firm, and went out for an evening of festivities—all paid for by DLJ.

The investment banking machine was beginning to suck us in with the lavish lifestyle that it would allow us to live.

Designated evenings out during our weeks of training were filled with baseball games, dinners at the Palm and Sparks, and nights out at dance clubs and, finally, strip bars. Most of it was paid for by our beloved firm. We were living large. The days were filled with lots of catnaps and free lunches. The firm was keeping us in an inebriated state so that we wouldn't realize what the hell we were getting ourselves into. If we had, we might have left immediately. But we were loving every minute of it. A

bunch of twenty-six-year-old self-important business
school grads wearing our best suits and ties and being
told that we would be the next big shots on Wall Street.
This was where Rolfe and I rekindled our friendship, sitting at the Crane Club drinking Jack Daniel's on the rocks
and discussing how we were going to be managing directors in five short years. We felt BIG. We followed up
our Crane Club fun with a visit to what would become
one of our favorite hangouts, Shenanigans—a second-
rate strip club right around the corner from DLJ's offices.

As the night wore on, the drinks all began running into
one another. We had no idea how much we—i.e., the
firm—owed on our bar bill. As the bill racked up, though,
something extraordinary began to happen. The alcohol
actually cleared our brains of all the clutter and set our
thoughts straight.

"Hey, Rolfe," I shouted over the booming Shenanigans
dance music. "You know, you were right, that second-
year associate was pretty bitter. Do you think he hates
what he's doing?"

"Yeah, maybe. Maybe his life really sucks. Maybe he
was told that he would work for the good people, but
then when he finally got to DLJ things changed."

"Shit. That wouldn't be so good. He did look pretty
tired, not to mention angry and about forty years old,
didn't he?"

"He sure did, Troobie. He sure did. Man, that's fucked
up. Do you think that'll happen to us?"

It was like we were finally sober for the first time since
we'd set foot inside DLJ as summer associates over a year
before. The alcohol had sent a bolt of lightning through
the gray matter, and we were realizing that we weren't

going to be treated like gold, and that we were going to have to pay some mighty painful dues. Dues that most of the senior guys had paid but that nonetheless were agonizing. If they had to do it, then so would we. Those were the rules. Maybe it was due to our drunken stupor, but it sure felt like we had been sold a bill of goods. We began to realize that we were in for a long, painful experience.

Then one of our favorite dancers, Angel, finished up on the main stage and headed our way to resume table dancing for us.

"What? I can't hear you, man. The music's too loud. I've got the next round. You want another scotch and water?"

"Yeah, make it a double."

The night went black. The next day Rolfe and I conveniently forgot the revelations we had come to the previous night. We were back in training class going for the gusto, and taking our place at the back of the queue.

The Food Chain

The higher a monkey climbs,
the more you see of his ass.
—General Joseph Stilwell

Within an investment bank there is a strict hierarchy. It's a pyramid, with each level of the pyramid resting on the shoulders of the level below. The further down you travel into the pyramid, the more primitive the species of banker becomes. Remember who built the great pyramids of Egypt? That's right, it was a bunch of sunburned slaves in loincloths.

The senior managing directors are at the pinnacle of the investment banking pyramid. They're the guys on the front line. They source business. They scour the world looking for ways to make fees for the investment bank. They approach companies in order to sell them on doing an IPO or raising money through a bond underwriting. They ask companies to buy other companies or to sell themselves. Every managing director's prime concern is to attract clients and bring fees into the bank. That's why they're paid the big bucks. Imagine a handsome gentleman in a twenty-five-hundred-dollar suit. He's neatly shaven, nicely manicured, and his shoes cost more than most people's living room furniture. That's the managing director.

The senior vice presidents are the next level down in the pyramid. At some banks they're called junior managing directors, but their role is the same. They attempt to bring in some business in order to justify their high-paid existence, but much of the time they simply process the deals. They inherit the business from the managing directors and with their team they process the hell out of it. They make sure that whatever deal was promised to the company is done quickly. Sometimes they even make sure it's done correctly. All the t's are crossed and all the i's are dotted. They are so close to the brass ring that they can taste it. Imagine a used-car salesman wearing a polyester leisure suit. Maybe he hasn't shaved for a couple of days and he's starting to smell a little gamey. That's the senior vice president.

Next come the vice presidents. The vice presidents are a crew of processing robots, few with any life outside the office. The vice presidents are making roughly half a million bucks a year, but they don't have any time to spend it. When and if they do get out of the office, they sleep. This turns them into a hapless bunch of angry young men and women who can't understand why they're so frustrated. They want to have relationships and become functioning members of the human race, like their friends outside of the investment banking realm, but they don't have the time. Usually, the only dates they can get are with the gold diggers who want to get their claws into a piece of that healthy paycheck. The nice boys and girls in the city, the ones that the vice presidents wish they were dating, are busy screwing the unemployed artists and musicians who have no money but plenty of time.

The vice presidents are making too much money to change careers because no other organization, with the exception of another investment bank, will hire a vice president and pay him half a million dollars a year to process deals. The vice presidents don't really take any financial risks. If they're willing to shamelessly kiss every upper-level ass they see and run around all night churning documents, they know that they'll continue to get a fat paycheck. The problem is that the vice presidents are making all this money, but they're not content. They're a miserable crew because they're trapped. Like caged animals. Imagine a prisoner of war kept shackled in a moldy basement for five years with no light, nothing but shoe leather to eat, absolutely no bathing privileges, and occasional doses of electroshock therapy. That's the vice president.

At the next level in the pyramid are the associates. Lots of them. The associates' lives suck. The vice presidents take out their aggressions on the associates all day and all night. It doesn't end until the associate either becomes a vice president, leaves, or commits suicide. The associate kisses the vice president's ass because the vice president helps determine the associate's bonus. Here's how it works: the managing director says "Jump" and the senior vice president says "How high?" The senior vice president then perpetuates the panic attack by sending a voice mail that conveys a false sense of urgency to the vice president. He basically kicks the dog. The vice president looks at the associate, takes a hot poker, and shoves it up the dog's ass. The associates are barely human but at times are brought to client meetings and are expected to act human. The associates are the Cro-Magnon men. They live in caves, have trouble walking upright, and have a lot of hair on their backs. Usually, they communicate by grunting. Those are the associates.

Finally, there are the analysts. Monkeys. Tons and tons of little monkeys. Not humans, just monkeys crawling all over each other and pulling lice out of each other's fur. Those are the analysts.

With all these different kinds of investment bankers, the investment banking department appears to be a huge place. It is. Goldman Sachs, Morgan Stanley, and Merrill Lynch each have their own investment banking army with thousands of soldiers. Then there's Lehman Brothers; Bear, Stearns; and First Boston. The list goes on and on. In reality, though, the investment bankers are just one small part of the broader investment house. They're just one little cog in a much grander machine.

Within each investment house there are capital markets desks, an institutional sales force, a trading operation, a research department, and a retail brokerage arm. Each department has a function, and they all work together. First, the bankers go out calling on companies, looking for the ones that need to raise some money. Once they find one, the bankers call up the capital markets desks and tell them to get the wheels rolling. The bankers tell the capital markets guys, "Look, man, we gotta raise some dough. What's it gonna take?" The capital markets desk tells the bankers, "We can raise your money. Here's the terms our buyers are gonna want."

After that, the capital markets desk calls the institutional sales force and tells them to round up some customers. The institutional sales force then begins calling the mutual funds, the hedge funds, the pension funds, and the university endowments—any and all institutions that control money that needs to be invested. These customers give the investment house some money to buy the new securities, the investment bank keeps a piece as their cut, then they pass the rest on to the company. A few weeks later the research department writes a report on the company that extols the virtues of the newly issued stocks or bonds. Eventually, the retail brokerage arm gets into the picture, calling on the retail investors with their latest and greatest investment idea—those same newly issued stocks and bonds. It's a profitable operation.

There are many other types of financial institutions in the Wall Street universe as well: clearinghouses, hedge funds, mutual funds, commercial lenders, and commodities trading operations. The investment houses are just a small part of the greater Wall Street universe. The associate is smaller than a piece of dust on a wart on the ass of a large male African elephant. The inside of the cheek of the ass, not the outside.

The Business

*The brain is a wonderful organ. It starts working
the moment you get up in the morning and does not
stop until you get into the office.*

—Robert Frost

So, how does a banker justify his or her compensation?
When it comes down to it, bankers really only provide
two services for companies: they provide advice on matters of corporate finance and they raise money. The
banker stands at the vortex of the capital flows, siphoning
off a portion of the swirling funds. For providing these services, the average upper-level investment banker can expect to earn about $750,000 in an average year. Is the
average banker worth five times the average executive in
most other industries? Does the average banker add five
times as much economic value to the greater good of the
common whole? Given that investment bankers carry a
disproportionate share of civilization's unjustified attitude
and hubris, the world would arguably be a better place
with fewer bankers and more guys selling soft-serve
twisty cones down on the corner. Shit, take away some of

the investment bankers, the terrorists, and the tax authorities and you're coming darn close to Shangri-la.

The investment bankers, of course, would disagree:

"We make the capital markets more efficient!"

"We bring together buyers and sellers!"

"We help maximize business value!"

Is it true? Do the bankers really do anything but suck the fat out of an overindulgent capitalist economic system? Yeah. The capital markets aren't perfect. Those who need money, and those who have the money, can't always identify each other. The buyers of businesses don't always know the sellers. Independent third parties are sometimes needed to confirm business value. What many of the bankers don't grasp, though, is the tenuous nature of the value of the services they provide. As the number of available information sources continues to proliferate, and access to that information becomes less proprietary, the bankers' ability to extract excess fees from that information will inevitably dissipate. It may happen slowly, but the bankers' value will diminish and melt away as surely as the Wicked Witch of the West in a South Florida rain shower.

Advisory Work

Historically, the investment banker's job was to advise companies on their financial alternatives. The investment banker was a confidant to the company's highest executives, and the relationship between a CEO and his banker spanned an entire career. The banker provided analysis and advice on possible merger and acquisition candidates, guidance on capital structure issues, and even occasional counsel on matters of business strategy. The banker was also the introduction person, the one with the relationships. If the CEO wanted to initiate merger talks with a competitor's CEO, or wanted to sell a division of his company, the banker was the go-to guy. The banker usually knew somebody at the other company, or knew somebody who knew somebody, who could get the CEO through the door and into the other CEO's office. The two CEOs would initiate talks, they might get a framework for a deal hammered out, and then the banker would tell the client whether the deal made sense from a financial perspective. All in all, it was exciting work. Bankers didn't have to spend a whole lot of time chasing new business and could go to sleep every night knowing that they'd added some value for their clients. Moreover, the work was steady. In both good times and bad, there was corporate finance work to be done. If the economy was booming and businesses were building up cash reserves, the mergers and acquisitions side of the business would likely be going gangbusters. When things got tight, the restructuring and strategic advisory piece of the business would compensate.

Bankers still perform advisory work. They still make recommendations to companies on possible merger and acquisition candidates. They still propose levered recapitalizations, stock buybacks, and other restructurings of a company's capital structure. They still write reports advising a company's shareholders as to whether an offer that has been made to purchase the company should be considered "fair" from a financial standpoint. There are still a few small, highly focused investment banks that continue to provide good strategic business advice.

In general, though, the advisory side of the business has become much more commoditized. The banker no longer has the lock on relationships. The banker's information is no longer highly proprietary. Information on companies is now so widespread that there's very little company-specific knowledge that bankers can truly call their own. The banker no longer brings enough unique added value to the table to necessarily merit a CEO's granting him a lifelong mandate to provide paid advice on matters of corporate finance.

This shift in the nature of the bankers' advisory business is illustrated by what, today, is a much more typical advisory assignment—an exclusive sale. In an exclusive sale a company that wants to sell its business calls up every investment banker that it knows. Usually, all the big banks with the well-known names make the list. Sometimes a couple of smaller banks will be on there as well. The company asks each of them to make a fee proposal. Some banks might offer to arrange the sale for 1.5 percent of total sale proceeds, others might offer to sell it for 1.25 percent of total sale proceeds. Some banks might structure a more innovative fee structure that includes a sliding fee scale, incremental incentive payments, or any number of other variations. Ultimately, though, since there's no longer any meaningful information differential between the different banks, the company will retain whichever bank agrees to make the sale for the lowest fee. It's a Kmart blue-light special in aisle five.

Once retained, the bank conducting the sale puts together an information booklet on the company being sold and mails it out to all the potential buyers. The information booklet describes the company's business. It's full of lots of colorful graphs and fancy fonts. That's the extent of the banker's value-added—making the information booklet look pretty. The potential buyers all get to submit bids on the company, and whoever puts in the highest bid walks away with the prize. Just like selling an old Dodge Dart, or a house, or a used diaper pail at a yard sale.

As the bankers' competitive information advantage has waned, the bankers have gradually been forced to change their approach. They can no longer rely on a relatively small number of loyal clients to generate advisory business for them year in and year out. They now have to spend a much larger portion of their time scrambling to find new clients and new business. To justify their existence, they now have to go out and pitch ideas to whomever will give them an audience in the hope that just a few of the potential clients will sign on for the program. And when those clients sign on, the bankers have got to assume that the next time there's advisory business to be had with that company, it might not necessarily be them providing the advice. In short, the banking business has become a whole lot more like most other businesses out there—competitive.

Capital Raising

The banker's second primary function is capital raising. Most growing businesses have an insatiable desire for capital, and few are able to generate enough cash through their ongoing operations to fulfill that desire. That means they have to go somewhere else for the money.

They have to go to the capital markets. In the most basic terms, a company that wants to raise money has only two choices; it can either borrow the money or it can sell an ownership interest in the company. Debt versus equity, that's the choice. There are all kinds of arguments for why a company, the issuer, might want to choose debt over equity, or vice versa, but the fundamental differentiators are cost and risk. The debt is a less expensive means of financing for the issuer, but if the issuer screws up and has trouble paying back the debt when it comes due, then the debt holder gets to keep the company. In other words, if the issuer fucks up they lose it all.

American-style capitalism puts a high premium on broad market discipline, and this has led to the development in America of the largest and most sophisticated capital markets in the world. The investment bankers have positioned themselves squarely at the crossroads of these public capital markets. They're the toll collectors. They make it difficult, nearly impossible in fact, to access the public markets without traveling on their parkway, and their parkway ain't a cheap road to travel.

The investment banker is the consummate middleman. A company comes to the investment banker and says, "I need money. I need lots of money." The banker replies, "No problem, I'll go out and find you some money. I'll give you most of what I find, but I'm gonna keep a little bit for myself." The investment banker then goes out with his or her colleagues from the bank and talks to the people with the money. That means the institutional investors—the mutual funds, the pension funds, the hedge funds, and the endowments.

The investment banker goes to the institutions and tells

them, "Look, I know this great company but they're a little short on cash. They've got this great new product, the best you've ever seen, but they don't have enough money to develop it. It's going to be the next big thing. The guys at this company, they're really a bunch of swell guys. If you buy some of their equity you're gonna get rich. I promise."

The institutional investors cut the investment banker a check so that they can buy a piece of the deal. Sometimes they'll buy a piece of the deal even if they don't like it too much. They do that because they're worried that if they don't buy into the latest deal, then the bankers might not come back around the next time with the *really* big deal. No institutional investor wants to be the only one to miss out on the next big thing. The banker collects the checks, cashes them, keeps a percentage, and gives the company raising the money whatever is left over.

The size of the chunk that the investment banker keeps depends on what kind of deal is being underwritten. A banker might keep as little as 1 percent for a high-grade debt deal and as much as 7 percent for an initial public offering (IPO). Originally, the investment banker kept a bigger percentage on some deals to compensate the investment bank for taking on greater risk on those deals. It used to work like this: (1) a company would tell an investment bank that they needed to raise money (2) the investment bank would write the company a check and buy the equity or the debt directly from the company (3) the investment bank would turn around and try to find buyers for the company's securities, and (4) the investment bank would hopefully be able to sell the securities and, in the process, get back not only all the money that they had paid the company for its securities but also something extra to compensate them for their work. The investment bank was taking on risk because they were exposed for the period of time between cutting the check to the company and selling the securities to the ultimate buyers. If the market headed south in that time period, or the investment bank hadn't valued the securities accurately, the bank could stand to lose money. Equity is inherently more difficult to value than debt, so the investment bank got a larger fee for underwriting the equity than they did for the debt.

Things don't generally work like that anymore. Nowadays the investment banks limit their risk by going out ahead of time and finding buyers for the company's securities. They no longer have to hold the securities for the period of time between when they buy them and when they resell them. If the bank can't line up enough buyers for the securities ahead of time, they tell the company, "No go, the market's not right, we can't do your deal." The equity or the debt being sold effectively goes straight from the company to the ultimate buyers. The investment bank just stands in the middle peeling off its percentage for having arranged the deal. The banks have managed to cut out most of their risk, but they continue to take the same spread that they've always taken.

If the market for investment banking services was an efficient one, the spreads would be a lot lower than they are today. They've stayed high, though, because there has always been an unspoken agreement among the bankers that when it comes to underwritings they won't compete on price. The spreads are sacrosanct. He who cuts spreads will himself become an outcast, condemned to a life of squalor among the filthiest of dogs. The investment banking community has long been an oligopoly, with only a handful of real players with the size and scale to drive through the big deals. The community of investment banks has always been small enough so that if one bank were to break ranks on the pricing issue, the others could quickly join forces and squash the offender like a june bug on the grill of an 18-wheeler. Every banker knows that the pricing issue is a slippery slope best avoided because once the price cutting begins, there's no telling where it will end.

Until recently, there weren't many new entrants to the underwriting business. Because an investment bank needs a certain minimum scale to operate profitably, there haven't been many new players willing to make the necessary up-front investment. Increasingly in recent years, though, as the risk of underwriting has come down and fee spreads have stayed constant, the economic return has appeared increasingly compelling for potential entrants to the business. As this has happened, the new entrants have begun to make their appearance.

The first new competitors through the door have been the U.S. and foreign commercial banks. Increasingly, the large regional commercial banks have begun to set up securities underwriting subsidiaries and have begun to hire away investment bankers from the DLJs, Morgans, and Goldmans of the world. New investment banks have begun to pop up with an operating model based on on-line distribution of IPOs direct to retail investors. As the number of underwriters competing for each piece of underwriting business has proliferated, the spreads have begun to come down. With more competitors, it isn't as easy anymore to close ranks on the offenders who dare compete on price. There's always somebody now who's willing to tell the other guy to fuck off. The underwriters' world has gotten more competitive, more complicated, and less capable of being controlled. A crack has developed in the underwriting foundation and each year now, as the aggregate amount of capital raised in the public markets increases, the average spread taken in by the investment banks decreases. The fees are coming down. Slowly, right now, but they're coming down.

One day, in the not-too-distant future, an old-school corporate executive may beckon his banker. The banker will walk in unkempt, unclean, and wearing a $99.99 poly-blend suit from the Burlington Coat Factory.

"My God!" the executive will gasp. "What happened to you? The ties, the suits, the shoes, the gold cuff links . . . where did it all go?"

"Away, my friend, away," the banker will reply in a subdued voice. "The times have changed."

The Sizzle

Don't sell the steak; sell the sizzle. It is the sizzle
that sells the steak and not the cow, although the
cow is, of course, mighty important.
                                        —**Elmer Wheeler**

As both the advisory side of the business and the under-writing side of the business have become increasingly competitive, the new business pitch has gained impor-tance as the bankers' core activity. As Rolfe and I found out, there's not much business anymore in the banking world that can be taken for granted. Pitching became our existence.

The most telling evidence of this shift in banking activ-ity has been the birth of what's known as the "beauty pageant." The beauty pageant is a head-to-head competi-tion among a bevy of investment banks for a new piece of business. The phrase is a misnomer. Unlike the contes-tants in traditional beauty pageants, the bankers aren't normally required to wear bathing suits at the pageant, but if the client asked them to, they'd come in wearing the tightest nut-hugging Speedo ever seen. In today's ultracompetitive environment, bankers will do anything for a piece of business.

The company conducting the beauty pageant sends out word to a whole slew of banks that it's looking to do a deal. The company sets aside a day for the pageant, and each bank gets to select the slot that they want. Just like making an appointment to get a cavity filled.

Bankers from each bank show up at the beauty pageant at their appointed time to meet with whoever is going to be running the deal from the company's side. The bankers always travel in packs. Even a crappy little deal usually merits the presence of a managing director, a vice president, and an associate. The senior bankers like to arrive at meetings flanked by a few junior bankers, like General MacArthur with his staff in tow. They think that the strong presence will impress clients and win business.

If the pageant is for an underwriting the bankers might also bring a guy from the capital markets group to the party. The capital markets guy is a cross between a banker and a trader—he's the illegitimate offspring. The bankers bring the capital markets guy along to show the company that everybody at the bank, not just the bankers, is going to be involved in the deal process. The capital markets guy always does the part of the pitch that focuses on the current state of the markets. It's usually something that's straight out of that morning's *Wall Street Journal,* but if he's a smooth talker it sounds like he's a real expert.

The capital markets guys are a double-edged sword. They're notorious for behaving like chronic Tourette's syndrome sufferers by unpredictably spewing out random vulgarities and filthy jokes in the middle of the pitch. It's the trader part of their mentality that makes them so dangerous. Sometimes the clients appreciate the debauchery, but other times they get offended and decide never to invite the investment bank back for another beauty pageant. The senior banker always hopes that the presence of the capital markets guy will help them win the business, but then they spend the whole pitch worrying that the capital markets guy is going to say something so offensive that it makes them lose the business.

The whole idea of a pitch is to convince the client that the bank delivering the pitch is the right investment bank to lead the deal. Every bank makes the same pitch. They all go into the beauty pageant and tell the company "We're the best. Our investment bank does all the big deals for companies in your industry. We know all the big buyers and we're the guys. We're the only investment bank qualified to lead manage your business."

Although they all start out the same, every pitch turns out differently. Some go well, some don't. Some are interesting, most aren't. Some managing directors light up the room when they're making the pitch. Others go over about as well as Jesse Helms at a gay pride rally.

At DLJ there were some managing directors who would make the pitch, win the business, and then wouldn't show up again until the closing dinner. We called them the Phantoms. They didn't need to be around while a deal was getting processed because there were hundreds of mindless vice presidents ready to do the processing for them. The Phantoms took the art of the sale to the highest order. They were able to instill so much confidence in a new client at the outset that they completely neutralized the need to hold the client's hand along the way. Fucking amazing.

There were other managing directors, though, who got up to make a pitch to potential clients and froze up like a born-again preacher in a Tijuana whorehouse. The pitch book was their security blanket. They read it aloud to the client like a kindergarten teacher at story time, physically unable to deviate from its sequence of pages. Watching these managing directors deliver a pitch was as painful as getting a steaming hot chocolate enema.

An associate's primary job is to put the pitch books together, carry them to the meeting, and pass them out. Associates routinely fly five hundred miles just to be the bellhop at a meaningless pitch. For a while, when associates are new, they'll try to convince themselves that things will change and that eventually they'll be asked to take a more active role, but it never happens. It's nothing but a pipe dream.

When associates finally reach this realization, they no longer waste time during the pitches conjuring visions of greatness. The pitch becomes nothing more than a routine to be suffered through. Since associates have typically been working on the pitch for the entire previous night, their primary activity becomes a struggle to stay awake. Every associate has his own techniques. I used to stick my hands into my pockets and try to pull hairs out of my legs. Rolfe once considered attaching clothespins to his nuts.

Being assigned to create a pitch book is a punishment. It's the pinnacle of mindless processing. Associates start out believing that they're going to create the Magna Carta, the masterpiece that will bring in the big deal, and that their pitch book will move mountains, convert heathens, and generate enormous fees. They end up realizing that the pitch book is an unholy creation, a mixture of three-week-old potted meat and smelly cottage cheese with just enough curry powder added to cover the latent rottenness.

A pitch book is never original. It's three sections from each of five other pitch books mashed together with a new overview in the front. The general outline is always the same. There are four main sections: Overview, Capital Markets Update, Valuation, and Expertise.

The first section is Overview. This section explains why the company that's getting the pitch is such a great company, and why they should think about doing a deal now instead of later. It shamelessly strokes the company's ego. Overview utilizes the classic technique of buttering up the client. It gets the client to spread their legs before the banker jams home the bacon.

If the pitch is for an underwriting, the second section of the pitch book is Capital Markets Update. This is the section where the capital markets guy chimes in if the bankers have brought him along. Capital Markets Update gives the client an overview of either the equity market or the bond market. If the capital markets are in good shape, this section provides the bankers with the ammunition to give the client inflated expectations about how successful their offering is going to be. If the capital markets are in a funk, the bankers gloss over this section quickly, and then use it as an excuse when they later fail to get the deal sold: "We warned you. We told you that the capital markets were bad . . . remember the Capital Markets Update section? Don't blame us!"

MONKEY BUSINESS

If the pitch is for an advisory deal, then a Strategic Considerations section replaces the Capital Markets Update.
Strategic Considerations is supposed to justify for the
client the need for a merger, acquisition, recapitalization,
or whatever other flavor of the day the banker is peddling.
In reality, this section is a lot like a game of Boggle. The
associate puts a bunch of sexy-sounding financial words
into a shaker ("capital," "synergy," "efficiency,"
"value" . . .), then shakes the words up and peppers them
randomly through a bunch of sentences that contain
other random words. None of it makes any sense, but if it
begins to sound enough like it's out of a business school
textbook, then the potential client will sometimes buy off
on it and retain the investment bank to do a deal.

The third section of the pitch book is Valuation. This is
the heart of the book, and it's the part that the client really
cares about. This is the part where the banker pleasures
the potential client with a high hard one. This is the section that either tells the client how the market will value
their company, or how much money they stand to make
from the transaction that is being proposed. It's the main
course. The experienced clients turn directly to this section as soon as the pitch books are handed out so that
they can get to the answer quickly. They look for the answer on their own and ignore the bankers. If they don't
like the answer that they find, they sometimes throw the
bankers out the back door into the alley.

The fourth and last section of the pitch book is Expertise. This is the part of the pitch book where the investment bank making the pitch attempts to demonstrate why
it's the logical choice to lead the transaction. The marketing approach in this section generally focuses on size and

quantity, as in the pie-eating contest at the county fair. If a bank has done a lot of a certain kind of deal, their bankers figure that it implies that they must be good at them. Quality is of no consequence, it's all about size and quantity. The Expertise section gives the bankers a chance to perpetrate one of their favorite deceptions—the spinning of the league tables.

The league tables are lists detailing how many deals, representing what total dollar amount, an investment bank has done in a given category. They're included in every pitch that's ever been made for an underwriting. If the pitch is for an IPO, the league tables will trumpet the bank's IPO experience. If the pitch is for a high-yield offering, the league tables will focus on the bank's experience in issuing high yield. The problem is that only one investment bank can truly be number one for any given type of deal, so the bankers have to get creative. It becomes the associate's responsibility to maximize this creativity.

When spinning the league tables, a banker will steadily whittle down the universe of "appropriate" deals until the bank comes out number one. There are a million ways to do this. First, the banker might narrow the list of deals down to only those within a certain dollar-size range. Next, he might narrow the universe down further to include only those deals in a certain industry sector. Still not number one? Try throwing out all deals for foreign issuers, or maybe excluding deals that were done concurrently with other kinds of deals. The possibilities are nearly limitless. With enough trips to the plastic surgeon, just about any bowlegged trollop can come out looking like a supermodel.

At the end of the day, when the league tables finally make it into the pitch book, the only evidence of subterfuge will be discreet. The heading of the league table will trumpet, "Our bank is the top underwriter of IPOs for companies similar to Acme." The caveat, in the form of a footnote in barely legible type at the bottom of the page, will tell the whole story.*

I once met a guy who told me that he'd had sex with seven different women. I told him that I didn't think that was so many. Then he told me that five of them had been Scandinavian hookers. Well, that changed the picture a little bit. If he was a banker, he could have made a league table for "Most Sexually Active" that would have had him as number one and Wilt Chamberlain as number two. That would have looked impressive, as long as you didn't read the footnote.†

In concept, the creation of pitch books shouldn't be the bane of the associate's existence. Mix up a cup of hyperbole, a dash of fabrication, a healthy dose of plagiarism, and a saucerful of aggressive valuation, shake well, and it's complete. In practice, it doesn't work like that. When it comes to pitch books, there's a long-standing tradition among bankers that it is all about pain, suffering, deliverance, and learning who's in charge.

The associate can deliver the first draft of the pitch book to the managing director a week ahead of the pitch. The associate can deliver the pitch in person or can have a eunuch in a loincloth deliver it. The associate can put

---

*For IPOs between $50 and $150 million in the telecommunications sector, and excluding foreign issuers, real estate investment trusts, and offerings done concurrently with debt issues. Full credit given to all managers.
†Includes only Scandinavian hookers.

on a Lycra body suit and a pair of gold lamé pumps, and deliver the draft with his head spinning like Linda Blair in *The Exorcist*. It won't make any difference. Regardless of the delivery time, regardless of the delivery mechanism, most managing directors in charge won't look at the pitch until the night before the pitch is due to be delivered and then they'll decide to futz with it. Why? Because like the rest of us, they procrastinate, and it's imperative that the associate fully experience the rite of passage.

The associate will spend the first half of the night before the pitch, up until about midnight, faxing copies of the pitch book draft back and forth between the homes of the vice president, the senior vice president, and the managing director. Each of them will continue to make changes to each other's drafts and comments until they're too tired to play their little game anymore. Throughout this part of the process, the associate plays the role of master fax operator and word processor, making sure that each of them sees the changes that each of the others has made. After they go to bed, the associate begins working full-time with the word processing and copy center departments to get the actual pitch books made in time for delivery to the pitch the next morning.

Only about one pitch out of ten ever hits the mark. Sometimes the bankers know when they walk out of the room that they aren't going to get the business, the karma's just not right. Other times, it's a couple of days before they find out. The worst possible outcome for the associate is when the potential client can't make up their mind. They hem and they haw, and they tell the bankers that they haven't reached a definitive decision as to whether they want to do a deal or not. They leave the door open just a crack, and give the managing director hope that if the bankers just keep pushing a little harder, they'll be able to convince the client to go through with the transaction. We used to call these clients the Living Dead.

The Living Dead were evil. They sucked out our brains and destroyed our spirit. They wouldn't die, no matter how many bullets we tried to pump into them. There was one managing director, Jack Gatorski, who was infamous among the associates for his ability to spawn the Living Dead. Gatorski rarely allowed any potential opportunity to die an easy death.

Gatorski was a rail of a man who looked something like a retarded scarecrow. His crowning glory was an egregious pointy tuft of hair on the top of his head that made him look as if a flying squirrel had just used his cranium as a landing strip. Associates used to place bets as to whether this shaggy curiosity was actually a rug or not. On the one hand, some believed that something so ill-fitted and so poorly maintained couldn't possibly be natural. Another school of thought, though, argued that a man making the kind of coin that Gatorski made wouldn't possibly subject himself to the humiliation of wearing such a disgraceful accessory. An associate classmate once deliberately rented a convertible while on a diligence trip in Florida with Gatorski in order to once and for all end the rug-or-not-a-rug controversy. However, it rained and the top stayed up, thereby scuttling the fact-finding mission and ensuring continued debate.

Rolfe had spent a lot of time working with Gatorski, so he had firsthand knowledge of why the guy was known as Gator. Gator was a prehistoric lizard in banker's pinstripes. He attacked potential deals like a Louisiana swamp gator going after a fatted calf. Gatorski would lie quietly in wait in the shallow water anticipating the arrival of his next hapless meal, and when it finally stumbled by he would attack in a flurry of churning water and sharpened teeth. Before the unwitting client knew what had happened they were firmly locked between Gator's muscular jaws, and the only way out was through a generous disgorging of fees. Tasty fees weren't the only satisfying feast for the wily reptile, however. A plump piece of fresh associate ass was nearly as pleasing for Gator, as it represented an untapped resource that could be molded into a potent weapon for use in the client attacks. That's why many associates had grown to fear Gator. Rolfe had done more than one tour of duty with Gator, and he had the battle scars to show for it.

Gator was one of a kind. He was the most persistent son of a bitch any of us had ever known. That was a good trait for a banker but spelled trouble for an associate—in this case, me. He refused to ever admit defeat. He thrived on rejection, it empowered him. The man was scary because he never took no for an answer. A client could tell him, "You suck. Your firm will never, ever do business with us. We hate you." Gator would be calling the guy up the next day with new alternatives and new ideas. It was rumored that there were actually clients who had specifically requested that Gator not be allowed into their offices because it was so hard to get rid of him. He was like a bad case of jock itch, only he could walk and talk. The only way to stop him was to either physically restrain him or kill him. Both options had been given serious consideration.

When you first did a pitch for Gator the work had only just begun. He would force you to create, rearrange, and explore literally hundreds of permutations of the original material after you'd made the pitch. The work that any given project generated was completely independent of the likelihood that the project would yield an active deal.

Gator's persistence wasn't just directed at associates and clients, it was directed at everybody. His whole promotion from senior vice president to managing director a couple of years before had allegedly been a direct result of his persistence with one particular client, Universal Wavelength. His performance on the Universal Wavelength deal was legendary. He had hounded the company for a full two years, almost nonstop, before they finally agreed to let DLJ underwrite a junk bond offering for them. Once the offering was under way, he had proven to be so persistently annoying that the only co-manager on the deal had walked away from the table leaving $1 million of extra commission dollars for DLJ. It was unheard of, a miracle in the world of investment banking, for a co-manager to leave a $1 million fee behind. When the head of DLJ's banking group saw that, he must have decided that he better promote Gatorski quickly to harness the full moneymaking potential of his abrasive ways.

The whole thing was, Gator's craziness may have been the result of a supercharged adrenaline rush coursing its way through his veins. Rob Katz, a vice president who used to spend a lot of time working with Gator, told me that he'd once been on an airplane trip back from Asia with Gator and he'd been having some difficulty sleeping. Gator told him to "try a half of one of these pills that I have." Katz asked for a whole pill, but Gator told him that he'd probably better stick with a half. "They're kind of powerful," he said. Katz claimed that he took half a pill and then watched Gator down two of them. Katz reported falling into this incredibly deep dreamless sleep immediately thereafter.

The next thing Katz remembered, all the passengers were getting off the plane and hitting him in the head with their luggage as they passed him in the aisle. Gator was still going full speed two seats over, cranking through a huge pile of work. The man couldn't be slowed.

Gator knew that he was a pit bull. It made him proud. He used to tell stories that perpetuated the myth. The best one came my way as I was cruising through the woods of Minnesota with him in the back of this late-seventies Cadillac stretch limousine. We were on our way back to the airport from a closing dinner, and the two of us were smoking some stogies and stinking up the entire limo. We started bullshitting about stupid things we'd done through the years, and Gator let loose with a classic.

"When I was in college, I was on a road trip with a buddy of mine. We were traveling from South Bend, Indiana, to Ann Arbor, Michigan. It started to get kind of late one night, and my buddy saw this quick-stop store up ahead, so we pulled in to grab some coffee and get something to eat. Well, while we were in there my buddy saw this *Penthouse* magazine, so he decided to buy a copy so that he would have something to do once we were back on the road.

"We were taking back roads most of the way, and the sun had gone down, so the roads were pretty dark. On top of that, my buddy had the dome light on in the car so that he could get a real good look at all these naked chicks who were in the magazine. You take all that, plus the fact that I was listening to my buddy read the *Penthouse* "Forum" submissions to me, and you ended up with me not paying real close attention to everything that was happening on the road in front of me. Next thing I knew, there was this fucking cow standing right there in the middle of the road, right in front of me, and it was too late for me to stop. We hit the cow.

"Well, now, this cow was a big fat one, and when it came down to this collision between our car and the cow, the cow came out ahead. He rolled up onto the hood, rolled over and crushed the front windshield, and then rolled right off the side of the hood and landed next to the car standing on all four legs. It was amazing. He stood there dazed for a minute, let out a belch, and walked off toward the side of the road into the darkness.

"I think that me and my buddy were more shocked than the cow was. We were sitting there in the middle of nowhere, and now we had a crushed hood, a windshield that we couldn't see out of, and we still had another fifty miles to go until we got to Ann Arbor. There was one other small problem. When we had hit this cow it was so shocked that it had spontaneously emptied its bowels all over the front of the car, so we now had not only transport problems and vision problems but stench problems too. My buddy was all flipped out about the car, and he kept saying that we needed to wait for another car to come along so that they could drive us to the nearest place with a tow truck. Well, I told him 'Fuck that, we don't have any idea when somebody's gonna come help us out, I'm gonna get us to Ann Arbor one way or another.'"

I often thought about the remainder of Gator's trip to Ann Arbor after he told me that story. I pictured him starting the car back up, sticking his head out the window like a dog, and driving down the road. I could see him, like the Red Baron, piloting a big whale of a cruise-mobile up to about thirty-five miles an hour before pieces of cow crap started peeling off the hood and flying back to hit him in the face. I could picture his buddy in the car hearing the slapping noises of the doody chunks hitting Gator in the face, and I could picture him pulling into Ann Arbor covered in cow shit, looking like something out of a grade-B horror movie. It didn't paint a pretty mental picture, but it helped me understand how Gator operated.

An associate didn't stand a chance with a guy like Gator as his managing director. He may have been a great guy out of the office, he could have even been the Messiah, but when it came to banking the guy was an animal. Getting staffed on a pitch with Gator was a sure death sentence for the associate, and there was no appeals process. The electric chair was ready and waiting and the power was turned on.

Fishing for Value

A lie can be halfway round the world before the truth has got its boots on.
—James Callaghan

The investment banking associate devotes a significant portion of his or her existence to performing valuation work. Theoretically, every transaction involves a valuation. If the bankers are selling a company, then they need to do a valuation to figure out what a fair sales price is. If the bankers are doing an equity offering, then they need a valuation to tell them how much money the market will give them for the equity. If the bankers are doing a bond offering, the bond buyers will want to know what sort of value the assets backing the bonds have.

The valuation work begins at the very first stages of the pitch and continues throughout the entire process until the deal is actually consummated. The valuation will go up, down, sideways, and backward. The valuation will start out looking like Little Bo Peep and end up looking like Quasimodo.

Any associate who has graduated from business school

knows all the different valuation techniques. There are market-based methods and theoretical methods. There are trading values and takeout values. There are going-concern values and liquidation values. Troob and I knew all this, but what we didn't know was how the valuations in an investment bank usually got done. After we learned, we called it doggy-style valuation because it was done backward. In an investment bank, the managing director figures out what reasonable valuation number he is going to need to tell the client in order to win the business. It then becomes the associate's job to work backward to figure out a way to display analysis that will validate the target value. In the process, associates try to convince themselves that what they're doing is solid analysis and not simply pure pretzel logic or high-level finance magic tricks.

We had a lot of valuation techniques at our command. It would have been nice if we could have tried out a few techniques, and then used the one that gave us the target value we were hoping to reach. The problem was that usually our valuation techniques didn't give us the numbers we needed. The numbers we had to give the companies during the pitch in order to win the business were usually bigger than we could reasonably justify. This was problematic, but it wasn't insurmountable. As long as we were willing to push the limits of our optimism, we could come out where we needed to be. As long as we were willing to take a second mortgage on our integrity, everything would be Dy-No-Mite.

This is how we did it.

Comparable Multiples Analysis

The quickest method of valuing a company is through use of a comparable multiples analysis ("comp analysis"). In a comp analysis the associate identifies a group of companies, the comps, that are similar to the company being valued, then he looks at what prices the comps are trading for in the public market. For instance, the group of comps might be trading on average for ten times cash flow. If that's the case, then the associate simply has to take the target company's cash flow and multiply it times ten in order to derive a value for the company. It's as easy as pie, and the principle behind the comp analysis is simple: if your neighbor's 1975 Chevy Nova sold for three hundred dollars, your 1977 Chevy Nova should probably sell for about the same amount.

The problem with the comp analysis is that most of the time the banker wants to have a group of comps with the highest multiples possible and that, in turn, means that the bank may have to use companies as comps that are completely different from the company being valued. The associate's job then becomes figuring out a way to make all the companies seem similar, even though they're not. I once worked on an IPO for an engineering company that had a lot of clients in the broadcasting industry. Broadcasting companies were selling at huge premiums to engineering companies in the market, so we convinced the buyers that the company going public was actually a *broadcasting* company that just happened to employ a lot of engineers. It worked like magic. On the comp analysis, any company with even the slightest justification for inclusion is considered. It can be a red-headed stepson, or a second cousin through marriage three times removed, and it'll still get invited to the family barbecue.

Bankers, in general, love comp analysis. A well-executed comp analysis contains lots of data, and that gets most bankers hotter than a plate of Louisiana crawdads. Our associate comrade Slick once worked on a deal for DLJ's merchant bank. The merchant bank wanted to sell one of their portfolio companies and they needed a comp analysis to figure out what sort of price they could expect to get in the public markets. The portfolio company was a textile company. The managing director said that he needed a very thorough comparable analysis; he didn't want to leave any stone unturned. Our man Slick had to put together a comparable analysis with one hundred companies on it. We called it the "100 Company Under-wear Comp" because a lot of the companies made underwear. Four times a year each of the companies on the comp released their quarterly financial statement and Slick had to update all one hundred companies. It took him two entire days. That was when he realized he had hit it big as an investment banker. Nobody knew as much about the trading multiples of underwear companies as he did. He had found his niche.

Discounted Cash Flow Analysis

Another key weapon for the creative banker is the discounted cash flow (DCF) analysis. The DCF is the grand-daddy of all crocks of shit. It's the technique that makes

MONKEY BUSINESS

Linda Lovelace look like a Catholic schoolgirl and Richard Nixon look like Abe Lincoln. In a DCF analysis, the banker projects the company's cash flow for a bunch of years into the future, then he figures out what all those future cash flows are worth today.

The DCF analysis is especially useful for valuing companies with no real business. A comp analysis, at least, requires that the company being valued have some revenues, cash flow, or earnings *today* in order to have any value. The DCF analysis does not. It finesses the problem by only attributing value on the basis of how the company is projected to do in the future.

The associate always takes the first pass at developing the DCF model. The associate has a quick rule of thumb—reality is irrelevant. The projections should always show revenues going up and expenses going down. That makes the DCF model spit out a big fat value for the business. Big fat values make CEO's happy.

When the associate finishes taking wild stabs in the dark on the DCF model, the more senior bankers will get involved. The senior vice president will decide that the revenue growth should be 11 percent per year instead of 8 percent. The vice president will have the associate take the gross margin up a percentage point. There are standard investment banking reasons why any given margin should improve. They always involve phrases like "operating efficiencies," "synergies," and "economies of scale." Everyone on the deal team will pull a few of these phrases out of the hope chest, and tweak the model a little bit so as to put his own special mark on it. It's like animals marking their territory. At the end of the day, there's only one immutable goal. The team has to reach the valuation target that the company will be happy with.

Over and over again associates tweak their DCF models. Over and over again they have models that show the company growing at a rate that, if continued, would allow the company being modeled to take over the entire planet within a generation. Over and over again the investors buy securities that are overpriced based on inflated and unrealistic expectations. For some reason, nobody ever learns. It's part of the magic of the DCF.

The Research Analysts

There is one final line of defense after the bankers have marked their valuation territory. This is the research analyst, the person who will be expected to write research reports and provide coverage of the company being valued. In theory, the research analyst is supposed to operate as a check on the overly optimistic bankers and is supposed to bring some incremental level of industry expertise to the entire valuation process. While some of them do, there are plenty of others who aren't truly independent anymore. These analysts operate as extensions of the investment banking operation, helping to win deals and generate business.

Research analysts have a mixed set of incentives. On the one hand, they need to maintain some credibility because long after the bankers have headed for the hills following a deal's sale, the analysts will continue to answer to the institutions whom they convinced to buy the deal in the first place. On the other hand, the bank is in the business of making money, and the investment banking fees associated with underwriting and advisory business are a prime contributor to the institution's profitability. Anybody who isn't a contributor to that profitability isn't going to be kept around for long. There's always the distinct possibility that the "cooperative" analyst will become accustomed to eating steak tartare at The Palm, while the less cooperative analyst will end up eating Salisbury steak at the Denny's buffet.

During the underwriting process, bankers and analysts spend a lot of time working closely with each other. They work out the details of a company's valuation, and debate what approaches should be used to position and market the company to the prospective buyers. In this close, intense atmosphere it's not unheard of for a banker and an analyst to begin a deal as nothing more than professional acquaintances but end up as lovers or, better yet, serial copulators. DLJ certainly wasn't immune to these semiprofessional trysts, and Troob and I heard scuttlebutt regarding bawdy romps, and subsequent spread-eagle delight, in darkened boardrooms after hours between members of the banking teams and their research analyst counterparts.

The thing is, these romps had the potential to be seriously controversial. By design, bankers and analysts are professional adversaries. Typically it is the banker's responsibility to represent the client by pushing for the richest valuation, while it is the analyst's responsibility to defend the bank's integrity by putting out unbiased valuation reports and buy/sell recommendations. It wouldn't be *too* much of a stretch to imagine that a devious banker might dangle the promise of some steamy sex in front of an undersexed, eager-to-please research analyst in exchange for just a few extra multiple points on a valuation.

No matter what sort of research analyst support a banker has on a deal, it's always the market that drives pricing at the end of the day. The bankers can take management teams out on the road, and they can have their research analysts telling the accounts that a new issue should be priced at fifteen times earnings, but if the market is unwilling to sign off on the proposed valuation, the company won't get the pricing and valuation points that they've been led to believe they can get. Since the bankers are known to regularly overestimate the market's willingness to pay a given price for a new issue, the banker's job uncomfortably becomes one of trying to figure out how to explain to the client at pricing time that the bank is going to be delivering less money than they originally promised. That reality exists whether or not the banker on the account is banging the research analyst.

Overall, investment bankers spend hours, days, and sometimes weeks of their lives trying to figure out a way to show a company what a tremendous amount of money the company is worth. Then, if they're lucky enough to win the business, they spend more hours, days, and weeks slowly persuading the salespeople, the capital markets guys, and the markets that the company is truly worth the value that the bank attributed to it. It's like catching a fish and then trying to hold on to it with your bare hands. Some investment bankers are just better fishermen than others.

The Merry-go-round

No passion in the world is equal to the passion to alter someone else's draft.

—H. G. Wells

As Rolfe and I learned, the initial rounds of valuation work are just the first steps in the investment banking process. These inaugural throes are the opening volley in what will become a barrage of documentation necessary to, first, win the business and, second, process the deal. The associate has the task of making all the valuation numbers look good and the reasons behind the numbers look even better. The bullshit is set to accelerate. This is where the word processing department comes in.

Professional word processing is performed on any and every document an investment banking associate works on. When an associate does a pitch there is word processing, on internal memos there is word processing, on anything that leaves the investment bank to be seen by a client or prospective client there is word processing. Every sole, single, solitary document has to look good because this constitutes 90 percent of the associate's value-added. If an investment banking associate is able to word process effectively and efficiently, then he or she will be successful for at least four years on Wall Street.

The word processing portion of an associate's work is like the boxes of Raisinets at the movie theater. They're a staple across the country, no one likes them and they should be rid from the planet, but they're still there. Every associate detests word processing, but it's a necessary evil in investment banking.

Unfortunately, that necessary evil occupies 40 to 50 percent of an associate's time. This equates to anywhere between thirty to fifty hours per week of word processing per associate. The amount of time associates on Wall Street spend submitting documents to word processing, proofing the documents after they come back from word processing, reworking the drafts that were first submitted to correct some of the errors the word processing gnomes made, again submitting the documents to the word processing department, and then again proofing them is mind-boggling. After completing all this work, the vice president on the deal usually scraps 80 percent of the stuff the associate wrote, and the word processing cycle begins all over again.

At DLJ, the word processing department was staffed by a crew that seemed like they belonged on the brig of the good ship *Lollipop*. Rolfe boarded this ship many times and got to know the crew pretty well.

There were two basic groups of word processing people. The struggling actors and actresses and the Christopher Street fairies. All of them were temperamental and refused to take shit from any junior bankers. They were competent, but if they didn't like us it seemed as though they would make lots of mistakes on purpose. They would fuck up fonts and underlines and paragraphs and make any long night even longer. It wasn't easy to get on their good side. We had to be nice. We couldn't pay them off. They got paid about twenty bucks an hour and didn't give a flying fuck about money. They just wanted respect. It was a beautiful thing to watch a snot-nosed, stuck-up banker groveling to a guy who only wanted to go down to Christopher Street to pick up his boyfriend. Usually, the banker had a hard time relating to the word processing guy, but the word processing guy held the associates' balls in his hip pocket. To cross the word processing department was one of the worst mistakes any of us could make.

The best way to convey the futility of the word processing merry-go-round is through an illustration. But keep in mind this won't give full justice to the actual pain inflicted upon us by the word processing merry-go-round. We had to deal with this crap on a daily basis for just about everything we did.

An Example

On most pitches, when the initial valuation work is complete, the vice president tells the associate, "Take a crack at writing the executive summary." The executive summary is used to state the business that the company being pitched is involved in, and to tell the company that the investment bank making the pitch should be chosen to lead manage the deal. The rest of the pitch book shows why the investment bank doing the pitching should get that business.

"Taking a crack" at something in investment banking is like jerking off on yourself in the corner. It's bad enough that you've got to go and jerk off in the corner, but to add insult to injury you have to do it on yourself and it's a mess to clean up. The associate works on the executive summary and sends it through the word processing department. When it comes back, the vice president rewrites the executive summary and the associate sends it back through the word processing department, gets it back, and proofs it. Then the senior vice president rewrites the executive summary once again, the associate sends it back through the word processing department, gets it back, and proofs it. Eventually, the managing director rewrites the executive summary for the fourth time. You get the idea. The shit continues ad nauseam. Rolfe experienced this clusterfuck firsthand while he was writing an executive summary for a telecommunications company:

I wrote

CELLULARNET, INC. (THE "COMPANY") IS A LEADING PROVIDER OF CELLULAR PERIPHERALS WITH OVER $150 MILLION IN REVENUES AND A STRONG BACKLOG.

THE COMPANY IS PLANNING TO RAISE $100 MILLION TO PURCHASE COMPANIES IN THE CELLULAR TELECOMMUNICATIO INDUSTRY THAT WILL PROVE TO BE SYNERGISTIC.

DONALDSON, LUFKIN & JENRETTE IS ABLE TO EFFECTIVELY RAISE EQUITY OR DEBT FOR THE COMPANY AND BELIEVES THAT THE ROLL-UP STRATEGY THAT THE COMPANY IS EMPLOYING IS AN EXCITING STORY THAT DLJ WILL BE ABLE TO SELL TO INVESTORS

DLJ IS ONE OF THE PREMIER INVESTMENT BANKING HOUSES ON WALL STREET AND THE COMPANY WILL HAVE THE FULL SUPPORT OF MR. Howard Isenstein, THE NUMBER ONE TELECOMMUNICATIONS ANALYST ON WALL STREET.

DLJ IS THE PREMIER INVESTMENT BANK IN SELLING "STORY COMPANIES."

I walked up to the word processing department so that I could submit the document and get the ball rolling. Fausto was sitting there looking haggard when I walked in. Fausto was the Grand Poo-Bah of word processing. He was responsible for allocating all the work in the word processing department. I don't know why he looked so haggard. Maybe he'd had a long night at the Vault, a sex club, or maybe he was just tired. I wrote out a word processing ticket and clipped my handwritten document to it. I was neither nice nor mean to Fausto. But I think he thought that I was a little curt with him so he gave my job to Elena. Elena was a beauty, but she hardly spoke English and I believed that if she tilted her head too far to one side pebbles would fall out. Two hours later a document came back that looked like this:

Executive Summary

Cellular-net, Inc. (the "Company") is a leeding provdier of cellulare periherals company with over $150 million in revenues and a strong backlo.

The Copany is planning to raise $1000 million to purchas companies in the cellul telecommunicationss industry that will be. Don aldson, Luskin & Jenrette is able to effectively raise equity or debt for Company and believes that the roll-up strategie.

DLJ is one of the premier investment banking nhouses on Wall Street and the Copany will have the full support of Mr. Howerd Isensteen, the number one telecommunications analyst on Wall Street.

DLH is the premier investment bank in selling "Story Companies.".

I was pissed off. I made the corrections and submitted the marked-up document. I spoke to Fausto very nicely and told him that I appreciated all his hard work throughout the year and that I really didn't know how he did it. This made him happy. An hour later a perfect document came out.

The following day I gave this "first crack" at the executive summary to the vice president and he scrapped it. He marked it up like this:

MONKEY BUSINESS

Make sure this is <u>Times New Roman</u> font.

one font size larger

<u>**Executive Summary**</u> *the foremost*

underline

MM

Cellularnet, Inc. (the "Company") is ~~a leading~~ provider of cellular

peripherals with over $150 ~~million~~ in revenues, and a strong backlog *and long term contracts.*

stet The Company is planning to raise $100 ~~million~~ to purchase *MM*

~~companies~~ *industr.* in the cellular telecommunications industry that will prove to

be synergistic. ~~Donaldson, Lufkin & Jenrette is~~ able to effectively raise *Company's*

~~equity~~ *debt* or ~~debt~~ for the Company and believes that the roll-up strategy ~~that~~

equity ~~the Company is employing~~ is ~~an exciting~~ story that DLJ will be able to sell.

~~to investors.~~ *a*

DLJ is ~~one of~~ the premier investment banking ~~houses~~ on Wall

Street and the Company will have the full support of ~~Mr.~~ Howard

Isenstein, ~~the~~ number one telecommunications analyst on Wall Street.

DLJ is ~~the premier investment bank~~ in selling "Story Companies."

DLJ   *DLJ's*   *uniquely qualified*   *will be*

After he was done hacking at the executive summary it
was about 9:00 P.M. I submitted it to word processing. Inevitably what came out of word processing was not perfect, so I had to resubmit it.

I waited for it to come out of word processing and got
it back around 11:30 P.M. The vice president asked me to
fax the finished product to him after it went through

word processing. So I faxed it. Of course, he was awake because he only had left the office a half hour ago. When he answered the phone I heard his TV in the background. There was a familiar theme song playing and I was pretty sure that it was the *Robin Byrd Show*'s "Baby, Let Me Bang Your Box." I vowed to myself that if I ever made it to vice president I'd go ahead and spring for either Spice or the Playboy Channel, so that I could at least watch some quality hoochie while my associates faxed me pitch books.

The vice president made more changes and faxed them back to me and asked me to have it to him by the morning. I could have either submitted his changes to word processing, waited for them to be done, checked them, and left the finished product on his desk, or I could have submitted the changes, gone home for some shut-eye, and then come to work early the next morning and checked the job that word processing had done. Either way I wouldn't have gotten more than five hours of sleep.

The next day the draft clawed its way up one level in the hierarchy to the senior vice president. The senior vice president took a look at the executive summary and made his changes as such:

Executive Summary

Cellularnet, Inc. (the "Company") is the ~~foremost~~ *leading* provider of

cellular peripherals with over $150 ~~MM~~ *million* in revenues, *and a* strong backlog, ~~and~~

~~long term contracts,~~

The Company is looking to raise $100 ~~MM~~ to purchase companies

in the cellular telecommunications industry that ~~will prove to be~~ *are* synergistic. ~~DLJ~~ will be able to effectively raise debt or equity for the

Company and believes that the Company's roll-up strategy is a story that

DLJ will be able to sell ← to investors.

DLJ is the premier investment bank on Wall Street and the

Company will have the full support of Howard Isenstein, ~~DLJ's~~ number

one telecommunications analyst on Wall Street.

DLJ is uniquely qualified in selling story companies.

the

Donaldson, Lufkin & Jenrette ("DLJ")

Add a chart of DLJ's ability to sell story companies.
Add color graph of DLJ's ability to do equity or
debt offerings for telecommunications companies.

The senior vice president I was working for loved graphs and charts. He had already mastered the art of written bullshit in the pitch books and was pursuing a loftier goal of impressing companies with color graphs and charts. It was truly amazing.

I got the marked-up document back around 6:00 P.M. and the word processing marathon began again. I put the changes through word processing and when I was done the vice president wanted to see the finished product to make sure that it was OK to send to the senior vice president. This checking and double checking is a staple of investment banking. I then faxed the document to the senior vice president at his house. He made all these changes to the other changes and faxed them back to me. I sent it through word processing and proofed it. It inevitably wasn't right, so I had to send it through word processing again. Then the vice president wanted it faxed back to his apartment, and he made even more changes. By this time it was midnight and the ridiculousness seemed like it would never end.

The next day the managing director looked at the executive summary and changed it again. His edits looked like this:

Executive Summary

Cellularnet, Inc. (the "Company") is the leading provider of cellular peripherals with over $150 million in revenues and a strong backlog.

The Company is ~~looking~~ *planning* to raise $100 million to purchase companies in the cellular telecommunications industry that ~~are~~ synergistic. *WiLL Be* Donaldson, Lufkin and Jenrette ("DLJ") will be able to effectively raise equity or debt for the Company and believes that the Company's roll-up strategy is ~~a~~ story that DLJ will be able to sell to investors.

DLJ is *one of* the premier investment bank *ing houses* on Wall Street and the Company will have the full support of Howard Isenstein, the number one telecommunications analyst on Wall Street.

DLJ is ~~uniquely qualified~~ *the premier investment bank* in selling story companies. *an exciting*

Put chart in red, graph in violet and yellow.
Make sure that graph is not red and that
chart is not in yellow. Change to twelve
font and make sure bold is fourteen font.
Make boxes around graphs and make them bold.

This managing director loved presentation. Colors had to be right, fonts easy to read, bolding clear, and underlining thick. I sent these changes through word processing, showed it to the senior vice president who touched it up a bit, sent it through word processing again, showed it to the vice president, who changed a couple of nits like commas and fonts, and sent it through word processing yet again. Then I faxed the document to the home of the managing director. It was about 6:00 P.M. He made some changes and faxed the document back to me. I sent it through word processing and faxed it to the senior vice president. He put his stamp of acceptance on it and then I sent it to the vice president and he also stamped it OK. Changes had gone back and forth and forty-eight hours of my life were consumed, and the document hadn't changed substantially from its original form except for the addition of a couple of graphs and charts.

Executive Summary

Cellularnet, Inc. (the "Company") is the leading provider of cellular peripherals with over $150 million in revenues and a strong backlog.

The Company is planning to raise $100 million to purchase

companies in the cellular telecommunications industry that will be synergistic. Donaldson, Lufkin and Jenrette ("DLJ") will be able to effectively raise equity or debt for the Company and believes that the Company's roll-up strategy is an exciting story that DLJ will be able to sell to investors.

DLJ is one of the premier investment banking houses on Wall Street and the Company will have the full support of Howard Isenstein, the number one telecommunications analyst on Wall Street.

DLJ is the premier investment bank in selling "Story Companies."

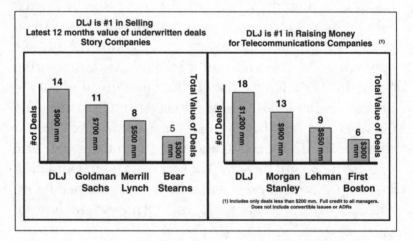

So, when is the word processing of a document really done? The answer is twelve hours before the time of the meeting with the company. If a pitch to a company was in a week, then the vice president, senior vice president, and managing director would come up with more charts, graphs, and drivel to put into the pitch until there were just twelve hours till showtime. When it's just twelve hours till showtime the associate has to put the pitch books into production.

Next stop: copy center.

The Bottleneck

*The trouble with being punctual is that there's
nobody there to appreciate it.*

This is a chapter about the copy center. It's not about
big, fat investment banking salaries. It's not about stocks
or bonds. It's not about leveraged buyouts or parties
where overpaid old men look for love from their secretaries. It's about the copy center. It's not intuitive, but it's
what matters. Before Troob and I ever became bankers,
if somebody had asked us what the most important areas
in the investment bank were we would have said "the
trading floor" or "the institutional sales department."
Maybe we would have said "the golf course." Under no
circumstances, though, would we ever have said "the
copy center." It wouldn't have made sense. We were
bankers. We did deals. We didn't make copies.

We learned quickly.

Our success, or lack thereof, in banking would be de-
pendent on a long row of Xerox copiers operated by a
platoon of patriotic Puerto Ricans. They were the revo-

lutionaries, capable of being either our greatest allies or our most heinous enemies. To get on their bad side was to commit hari-kari. A banker with no copy-making abilities is impotent, so the militants in the copy center became our best friends. There were times when we would have given a round of blowjobs to the entire copy center staff if they'd requested it. We would have done it with a big smile on our faces, and we would have swallowed. Anything for the copy center guys.

The word processing department is the brains of the operation. The brains are no good, though, without a pair of hands. A genius can think up brilliant ideas all day, but if he can't make them happen, then the ideas aren't any better than a clock with no key to wind it up. The copy center is that key. The copy center takes the ideas put on paper by the word processing department and makes copies of these ideas. The copy center disseminates the ideas so as to make them come alive. The copy center is the pair of hands that turns the brain's ideas into something real. It's where the ideas become actual, tangible things—big fat stacks of paper and pitch books that say "Donaldson, Lufkin & Jenrette" on the spine.

Some investment bankers measure their success by the amount of paper that they generate. They're known as the Paper Bankers. For the Paper Bankers, more is better. Paper Bankers make copies of financial statements, models, and research reports and pass them out to everybody, even people who aren't connected with their deal. That helps them cover their ass, and keeps people from screaming, "Why the fuck didn't you tell me about this!" later on. Sometimes the Paper Bankers don't even need a reason to make copies. They'll just send a stack of miscellaneous stuff to the copy center and get fifty copies made because they haven't gotten many copies done lately. It soothes their savage beast within.

At DLJ, the copy center wasn't actually run by DLJ employees. It was inside of DLJ, though, and anybody who wasn't paying attention probably thought that it was actually a part of DLJ, but it wasn't. The copy center function was outsourced to a service company that ran copy centers at a bunch of big companies in New York. Many bankers are rude to anybody who they think is making less money than them, and that includes all of the service people who help them get their jobs done. A lot of the DLJ bankers, though, figured that they could be *extra* rude to the copy center people since they weren't actually company employees. It was like they thought that they could be as rude as they wanted to, and if the copy center people lodged complaints, then the banker would threaten their big boss—"Those goddamned copy center employees of yours, if they don't get a better fucking attitude we'll take the service contract away." The good bankers didn't usually make that mistake more than once.

The copy center is where the bottlenecks always pop up in the pitch book–making process. Bottlenecks occur in word processing, but not to the magnitude of copy center bottlenecks. In word processing the fonts inevitably get screwed up or underlines are botched. Although annoying and time-consuming, all of these problems are easily fixed. Also, during the word processing stage the associate feels time pressure, but nothing like what the associate feels during the copy center stage.

By the time the copy center stage is reached, the associate knows that the pitch is going to occur the next morning. We believe that we're accurate when we say that never in the history of investment banking has a pitch book been sent to the copy center twenty-four hours in advance. If a banker has the time to dicker around with a document, then he will. So a banker will never allow a pitch book to be complete before it absolutely, positively has to be complete. And that is exactly twelve hours before the presentation of the pitch book to the prospective client.

Like clockwork, a junior banker with the most important pitch of his life will walk into the copy center at 2 A.M. with a pitch book ready and tell the guy behind the counter, "I need twenty copies by seven A.M." and the copy center guy behind the counter will say, "Join the crowd, my brother. Join the crowd." The copy center guy will then point to a huge stack of other pitch books that have to be made by 7 A.M. and tell the banker, "You'll be lucky if we get it done by noon tomorrow. Sorry."

Now, understand that it's not like the banker can run out to Kinkos to get the job done. This is a major production process—colors, bindings, inserts, acetates—the copy center guys, for all their shortcomings, are the only ones capable of cranking out these pitch book behemoths. Taking a job like this to Kinkos would be like trying to clean up an offshore oil spill with a dish sponge.

So at this point, the interaction can take one of two potential paths.

Path#1: The associate flies into an immediate rage. "You fucking idiot! This has to be done by SEVEN FUCK-ING A.M.! Do you read me? Comprende? My job, this here job, takes priority! This is the biggest goddamned deal this fucking bank has pitched in the past decade. Do you understand what that means? Do you have any understanding outside of that miserable little existence that you call a life what I'm telling you here? Of course you don't. Who the fuck am I fooling? Look, get this through your thick head—THIS JOB TAKES PRIORITY! Now goddamn it, get it done by seven A.M.!"

This is exactly what the copy center guy wants to hear. This is precisely the kind of respect that a guy making seven bucks an hour figures he deserves. An apoplectic born-with-a-silver-spoon-in-his-mouth asshole from Westchester County is telling the Pride of the Barrio that he's a fucking idiot. And, moreover, he's telling him that he's an idiot while concurrently begging for his help. The rich honkey banker has just made it clear through his very rage that he's in a pickle. Nobody gets that mad about something unless their ass is in a sling.

The world is an unjust place, and the inequities inherent in Wall Street's money game push the outer limits of that injustice. The copy center, though, is the one place on Wall Street where the little man has his day. When confronted with a livid banker demanding service, the copy center guy gets to give the rich pricks their comeuppance. It's a kangaroo court for assholes, and the copy center guy is judge, jury, and executioner. The copy center guy can turn to the raging banker and tell him, "So sorry, but your job doesn't have priority here. This is my shop, this is my decision. Your job'll get done when I get to it." The banker has no choice. He has no idea how to make copies, especially color copies, and he has no idea how to bind a document. He has no idea where the dividers are, the blue sheets, the covers, the acetates, the back covers, or anything else. Unlike word processing, which any half decent associate could do himself if push came to shove, the associate is unable to do the copy center guy's job. No way. The associate is screwed. He's up shit's creek without a paddle. The associate has no choice but to surrender to his destiny. The associate has to suck up his pride and develop a new approach. He must head down path number two.

Path #2: Money talks. The associate relies on his skills of negotiation and bribery to move the job to the head of the priority list. This isn't as easy as it sounds, because the sort of cold cash payments to the copy center guys that would provide incentive enough for them to push all other jobs aside are only allowed at holiday time. At all other times of the year, the bribery has to be more subtle and the associate has to be more crafty in the approach. The senior bankers don't understand this part of the game. A managing director has no idea how to build a relationship with the copy center guys. The managing director may be at home in the corporate boardroom talking turkey with eager CEOs with deal fever, but when it comes time to get a priority rush on some pitch books from Julio in the copy center they're useless. They have to rely on their lieutenants—the associates.

The good associate recognizes from day one the value of good copy center relationships. The good associate greases the wheels of progress, even when there isn't an imminent need for express service in the copy center. The good associate orders up five or six pizza pies for dinner every couple of weeks and sends two of the pies up to the copy center. The good associate runs around the corner to the deli once a month, picks up a case of beer, and delivers it to the copy center guys. The good associate stuffs a twenty-dollar bill into the pockets of the key copy center guys at Christmas time and engenders some goodwill, or he stuffs a fifty into those same pockets and engenders twice as much goodwill. And then, when the need for express copy service actually arises, the good associate finds his job pushed to the head of the line while the badly mannered bitter associate spews forth futile vitriol, and gets the job returned three hours after his deadline. One hand washes the other.

The copy center is a factory. It's full of big industrial-size copy equipment, the kind of heavy machinery that's not supposed to be operated by anybody under the influence of NyQuil. The copiers in the copy center are living, breathing creatures capable of tearing off a thousand copies in the time it takes to light a cigarette, and stapling those copies before the first soothing fix of nicotine hits the bloodstream. These aren't copiers where you punch in the number of copies you want and hit a big green "COPY" button. These are copiers with a command console that looks like something out of a nuclear submarine. They're scary, and the only people who know how to make them work are the copy center guys.

Copiers aren't the only equipment in the copy center. There are also big industrial hole punches, heavy-duty paper cutters, monster scissors, gigantic stapling machines, and huge, intricate binding machines. The binding machines have a big steel handle on the side. When you pull the handle, two rows of metal jaws pull the plastic binding apart so that the copy center guy can slip the pages into the binding. Like birth stirrups for a newborn book. The copy center's not the kind of place that you want to be caught naked in. There's too much opportunity for something to get caught, twisted, pulled, or cut off.

There are a million variations on the basic black-and-white copy available in the copy center. There are standard copies and there are color copies. There's white paper, beige paper, and blue paper. There's velo binding, staple binding, and spiral binding. There are horizontal covers and vertical covers, with and without little windows. There are acetates and back covers that are green or black, with the DLJ logo printed horizontally or vertically. The permutations are limitless. Copies can be grouped, collated, stapled, or hole-punched. The copies can be delivered to somebody's office or picked up. A banker can give the copy center a single sheet of paper and get back a copy of that sheet on laminated bond paper, bound into a booklet with an expensive-looking green cover with "Donaldson, Lufkin & Jenrette" embossed in gold letters. It makes that one sheet of paper look very impressive. That's what making the pitch books is all about—making mundane information look impressive.

When a job gets delivered to the copy center the associate has to fill out a requisition form. The requisition form includes spaces for all of the options. It looks like a test form for the SATs. It's important for the associate to mark the requisition forms very carefully, because the copy center guys do exactly what the requisition forms request. They aren't there to think, they're there to do. If an associate gets a job back, and is convinced that the copy center has screwed it up, he'll march into the copy center and start yelling. His copies are screwed up and he wants to see some heads roll. The copy center guy behind the counter will look beneath the counter for the requisition form. Most of the time, he'll pull it out and, with a big smile on his face, show the junior banker that the form was marked wrong. That makes the copy center guy feel good. If the copy center guy says that he can't find the requisition form, that's the secret code for "We fucked it up." The copy center will never openly admit that they fucked it up, though. They know how to cover their ass.

Troob knew how frustrating the copy center could be. Part of the reason for that was that he did a lot of work for Jack Gatorski, and Gator loved to get copies made. Troob once told me that he thought Gator had a strange thing for copies. It went way beyond just being a Paper Banker. He swore that he'd once seen Gator get a big stack of copies back from the copy center that were still warm, and that Gator had closed his eyes, leaned back in his chair, and started stroking the warm paper.

Gator was crazy when it came to getting copies made. He especially loved color copies. Charts, graphs, maps, pictures, he loved all that shit. Whenever I did a pitch for him we'd sit down to run through a draft of the pitch book and I'd be saying to myself over and over, "Please, God, not too many color copies. Please, Lord, not too many color copies. Just don't let him ask for too many color copies; please, please, please." My supplications were never answered. The good Lord never came to my rescue.

Gator's penchant for color copies always overcame whatever practical sensibilities he may have had.

The problem with the color copies was that they
gummed up the entire pitch book–making process. With
all the state-of-the-art high-technology equipment that
they had up in the copy center, the process of actually assembling the pitch books was barbaric. The black-and-
white copies got made on one machine, and the color
copies got made on another, much slower machine.
Whichever copy center guy was putting the books together then had to collate everything by hand. The copy
center guy would have fifty piles, each one a separate
copy of the book, spread out all over the room and he'd
be pulling copies off the color copier and sticking them
into each of the piles where they were supposed to go.
Well, if you've only got three or four color pages in each
book then there isn't all that much room for error, but in
one of Gator's books there were usually more color pages
than black-and-white pages, which meant that no matter
how conscientious the copy center guy was, chances
were that something was gonna get screwed up. Layer on
top of that the fact that the copy center guy was only
making seven dollars an hour so he didn't usually give a
fuck, and he had twenty other bankers calling him every
fifteen minutes to ask him when their more straightfor-
ward black-and-white jobs were gonna be done, and it
was a recipe for disaster.

What it all meant was that every time I got a set of pitch
books back from the copy center, I had to page through
every single copy by hand to make sure that all the pages
were in order, that all the copies had been made on the
same kind of paper, and that some random crap hadn't

made its way into my pitch book from somebody else's pitch book. It was like doing piecework for an Eighth Avenue sweatshop. When I did find the inevitable mistakes, I couldn't bitch and moan about them to the guy in the copy center who had screwed things up, because he'd just end up getting pissed off and fucking me over the next time I needed a favor. In fact, I usually had to take the books back up to the copy center and act like the mistakes were my fault, and beg and plead for the copy center guys to fix the books so that I could meet the deadline, which was usually within ten hours. The copy center guys hated it when I brought back jobs that they thought they'd seen the last of, so I usually had to provide them with some extra incentive to make things right. My big sales tool was lap dances down at Shenanigans. I'd offer to buy the guys a few lap dances each, and they'd usually take care of me.

There was one time when I got my pitch books back at 4:30 in the morning. The copy center guy who had just finished them up had taken off for home as soon as he was done and a new copy center guy was on call. Well, as usual, the pitchbooks were all fucked up. I had to be on a flight for Cincinnati with the books in three and a half hours so I had a little bit of a problem. To explain the problem to the new guy and go over what he'd have to do to fix it would take hours, and to do it myself was impossible because I didn't know how to use the machines. So a fifty-dollar bill emerged from my pocket and two pepperoni double cheese pizzas helped to cajole my new-found friend in the copy center—Manuel—to help me go through each book, book by book, and fix them.

Manuel and I went through each book and through

both pizzas. First, each book needed a new page twelve. Fourteen books and each one needed page twelve changed. Then the back cover needed to be put on each book, then page thirty-four needed to be replaced by a color graph. Page seven had to be removed and a new page seven had to be inserted. Pages twenty-four and twenty-five were inverted so they had to be switched around, and page forty-two was behind page forty-three, so that needed to be fixed. All of the books needed to be checked again.

It was 6:30 A.M. when we got done, or so I thought. When I checked the books some were still fucked up. The monotony of making the same changes in every book was mind-numbing and Manuel and I were incapable of keeping all the changes straight. So, back we went to the spiral binder and copy machine to fix the mistakes. Basically, everyone else's jobs got screwed, but I had forked out fifty bones and two pizzas. At 7:30 we were done. I had half an hour to get to the airport. I had packed a bag the night before and left it in the office knowing that something like this would happen. It inevitably did. I ran to a cab with fourteen pitch books, an overnight bag, my briefcase, a cell phone, and no sleep.

For the past year, I'd been dating this girl Marjorie. Since she lived in Chicago, we had been doing the long-distance thing. Lately, things between us had started to get more serious. I called her from the cab and left a message on her answering machine saying hello and "I'm sorry." I felt bad. The previous weekend she had come to New York to visit me and had ended up sitting in my apartment the whole time because I had to work. Thank God for 1-800-FLOWERS.

MONKEY BUSINESS

In the cab I checked the books and ten were good, two were slightly messed up, and two were completely fucked up. I took one of the messed up ones for myself and prayed that after giving one good one to Gator there wouldn't be more than nine guys from the company who wanted pitch books. I dumped the two fucked-up pitch books in the garbage at La Guardia.

I made it to the gate at the airport just as they were about to stop letting people onto the plane. I made my way to my seat, and there was Gator reading the *Wall Street Journal* and looking fresh as a spring daisy. He glanced up at me and said, "It's a good goddamned thing you made it, because if you hadn't there would've been hell to pay. You look like shit. You're an embarrassment."

Gator and I had gone through a lot over the previous year. I had a grudging respect for him. I can remember him being a good guy—at times—but this time he was an asshole. Maybe the pressure to perform pushed him to be a fuckhead. Whatever the case, I almost yanked him up, pulled his trousers down, and shoved that whole bag full of pitch books straight up his ass.

There wasn't a lot of love lost between Troob and Gator after this incident. I think that in another life they might have been friends. They might have enjoyed each other's company. They weren't in another life, though. They were in a life that involved color copies. For the time being that made them enemies.

The Holiday Party

*Between two evils, I always pick the one
I never tried before.*

—Mae West

The first weeks and months that Troob and I spent at DLJ as full-time associates were painful. The constant pitching, the endless valuation shenanigans, the long nights spent kissing the asses of the coterie of word processing pixies, and the gifts to the copy center Barrio. These exercises in futility clearly weren't the activities that a young investment banker's wet dreams were made of. We continued to hold out hope, though. Hope that we'd turn into deal doers and rainmakers. Hope that we'd have a compensation review session where the head of our department would bestow upon us a zillion-dollar bonus. Hope that John Chalsty, DLJ's CEO, would call us into his office and tell us, "You're my guys. I need you. I'm gonna build the business around you." Selective perception was still operating at full tilt, and for the most part we were still seeing and hearing mainly those things that helped fuel the dream.

MONKEY BUSINESS

Deals came and went. Different companies, different needs, different industries, and different deal teams. The only real constant in our daily lives was that we walked into the office every morning knowing that our day was going to be completely different than the day before had been. We learned to expect the unexpected, and became accustomed to operating as if absolutely everything we worked on was critical to the future welfare of the free world. We were learning how to operate in a pressure cooker without getting basted.

Although each day was different there was a broad sort of daily routine that we all followed. Being a junior banker meant being a night person. That, in turn, meant that none of the associates usually rolled into the office before about 9 A.M. Inevitably, when we did roll in, there would be something that needed checking. Mornings were checking time. Maybe it was something that we'd left to get turned through word processing on our way out the door the night before. Maybe one of the analysts had built a new financial model and left a copy on our desks. Whatever it was, we'd spend the morning going through it line by line to make sure we weren't going to get our heads chewed off as a result of somebody else's screwup.

The checking routine usually lasted until around lunchtime. Now, at most jobs lunch divides the day into two. There's "before lunch" and there's "after lunch." Once the majority of corporate America has made it through lunch, it's a downhill ride. Investment banking doesn't work like that. An investment banking associate has four parts to his day: "before lunch," "after lunch," "after dinner," and "after midnight."

Lunchtime at DLJ meant that the day was just getting started. We usually ate lunch at our desks. That was the low-risk way to keep our heads down. Sometimes, if we were feeling adventurous, we'd round up a crew of our comrades and head down to the cafeteria. Eating in the cafeteria was a dangerous game, though. The big risk was that Doug Franken, the managing director in charge of staffing, would see us there and interpret our presence as a sign of sloth. It was a game of Russian roulette whenever Franken caught us down in the cafeteria. We knew that one of us would end up having to take a bullet for the team, we just never knew which one of us it would be.

The "after lunch" part of the day was usually taken up with meetings. Meetings with clients. Meetings with potential clients. Meetings with deal teams. Meetings with lawyers and accountants. If we couldn't meet in person, we'd do it by conference call. We had deal team meetings before the client meetings to figure out what we were going to talk about at the client meetings. We had deal team meetings after the client meetings to talk about what we'd just gotten done talking about. As associates, we grew to hate meetings because meetings were the places where little ideas capable of generating huge amounts of work were spawned. The words "I've got an idea . . ." were anathema to us. When we heard them, our hearts dropped into our loafers.

There were some managing directors who didn't confine their idea generation only to meetings. Some of them preferred to perpetrate evil through the voice mail system. The Widow used to use the voice mail system to avoid human contact altogether. He would sit in his lair and create voice mails full of new ideas, and then send them to my mail box without ever actually calling me. Many an afternoon I sat at my desk and saw the message light go on without the phone ever ringing. Whenever that happened, I knew that it was one of the Widow's insidious mail bombs.

It was tough to get any real work done while the senior bankers were still around. That's why so many days included "after dinner" and "after midnight." The managing directors usually took off by dinnertime, which meant that the phones would finally stop ringing and that we'd be able to get cranking on the latest fire drill. Before we did, though, we had a nightly routine whereby Troob, Slick, and I would corral three of our other comrades-in-arms for a tête-à-tête. These three other regulars were Isaac "Big Man" Johnson, who worked in the high-yield group and who had once walked straight into a wall as a result of sleep deprivation; Mike "Wings" Roganstahl, who always dressed to the nines and thought he worked in the merchant banking group but in reality was a generalist peon like the rest of us; and our friend Deepak "Tubby" Verma from the M&A group whose fat gut and tiny ass usually made his suit pants look like an opera diva's muumuu. Each night we would commandeer a conference room, order dinner, and spend at least a half hour crapping all over everybody who'd crapped on us earlier that day.

Dinner was full of insults and profanity. Nobody was called by their real name. Everybody was "pricko," "fuck-face," or "jackass." We reveled in insulting each other's dignity. The free-for-all at dinner was the glue that held us all together. On a nightly basis, it gave us the opportunity to try to convince each other that the dream was

still alive, while we collectively came to the dawning realization that we were investment banking automatons
marching in lockstep to the same inevitable fate. Dinner
was our group therapy.

Dinner wasn't just five nights a week. We were usually
there on weekends, too. Every night at dinner there was
one thing we could rely on—Slick's dinner order. Slick
ordered the same thing every night: penne bolognese,
tiramisu, and two small bottles of San Pellegrino
sparkling water. The rest of us would mix it up a little,
but not Slick. He never deviated. In our first year at DLJ,
Slick was probably on the road a total of fifty days. There
were probably a total of another twenty days that fell on
weekends when he was out of the office at dinnertime.
That means that we sat in a conference room watching
Slick down penne bolognese, tiramisu, and two little bottles of San Pellegrino sparkling water 290 times in that
first year. That's a lot of bolognese. Troob and I think
that penne bolognese was Slick's emotional anchor. No
matter what happened during the day, Slick always knew
that the penne bolognese would be waiting for him at
night. It was like a girlfriend, only better, because the
penne bolognese was always on time, didn't get mad at
him for being at work all night, and didn't yell at him
when he had to cancel a vacation.

"After dinner" was creation time. God may have created first and rested later, but an investment banking associate rests first—at dinner—and creates later; 8 P.M. to
midnight was prime time. We drafted pitch books, built
models, updated comps, and wrote memos. Computers
cranked, pencils flew, and steam came out of our ears. It
was the one time of the day when we felt like we were ac-

tually moving ahead and weren't either treading water or slowly sinking. If we were lucky, if the fire drill wasn't so urgent that something had to be created for the following morning, we'd be able to head home by midnight. Often, though, that wasn't possible.

If the fire drill was real, then the day rolled into the "after midnight" segment. After midnight the associate became a conductor. The creation of the raw material was complete, but the transformation of that raw material into something presentable was only beginning. After midnight the associate stepped up to the riser, raised a baton, and brought the orchestra to life. Word processing, copy center, and the young analyst monkey boys each played their part in the symphony. Some movements played fast and furious, others slow and serene, but the music rarely stopped. If it did, the associate would slip into an adjustable chair and close his eyes for a few moments of bliss until the music began again. The after-midnight segment could end at 2 A.M., 5 A.M., or it could end at 8 A.M. All we could hope for was that it would end at least a few hours before the routine was all set to begin again the next morning. Spending two, or even three days straight on the Ferris wheel with no sleep wasn't easy.

So with all this crap, all this garbage that we were piling through, what was the bottom line? A lot of anguish, never saying no, and about 100 hours a week spent in the trenches. There are only 168 hours in a week, and working 100 of them meant that we had to work every day, seven days a week. Taking corporate car rides home, showering in the mornings, and searching for our lost identities before we went to bed at night enveloped 20 hours of our week. Making a lame attempt at a social life engulfed 15 hours of the week. So that left 33 hours of our week for sleeping. That meant an average of four and a half hours a night. So with this little sleep, there are two obvious questions: (1) Were we productive? and (2) Weren't we constantly tired?

The answers to these questions are simple. We shouldn't have been productive, but we were, and yes—we were always tired. Investment banks are savvy. DLJ was no exception. It knew how to squeeze every drop of productivity out of our little bodies. The investment banks keep the climate perfect for an around-the-clock working environment. Within DLJ the lighting and air-conditioning systems were like a Las Vegas casino. The lights were bright and fluorescent. The air was kept cold, crisp, and dry. It always felt like the middle of the day, even at five in the morning. When we finally left our investment banking casino and stepped into the outside world we came crashing down. But while we were inside the walls we were as productive as little beavers building a dam. We scurried around like lab rats in a cage and were full of nervous energy. Like casino gamblers, we had a lot to give and expectations of much in return.

DLJ tried to lessen the pain of this grind through the liberal application of its own corporate narcotic— money. Unlike a lot of other firms, DLJ was clearly with the program. What that meant was that DLJ didn't nickel-and-dime us to death on our expenses; the firm knew how to keep our appetites whetted. When we had business dinners they were always first class—the 21 Club, Aureole, Le Cirque 2000. When we traveled, the charges didn't get questioned. The firm knew that extravagant tastes were the best defense that they could ever hope to have against our departure. And when it came to purely social events, the firm threw just enough corporate clambakes to keep the junior bankers from engaging in open rebellion.

The premier DLJ party each year was the holiday party. When DLJ threw its holiday party it was no joke. We're not talking about paper tablecloths, folding chairs, and spiked punch in plastic cups. The DLJ holiday party was the real deal. It was an opportunity for the top dogs to loosen the purse strings, pull out a few gold coins, and impart a brief evening of unrestricted hedonistic pleasure to the masses.

When DLJ threw a party it was always done with style and with no regard for expense, but the holiday party was special for another reason. The myriad dinners, receptions, and dances that we were becoming accustomed to as associates at DLJ were the exclusive province of the bankers, brokers, salespeople, and traders. For many of the thousands of DLJ employees, however, the ability to live large on the firm's nickel was nothing but a fantasy. Once each year, at the holiday party, that changed. Every secretary, banking assistant, and receptionist was given five hours in which to taste the good life. It was an opportunity for them to develop a sense for just how much money an investment bank was capable of generating, and how well paid those higher up the food chain actually were.

In the weeks leading up to our first holiday blowout, the senior associates schooled us in the essentials of DLJ holiday party tradition. The rules were simple: (1) get stone drunk (2) avoid vomiting on any managing directors, and (3) make every effort to get a banking assistant into bed by the end of the night. As legend had it, fishing off the company pier at the holiday party was more than just a time-honored tradition, it was an obligation that was borne by all. For me, the possibility wasn't just a challenge, it was a burning necessity. To start out with, I'd never been a guy who got a lot of play from the ladies. Now that my every waking hour was spent at the office, short of paying a hooker, the only way I'd ever get any loving was if a generous BA decided to take pity on my sorry state and provide me access to her honey pot.

The DLJ holiday party was traditionally held in the middle of the week. This was far from ideal from my standpoint, since it inevitably meant that the day following the party would degenerate from a typically wretched banking day into one made all the more evil by a pounding headache and probable bouts of dry heaves in the toilet stalls. Those responsible for the welfare of greater DLJ, however, were convinced that holding the party in the middle of the week would somehow cause the riffraff to exercise some degree of moderation in their pursuit of joyous holiday spirits. They should have known better. In practice, the midweek scheduling merely meant that the majority of the junior bankers and support staff would be taken completely out of commission for the day following the party. They'd all be hunkered down in the stalls next to me noisily heaving their own innards out in supplication to the porcelain gods.

On the day of the party, the end of the working day for the secretaries and BAs signaled a mass migration to the women's bathroom for the grand transformation. Most of the women brought either cocktail dresses, evening wear, or other seductive clothing—all of which had the potential to cause me and the other sex-starved young bankers to work ourselves into a hormone-soaked lather. Due to the quantity of hair spray that was applied during the preparation period in each of the women's bathrooms, it was widely believed that the introduction of an open flame anywhere in the vicinity could prove deadly.

DLJ's holiday party was traditionally held at the Rainbow Room, a New York City landmark that takes up an entire floor of 30 Rockefeller Plaza and provides spectacular views of Manhattan. For one evening each year in mid-December it belonged to DLJ. The date of the holiday party was always known well in advance by everyone at the firm. In any sane profession every opportunity would have been made to clear the decks beforehand to enable everybody to attend. This was investment banking, though, and the masters of game theory were at work.

The more naive of my first-year associate classmates worked hard that week to finish the work that they knew would be coming due later in the week. In their ignorance, they actually believed that doing so would increase their chances of being able to attend the famed holiday party. If, in fact, all the other associates had been operating under the same set of assumptions, and if, in addition, the workload distribution among the associate class had been anything close to fair, the strategy probably would have been a good one. There were smarter, more devious forces at work, however.

The optimal work strategy leading up to the evening of the holiday party was really no different than the optimal work strategy on any other given day of the year, the stakes were just higher. The naked reality was that there was absolutely no benefit to making an effort to get work done ahead of time. There were two reasons for this.

First, completion of work well ahead of a deadline simply gave the senior bankers that much more time in which to demand changes or additions to the work that had already been completed. These requested changes were rarely necessary, but there was a pervasive and deep-rooted belief that more analysis was necessarily better analysis. Reams of analysis had become a security blanket for many of the bankers, who had lost the ability over the years to make informed assessments of what was *really* necessary to get a transaction done. Instead of spending fifteen minutes to draw upon their experience and determine what the critical path for closing a deal was, their reflex was to demand analyses covering every possible contingency in a deal. Delivering work significantly in advance of a deadline, then, usually just resulted in a bout of self-doubt for the senior banker on the deal, which inevitably just resulted in requests for unnecessary additional analysis and more trips back to the word processing department.

The second reason to avoid completion of any work ahead of time was a result of the vagaries of the staffing process. There was no monitoring of the parity of the workload among the associates. When a managing director needed to staff an associate on a deal, he would begin making the rounds to determine who had the capacity to take on additional work. It made no difference whether a given associate had done two all-nighters over the previous four days, all that mattered was what was on everybody's plate over the coming couple of days. So, completion of work ahead of schedule exposed the ambitious offender to the likelihood of having to take on even more work. It was an insidious catch-22.

These two realities resulted in a system in which the only way to maintain a manageable workload was to push everything off to the last possible minute. When a senior banker came looking for an associate, the only acceptable line of defense was to rattle off multiple last-minute projects that had to be completed and that would prevent the associate from working on any new assignments. The downside was a perpetual state of acute urgency that was contributing heavily to our rapid burnout.

By the time our first holiday party rolled around, some of my associate classmates hadn't yet figured all this out. These unfortunates were still operating under the mistaken belief that timely completion of their work was the responsible course of action, and that by working hard ahead of time they'd ensure their ability to attend the glorious holiday bacchanal. And so it was that when calls for associates went out on the afternoon of the party, these poor souls were the ones who had to answer the call of duty, while those of us hiding behind our wall of last-minute deadlines were free to pursue our anticipated evening of debauchery.

Troob and I headed out to the holiday party together that evening, and as we exited the office on our way to the Rainbow Room we popped our heads into the offices of those we were leaving behind. "Tough break," we told them. "Too bad you're gonna miss the blowout." Inside we laughed, though, for their misery was our small triumph. The staffing process was a zero-sum game, and it was impossible to maintain our own sanity without send-ing some of our mates to the gallows.

DLJ's holiday party was owned by the associates and analysts. We were the ones in the middle—the only ones who knew people all the way up and down the banking hierarchy. The senior bankers lived in their own world, dealing only with other bankers, capital markets people, and company executives. The managing directors gave us our marching orders and expected us to get the work done, but most of them had not processed a deal in years. They couldn't have found their way to the word processing department or the copy center without a map. As for the support staff, they had no idea who most of the senior bankers were either. They knew them by name, and possibly by appearance or reputation, but they didn't have any direct dealings with them. They just knew them as the guys who made a lot of money and made life miserable for those of us in the middle.

The junior bankers were the only ones who played both sides of the system. We knew everybody: the senior bankers, the capital markets people, the BAs, the secre-taries, the copy center guys, the frolicsome thespians from the word processing department, and the mail room staff. This became obvious as Troob and I got into the line for the elevators that would take us up to the Rainbow Room. It was a textbook demonstration of the caste system, only we weren't in India.

The senior bankers stood in pairs talking quietly with each other. The word processing boys, for their part, chatted gaily among themselves. Half of the copy center guys stood in a group ripping maniacal rhymes with each other, while the other half cast furtive glances at the primping secretaries. Troob and I stood in the middle, directing the verbal traffic and drinking it all in. Small talk with the managing directors? Not an issue. Busting a move with the copy center guys? No problem. We were the Renaissance men, and we had visions of sugarplums dancing in our heads.

By the time the elevators finally made it up to the Rainbow Room, the party was already in full swing. Tuxedoed waiters met us with trays of champagne as we came off the elevators. Troob and I each grabbed two, chugged them down, and headed out to survey the scene.

There were a number of different rooms, each with its own distinct personality. Each had multiple bars, fully stocked with top-shelf liquor, and buffets laden down with an impressive collection of seafood, meats, pastries, fresh fruit, and other delicacies. The Grand Ballroom was at one end of the building and featured fifty-foot ceilings and a full orchestra playing big band music. This was where most of the managing directors and upper management were hanging out. Off one end of the Grand Ballroom was another room that ran the entire length of the building. It was filled with small cocktail tables and booths, an intimate setting in which I hoped, by the end of the night, to be engaging any number of passionate young ladies in sensual repartee.

The main event, though, from the associates' perspective, was taking place in another large ballroom at the opposite end of the building from the Grand Ballroom. In both physical location and atmospheric demeanor, it was about as far from the Grand Ballroom as one could get. The room was filled with analysts, associates, secretaries, and BAs. Instead of big band music, there was a DJ pumping out house music. Instead of muted conversation about professional matters, there was a race to inebriation and hopeful coupling. A buffet dominated one end of the room, and immediately adjacent to it was a large dance floor. The convenience of this setup can't be overstated. It facilitated every fool's ability to simultaneously demonstrate his or her disco dancing skills while grabbing slices of roast beef from the buffet and slinging them airborne across the length of the room.

When I first arrived that evening there was little dancing going on. The junior bankers, BAs, and secretaries were all focused first on getting ripped, so that their subsequent gyrations on the dance floor could be explained away afterward as the result of a drunken frenzy. I didn't have any problem with this approach to things, as it was a strategy I had often employed myself when hunting for love. There was, however, one sticking point in its implementation. There was a monster bottleneck at the bar. Fortunately for me, I was practiced in the fine art of maximizing my alcohol intake under adverse conditions, and a long line was not an insurmountable obstacle. When my turn at the bar finally came, I ordered four mixed drinks and a couple of beers. What the bartender didn't realize was that the entire stock was for me. If the price of inebriation was warm drinks with melted ice, so be it.

My rude, selfish actions were a model for others. The trail I blazed would not be a lonely one. Soon, double- and triple-fisters could be seen leaving the bar with smiles on their faces. I felt warm inside, knowing that I had done my small part to lead the way and bring alcoholic happiness to those who needed it most. The evening was starting well.

As the crowd continued to pour a river of liquor down its collective throat, the dance floor began to fill up. The spectacle that ensued was solid evidence that if there's one thing that money can't buy, it's rhythm. When it comes to pure foolishness, a room full of drunk investment bankers prancing around a dance floor pushes the limits of the imagination. To this day I pray that it's a sight the civilized world will never be forced to witness.

The scene that was unfolding was one only a limited number of the managing directors and senior officers of the firm would ever behold. For the most part, the senior bankers knew better than to penetrate this fortress of unfettered libido in the rear ballroom. There were a few, however, who were willing to try. In general, the MDs who made their way back to our province did so because they were themselves looking to scavenge up a little bit of young love for the evening. The large-scale search for young love by decrepit managing directors was, to my understanding, a yearly occurrence at the holiday party. Unlike many of the other work-related social events on the bankers' calendar, the holiday party was for DLJ employees only. No wives, husbands, or significant others were allowed. A licentious old managing director, then, could pursue a BA in her mid-twenties for the evening with no worry of the proverbial shit hitting the fan. The only people who would ever know would be the thousands of other DLJ employees who'd seen it happen.

As for me, I made a few trips out to the dance floor to show off my balletic talents but spent the better part of the evening parked at a table adjacent to the dance floor, knocking back glasses of warm gin and yelling vulgarities to my boys. It was fine entertainment to watch a fifty-year-old managing director and a twenty-seven-year-old associate sandwich a busty banking assistant between them and give her the bump and grind. If nothing else, I knew it would provide me with fodder for some gossip the following day.

There was a clear point of delineation that night before which I was a somewhat normal, functioning member of civilized society and after which some might have considered me a heathen. Physiologically, I probably crossed the bridge into chaos at some point between my eleventh and twelfth mixed drink. Mentally, though, my deliverance coincided with a spontaneous act of natural vitality, one that seemed entirely appropriate at the time.

I was sitting in my chair just off the edge of the dance floor mired in a mild alcoholic daze when I felt the heaviness of the last few drinks settling in down below the belt. I happened to be sharing my table at the time with two managing directors, each of whom was mired in his own alcoholic stupor, and one of whom had been a class-A prick to me when we'd worked on a pitch together a couple of weeks before. Given that I was in my late twenties at the time, I'd been potty trained for nearly twenty five years. Maybe it was just that after twenty five years I was sick and tired of having to relieve myself the way that everybody else did. In a toilet, that is. More likely, after only four months on the job at DLJ I was already yearning to piss on the shoes of some of the SOBs who'd been making my life hell. Whatever the case, as the pressure below increased, I began to contemplate alternative options to trudging to the bathroom for a quick draining of the plumbing. The managing directors on either side of me were no issue. I knew that it would be a stretch for either of them to believe that the associate sitting next to them was tinkling under the table. They'd have to be looking out for it to become suspicious. The table was covered with a white linen tablecloth whose edges hung halfway to the floor—a perfect shield for my lone act of defiance, and I had just finished a bottle of beer—a fitting receptacle for my golden gift. All the pieces were falling into place. I sidled up closer to the table, slipped the empty beer bottle down below, covered my lap with the tablecloth, and relaxed. . . .

The first five seconds of relaxation were pure bliss. Not only was the physical relief first-rate, but I was performing an act most unbecoming of an investment banker. That made me proud. Someday, I'd be able to tell my kids about this seminal moment in my professional life and they, too, would be proud of their father. As the bottle grew warmer and heavier, I realized that I should have put a little bit more thought into my plan up front. By the feel of things, there were only about two ounces of space left in the bottle. The problem was that there were at least twelve ounces of golden delight left inside of me, and far too much momentum to turn off the spigot. I let the bottle drop to the floor and continued to tinkle unencumbered, showering both the Rainbow Room's carpet, and the managing directors' shoes, with my goodness. If either of the managing directors to my sides checked their wing tips upon returning home that evening, they would have noticed a unique speckled pattern covering their lovingly shined shoes. It was my personal tribute.

Now through all these comings and goings I hadn't forgotten my original goal for the evening—the identification and pursuit of free love. In fact, throughout my evening of sedentary pleasure there at the table I'd had an ongoing dialogue with a number of prospects, but none of them had come to full fruition. As I saw Troobie walk by, I corralled him.

"Troobie, what's going on?"

"Not much."

"I'm all fucked up. I just peed underneath the table."

"You did what?"

"I peed underneath the table here."

"Well then why the hell are you still sitting there? Move your lazy ass somewhere else, you filthy pig."

"Yeah, I guess I'd better."

"Well, what do you want to do, Rolfe? The party here'll be going on for another hour or so, then they're gonna shut it down. The question is whether we stay here to take our chances or go and get a sure thing."

"What do you mean, sure thing? You mean a strip joint?"

"Yeah, what else."

Right there, Troobie and I should have realized how far we'd sunk. We were so hard up to get a peek at some ass that we were about to leave a fully paid, top-shelf party, full of all kinds of women just itching to get laid, so that we could hunker down in a seedy sex parlor and pay a bunch of gyrating Delilahs to let us fondle their anatomy. And while some might argue that perverts are born, not made, I'd take exception to that. The job had shifted reality for us. It was making us crazy. We had no life outside of work because we were working hundred-hour weeks, which meant that Friday nights, Saturday nights, and Sunday nights found us sitting in the office more often than not. We didn't have enough time on the weekends to go out on dates, meet women, and establish relationships. When we got the rare night off we wanted a guarantee that we could make the most of it. The only way we knew of to guarantee something was to keep throwing money at it until it happened. The night of the holiday party, that meant that there was no way we were going to waste time working on a 50 percent chance of getting one of the BAs to come home with us when we knew we could hit the peep shows, lay down some cash, and have a 100 percent chance of at least *seeing* some poontang. In our minds, there was no comparison.

Troobie and I put our heads together. The way we saw it, there were two alternatives. We could go to one of the usual upscale places like Scores, Tens, or the VIP Lounge or we could be more debaucherous, roll the dice, and go to the Vault—a sex club down in the meatpacking district. The Vault offered up the not so standard S&M fare: men with minor self-esteem problems lying in the piss trough, dominatrixes leading their subservient partners around the room on leashes, spankings, hot wax, and cat-o'-nine-tails. It was the Betty Crocker's kitchen of sadomasochism.

We decided to split the difference and go to the Harmony Theater. The Harmony was filthier than the strip clubs but not as low as the Vault. It was a Shenanigans meets Peepland—a full-contact booby bar where a single dollar could buy you a grope up on the main stage. When we got there, Troob and I parted ways for a while to find the women of our dreams. I saw Troobie getting a lap dance at one point while the stripper used his Hermès tie like a big piece of dental floss between her legs. Troob told me later that he had to barter the tie away for another lap dance after he ran out of money. As it turned out, Troob and I weren't alone in our desires. After about an hour our colleagues Tubby, Slick, and the Big Man all walked in. I guess that they were looking for a sure thing, too.

From my perspective, the only repercussion to come from our night of holiday bacchanal was a burgeoning realization that our lives were pathetic. For Troob, though, the effect of our night out was more profound. I walked into his office the following day with a huge smile on my face, despite a wicked hangover. I'd come to recount the previous evening with him, and revel in our naughtiness. What I found, though, was a chastened Peter Troob.

"Troobie, man, that was GREAT last night! We gotta do it again soon. I gotta get back down there to the Harmony. I love chasing the ladies with you."

"I don't know, man. I don't feel so good about it."

"You don't feel good about it? What the fuck is that supposed to mean?"

"It's Marjorie, man. Don't tell anybody I said this, but I feel guilty about last night."

Marjorie was the girl from Chicago that Troob had been dating. He had met her over a year before, and their relationship had seemed to stick. She knew he worked hard, and he had been forced to bail on her before, but since she lived in Chicago she didn't really know just how bad his work hours actually were. That was good. I knew that Troob liked her, but that hadn't ever stopped our debaucherous pursuits before. I could see that Troob was starting to get that look in his eye that you see in your friends right before they leave the bachelor brotherhood. That look scared me. He was my comrade-in-arms, my partner. Troob was already getting up the curve on developing a conscience. That was troubling.

Drafting

Sometimes I get the feeling that the two biggest problems in America today are making ends meet— and making meetings end.

—*Robert Orben*

Rolfe and I knew that meetings would be a major part of our existence as bankers. We never imagined, though, just how absurd the meetings could get. Banker meetings are a lot like the Ebola virus. They start out small, but they grow quickly. And they don't stop growing until they've consumed everything around them. At times, when it came to meetings, Rolfe and I felt like we were trying to play two-on-two basketball with twenty-five people on each team. We never really nailed down why banking meetings always seem to end up out of control, but we think it has something to do with how the new generation of bankers was hatched.

In the early days of banking, bankers were a lot like drug dealers. They told the potential customers, "My shit's the best, man, it'll really do the job for you." The customers told themselves, "This guy's dressed nicely, he's smooth, he must have the goods." They bought some of his shit and they took it home. They smoked it down, they shot it up, or they put it into their portfolio, and then they waited. Nothing happened. They weren't getting high. They weren't getting rich. Sometimes they even got a headache or, if they were really unlucky, they got some really bad shit that killed them. That was the nature of the beast.

Before the Great Crash of 1929, bankers were selling all kinds of bad shit to the public. They called the bad shit "securities." It was like the bankers were packaging up little dime bags of flour and telling the customers that it was high-grade cocaine. The customers didn't care, because they never tried it and didn't know what it was. There was always some bigger fool that was willing to pay them even more for their little bags of flour than they'd paid themselves. And then, one day, some random guy tried snorting up some of the flour and he realized that it wasn't cocaine at all. He realized it was crap. He sold his little bags of flour and told two friends what he'd figured out. Each of them, in turn, called their brokers, sold their bags of flour, and told two more friends about what was going on. Before long, everybody was trying to sell their flour, nobody wanted to buy it anymore, and the Great Crash had arrived. The game was up.

In the wake of this scandal, the federal government decided that somebody had to reign in the freewheeling bankers and their errant sales forces, who'd foisted the little flour bag scam upon the unsuspecting public. With this goal in mind, President Roosevelt's regulators jammed reforms through the legislative branch under the guise of the Securities Act of 1933 and the Securities Ex-

change Act of 1934. Among other things, these Acts created the Securities and Exchange Commission, or SEC,
which is now responsible for the monitoring and admin-
istration of most aspects of securities issuance in the
United States.

The SEC is pure government bureaucracy. Its policy is
never to approve any aspect of a new securities issuance;
its only "approval" of a given deal comes in the form of a
"failure to disapprove." In other words, when a company
and their investment bank come to market with a deal,
the SEC doesn't give a seal of approval that the deal's OK,
it merely states, "We're not saying that this deal's *not*
OK." It's one of those double negatives that guys use to
fool their girlfriends after they've done something wrong.

One of the requirements for securities issuers is that
they make a filing with the SEC every time they intend to
sell new securities to investors. The filings contain very
specific information about the company issuing the securities and the nature of the securities themselves. These
filings, which generally have to be made available to the
investing public, go by a number of different names: S-1,
S-3, S-4, the list goes on and on. The type of filing depends on what kind of securities are being issued. The important thing to remember is that the filings are required
by law, which means that the bankers don't have any
choice but to put these documents together before they
can go out, sell the securities, and earn their fees. They
can no longer just tell the buyers that their shit is the best
and the companies they are representing are high fliers,
now they have to put it in writing. That presents a problem for the bankers, because it creates a paper trail.

MONKEY BUSINESS

When things go awry, the buyers know where to point the finger and where to go looking for payback.

For the ever optimistic bankers, the filing requirements have created an opportunity. The bankers have decided that if they're going to be forced to create this public filing, then they're going to do it on their own terms. They're going to turn it into a sales brochure, complete with color pictures and promotional material about what a fantastic, once-in-a-lifetime investment opportunity the securities being sold represent. They're going to take that filing, print it up in a neat little package, and mail it out to all the potential buyers. Once it's in the buyers' hands, the bankers will take the smoothest, best-looking, most presentable members of company management, trot them out to all the big potential buyers, and put on a show. It's called a road show, and it's in the best tradition of the traveling medicine shows. Instead of traveling around and putting on the show off the back of a covered wagon, though, the bankers and the members of management use private jets. They stay in the best hotels, and put the show on in fancy restaurants, so that the buyers can have a nice meal while they hear about how wealthy they're going to get by purchasing the company's securities. It's critical to maintain the image of big money. The buyers have to believe that the management team knows how to make coin. They have to believe that this is the team that's going to make everybody rich.

Before the show can begin, the bankers and the company have to give birth to that sales brochure. It's called the prospectus. It's a tricky job, because at the same time that the prospectus tells the buyers what a great opportunity exists, it also has to cover everybody's ass and meet the letter of the law on SEC filing requirements.

A long time ago, somebody figured out that if he came up with an important-sounding name for these meetings where the prospectus is created, people wouldn't focus so much on what a waste of time they were. They decided to call them "drafting sessions." All associates experience their fair share of drafting sessions. Rolfe and I were no exceptions.

Drafting sessions involve a big cast of characters. Everybody gets together in a room. They spend long days disagreeing with each other on what should be in the prospectus.

The bankers are always there. They only want to say good things. The better they can make the company sound, the easier it will be for them to sell the securities. The easier it is for them to sell the securities, the more certain they'll be that the clients will be happy. That means fees. Fees are important.

The bankers have their lawyers there—the underwriters' counsel. The job of an underwriters' counsel is to make sure that the bankers don't put any lies into the prospectus that are going to get them into trouble later. They have to twist the language in the document around so that if the prospectus ever gets brought up as evidence in a court of law the judge and jury will be so confused that they won't have any idea what the language is claiming, or trying to claim, or maybe not even claiming at all. They have to be crafty.

Representatives from the company are there. The CFO almost always shows up; he's usually in charge from the company's side. Sometimes, depending on how important the transaction is to the company, the CEO may show up as well. If it's the company's first trip to the public markets for money the CEO usually comes in for lunch one day during drafting. There's almost always somebody more junior from the company there also, usually somebody from the investor relations department. The CFO needs to have somebody to pin the blame on in case things get fucked up.

The company has its lawyers there also. Similar to the underwriters' counsel's role, it's the company counsel's job to make sure that any half-truths that go into the prospectus aren't going to get the company into trouble. Sometimes company counsel is on the same side of the fence as underwriters' counsel; more often than not they're arguing with one another. If there's ever going to be trouble, the company and the underwriters both want the other guy to take the fall. That's usually why their lawyers end up arguing with each other.

The company's accountants are there. Their job is to provide a fair and impartial rendering of the company's financial health. The prospectus contains a lot of detail on the company's historical financial performance, and it's the accountants' job to make sure it's accurate. Before the prospectus gets finalized, the accountants have to provide "comfort" on the numbers. They usually spend a lot of time arguing with the company about what the right numbers should be, so their provision of professional comfort is generally accompanied by acute feelings of personal discomfort. At the end of the day, the company can fire the accountants if it doesn't like the position they're taking. This means that the accountants tend to come around to the company's point of view if they want to keep the business. Usually, they want to keep the business.

If there were only one representative from each participating organization at the drafting sessions, things would probably go pretty smoothly. Five or six people could get together in a room and hammer out the prospectus in a couple of days. The problem is that each organization sends its own small army. An army girded for war.

The lawyers show up with the managing partner on the account, an associate, and a paralegal. The managing partner's job is to argue, the associate's job is to make a lot of pencil marks on the master draft of the document, and the paralegal's job is to make copies and faxes. As junior bankers, whenever we were feeling low, we'd watch the junior lawyers and start feeling better. They worked just as many hours as we did, they made a lot less money, and their work was even more boring than ours. Three strikes, they were out.

The bankers show up with a managing director, a vice president, an associate, and, sometimes, an analyst. Having lots of bankers at the drafting sessions conveys strength and power. The clients are supposed to believe that with such an impressive array of financial talent, there's no way the deal can fail. If there is more than one investment bank underwriting the deal, which there usually is, each of the banks will send its own representatives. Only the lead manager will send the full array of bankers. The co-managers figure that they're not getting paid enough to have the whole cast show up. Sometimes the co-managers will each send only an associate, but usually they will send at least a couple of bankers.

There has to be at least one banker from each underwriter. There are two reasons for this. First, each underwriter wants to be absolutely positive that their firm's name is printed correctly on the prospectus cover. This is a major concern for all associates. The junior banker's most important job is to make sure that the firm's name is spelled and displayed correctly on the prospectus cover and that the colors on the cover and inside the cover are accurate and vibrant. Second, a co-manager has to send at least one banker to the drafting session just in case the other underwriters decide that they're going to try to get that co-manager evicted from the deal. Allowing a drafting session to pass without at least one banker from your bank being present is more dangerous than letting a hungry weasel into a nudist farm hot tub.

On the first day of drafting, everybody meets at the company counsel's office. The company counsel keeps control of the document. Everybody meets up in a conference room that has a big table in the middle of it. Usually, there are twenty to thirty people there. Everybody stands around drinking coffee, adjusting themselves, and billing their clients.

As associates, our first order of business on the opening day of drafting was to seek out the associates from the other investment banks. We'd find them, introduce ourselves, and size each other up. It was like two dogs meeting in the park and sniffing each others' asses to determine whether they were compatible. All the associates fell into one of two camps; those who got it, and those who didn't. You could look into any of the other associates' eyes and determine immediately which of the two species they were a member of. The ones who got it understood the game. They knew that an associate was little more than a yes-man, and that our role was to be as humble and subservient as a geisha girl. They were our allies, and we'd commiserate with each other throughout the deal process. The ones who didn't get it believed that they were hotshots and deal magicians. They thought they were driving the wagon train when in fact they were being ridden like an inbred pack mule. They didn't see themselves for what they were—street punks learning the business. They carried Mont Blanc pens in their front pockets so that everybody could see them. They had new Coach briefcases and shiny leather shoes. They shook everybody's hand in the entire room and told them how glad they were to make their acquaintance. It was embarrassing to watch. In our minds, they were there to be tormented and, if the right opportunity presented itself, terminated. They were the enemy.

In preparation for the first day of drafting, company counsel usually puts together a rough draft of the prospectus. The rough draft provides a reference point from which to begin working. It's easier than beginning work with a blank sheet of paper, but this rough draft is really rough, like that institutional toilet paper that feels like a sheet of sandpaper in your ass. The rough cut normally just includes a brief description of the company up front, and then a bunch of section titles in the back as placeholders. It costs the company a few thousand dollars, and by the time the final draft rolls around not a single word from the original will remain.

When it comes to drafting, there's no such thing as pride of authorship. The normal rules of literary law and etiquette do not apply. This is probably because the rules of literary law that address plagiarism only apply to prose worth stealing, and there's never been any text in a prospectus worth stealing. Bankers aren't known for their vivid imaginations, so the chances of them breaking any new ground in their descriptions of a company's business are slim. Furthermore, whatever mildly compelling prose any banker has managed to create to describe a company's business has inevitably gotten watered down by paranoid lawyers. There's no prime rib in the process; hamburger goes in, horsemeat comes out.

The various sections of any given prospectus are dictated both by tradition and regulatory mandate. The sections may differ slightly, depending on the nature of a given deal, but there are certain sections that are included in nearly all prospectuses. What follows here is our guide to prospectuses. For the uninitiated it will hopefully serve as a road map if you ever decide, against your better judgment, to actually sit down and read one.

Prospectus Summary—This is always the first section. It's what the drafting team spends 75 percent of their time working on, and it's often the only thing that prospective investors ever read. It's supposed to give the reader all the key information in two to three pages. It's supposed to tell the reader why the company doing the offering is the best, most successful competitor in its industry, why they're the ass kickers who take no prisoners. It's supposed to tell the reader how the company is going to take over its industry, and then its country, and then the world, so that an investment in the company will eventually represent pro-rata ownership in world domination. This sec-

tion usually contains more bullshit than any other section.

Reversion to the mean dictates that most companies
have to be average. There can only be a few standouts in
any given industry. This principle works against the goal
of presenting every company engaged in an offering as
the industry leader. Since, therefore, it is impossible to
present facts that actually support most companies' claim
to be the standout in their industry, the prospectus summary generally tries to confuse the readers through obfus-
cation. Those drafting the prospectus believe that if they
can layer in enough nonsensical prose, readers will become so confused that they'll be unable to realize how
mediocre the company actually is.

Risk Factors—This section is a lawyer's wet dream. It describes all of the things that could go wrong with the
company. Years ago, the bankers, the lawyers, and the
company all used to spend a lot of time fighting about
what went into this section. The bankers and the company didn't want to put too much in here, because they
thought that people might get scared and not buy into the
offering. The lawyers, though, were scared shitless and
just wanted to cover their asses. The fights raged on and
on. Then, one day, folklore has it, a brilliant young lawyer
came up with a most Machiavellian strategy. He decided
that if he overloaded this section with a bunch of irrelevant drivel, people would give up in frustration and ne-
glect to read any of it or, at the very least, stand a good
chance of missing the really important points. The strategy was pure genius. Today, there are maybe one or two

risk factors that are relevant, really relevant, for any given deal. The rest is window dressing, but there's so much of this extraneous window dressing that the relevant risk factors get ignored. The lawyer, the one who invented the strategy, has been immortalized as a charter member of the Prospectus Drafting Hall of Fame.

Use of Proceeds—Not too many people pay attention to this section, but they should. A careful reading of this section will tell you where the hell all the money from the offering is going. If it's not going into the company coffers to help grow the company, but instead is going to pay out existing owners and management, then stay away. If owners are cashing out, there's no reason for you to be cashing in.

Selected Financial Data—This section is also known to insiders as "Creative Presentation of the Company's Financial Performance." In it, the bankers and accountants put all their efforts into figuring out a way to make the company look like a real money machine. If a company's got good cash flow but no earnings, you'll see a cash flow line presented in a fat, bold font. If a company's got neither cash flow nor earnings, but it's growing like a weed, then you can bet that there's going to be a bold line at the bottom showing year-over-year revenue growth or unit growth or employee growth. The only situation that's difficult for even the most talented bankers and accountants to contend with is one where there's no revenue at all. Even Houdini can't mask the vacuum that a revenue line equal to zero creates. In this situation, the company is effectively fraternizing with the professional beggars on New York's subway lines—"Please, I need money right away. It's not for crack, I swear. Just soup and a sandwich."

Management's Discussion and Analysis of Financial Condition and Results of Operations (MD&A)—MD&A is the place where dreams are made, and mistakes justified. While the tables in the Selected Financial Data section can be spun and recrafted to focus attention on and present results in the best possible light, a good huckster needs a real soapbox to get out the vote. This is where MD&A comes in. In MD&A management gets the opportunity to justify its mistakes and take credit for its successes. In a painstaking narrative the management team explains just how things got to be the way they are. Revenues have dropped by 20 percent. Here's why. Costs are spiraling out of control? There's a valid explanation, and here it is.

Business—This section is an exact replication of the prospectus summary, but with twice as many meaningless adjectives and even more excruciating detail. If it wasn't boring enough the first time around, it'll become so in the Business section.

Management—This section presents biographies of both the management team and the board of directors. Members of management and/or the board of directors generally get only two to three sentences each to make themselves seem important, so they maximize the balderdash per sentence. The Management section also presents the reader with an opportunity to assess just how inbred the board of directors is. A good way to figure out how likely it is that the directors are sucking money out of a company is to draw a chart with each director's name in a box. Read through the Management section, and each time that you identify a professional or personal connection between two directors, connect their boxes with a line. If you also happen to know about other relationships between directors, for instance one director is married to another director's daughter, or one director is an old college buddy of another director, you can draw a line in there as well. If, upon completion, the chart looks like a spider web, then hold on to your wallet.

Principal and Selling Stockholders—This section describes who owns big pieces of the company and, if it's an equity offering, whether any of them are selling their stock. If there are relatively few stockholders, each of whom owns a large piece of the company, that's good because they're probably going to be just as pissed off as the minority shareholders if the value of their holdings starts going down the toilet. It's good to have a group of people channeling their fear, frustration, and greed to maximize the value of your investment.

If any of the large holders are selling their shares in the offering, stay away. As junior bankers, when institutional buyers would ask us why insiders were selling their stock in the offering, we'd volunteer numerous glib responses:

"Oh, it's a liquidity issue."

"Estate planning, nothing more."

"Diversification, they don't want to have all their eggs in one basket."

In general, if the people who know the most about the business are taking their money out, it's a safe bet that you shouldn't be putting yours in.

Underwriting—This section will indicate which banks or brokerage houses are getting allocated a portion of the offering to parcel out to their preferred accounts. Effectively, the relatively small number of investment banks that underwrite the deal (the managers) sell the entire deal to a much larger group of brokerage houses (the syndicate), which in turn sell the deal to investment institutions and individuals. Now it's much more lucrative to be a manager of a deal than it is to merely be a member of the syndicate, but a crummy free lunch is better than no free lunch at all. The syndicate is like the Treehouse Club—only the really bad boys don't get to be members. The investment banks all fight tooth and nail up front to be given the mandate to manage a deal, but there's an unspoken understanding among all the players that even those who lose out on the management mandate will get to be a part of the syndicate at selling time. Participation in the syndicate is the ever present booby prize of the public offering world.

Financial Statements—This is the real meat and potatoes of the prospectus. This is the section that should be up front. The problem is that this is the section with the least room for creative input, since disclosure in the financial statements is dictated by a well-defined set of independent accounting principles. The bankers don't get a vote here; it's the timid little bean counters who make the final decisions on what makes it into Financial Statements. In fact, it's not so much the fact that the bankers don't get to make the decisions on what goes into this section that drives them mad. It's that the guys who *do* get to make those decisions are the accountants. If a big hitter like a CFO were responsible for the decisions it would be one thing, but it's the frigging accountants. Call it the accountant's revenge, and chalk one up for truth and justice.

For the investor, the financial statements are the only unadulterated statement of historical fact that can be used as a justification for taking on risk. The prospectus should be read like a Chinese newspaper, start at the back and work your way forward.

The entire drafting process can take anywhere from five to ten full working days. With a working group of twenty to thirty people, that translates to somewhere between one hundred and three hundred equivalent work days. That's about a year's worth of work for the creation of a document that hardly anybody reads. If one were to add up all the man-hours that go into the drafting of prospectuses in a given year there might be enough to develop a cure for cancer. The cure probably wouldn't pay as well as writing prospectuses does, though.

As associates, our responsibilities at the drafting sessions were a function of the senior banker on the deal. Some senior bankers didn't want us to do anything but sit quietly. We were just there to provide a presence, and as long as we didn't fall asleep or wet ourselves we were doing our job. Other senior bankers gave us marginally more responsibility. They would stand up to leave the room and announce, "I have to go make a few phone calls. My associate here will lead the drafting while I'm gone." That meant that if the group spent more than ten minutes arguing about how a single sentence should be worded, it would be our responsibility to state loudly, "OK, let's keep things moving here." It was an impressive skill to be developing.

The associate's other responsibility once the document begins taking shape is to conform it to the bank's formatting style. Every investment bank has a style manual. It's a book that details every element of prospectus formatting—what size fonts to use in which locations, where headings should be placed, which lines in the financial tables should be underlined. This is important stuff, and being on style duty at the drafting sessions was exactly the sort of intellectually challenging work Rolfe and I had always dreamed that we'd be doing one day as investment bankers. We were determined to become the best damned style managers Wharton and Harvard had to offer.

Drafting sessions are utterly forgettable. They are slow, painful, and excruciatingly boring. Usually, the most difficult aspect of the drafting sessions is striking a reasonable balance between the amount of coffee one has to drink to stay awake and the number of trips one takes to the bathroom to mitigate the diuretic effects of the caffeine. Mealtime provides the only break in the insufferable monotony. I once asked Rolfe whether he'd ever enjoyed himself at a drafting session. He thought long. He thought hard. I began to worry that his brain might crack. After much reflection, he said no, he'd never actually enjoyed himself.

Rolfe and I had been to drafting sessions in Dallas, Los Angeles, Washington, D.C., Montreal, and New York. We could have had drafting sessions on the beach at Maui, or while flying in a hot air balloon high over the Amazon. It wouldn't have made a difference. They still wouldn't have been memorable.

The associate never knows for how many weeks the drafting sessions are going to drag on. Each drafting session ends with the scheduling of the next session. The associate understands that drafting is a lot like chemo-therapy. There are no guarantees that the drafting will eventually lead to a completed deal, but without it there's no chance for success. Each session is a necessary step in an evil, painful process. At the end of each session, the associate yearns for some indication that the process is drawing to a close. One day, he gets it.

The senior banker on a deal is the one who pulls the trigger and decides when the drafting sessions are done. This determination is not an objective process. The members of the drafting team don't dot the last "i," cross the last "t," look around at each other, and exclaim "by God, we're done!" It's much more subjective than that. The lead banker uses an internal productivity gauge, developed over years of experience with both human nature and the tendency of attorneys to generate as many billable hours as possible. The lead banker assesses each drafting session's accomplishments. When the number of accomplishments per dollar of billable legal time for a given drafting session falls below some minimum threshold the lead banker pulls the trigger. The banker decides that the time has arrived to light a fire under everybody's ass. The time has arrived to start making it *really* expensive to continue wasting time. The lead banker decides to crank up the momentum, and take the drafting team to a place where dillydallying is not allowed. The lead banker speaks the words:

"It's time to go to the printer."

Push the Button

It is a riddle wrapped in a mystery inside an enigma.
—*Winston Churchill*

From the time fledgling bankers first begin their descent from on high, they hear about going to the printer. Until they get the chance to go, it's one of banking's biggest mysteries. They don't know what actually happens at the printer. They don't know what they're supposed to do at the printer. They just know that a trip to the printer is important, really important, so important in fact that any of the other deals they might be working on take a backseat. They know that if a vice president or a managing director calls them up and says, "I need you to be at this pitch with me tomorrow," they can tell him, "Fuck you, I'm gonna be at the printer." The printer always takes priority, even over the calls of senior bankers.

Going to the printer is a classic investment banking clusterfuck. Young bankers who haven't ever been to the printer don't know what they're supposed to do there—they're expecting the associates in the know to give them some guidance. The problem is that the associates who *have* been can't remember anything of substance they've ever done there, so they've got nothing to tell the associates who haven't been. Nobody knows anything, nobody wants to look like an idiot, and nobody will admit their ignorance. It's a self-perpetuating cycle of stupidity spiraling into a black hole.

When we first started working at DLJ I cornered Troob one afternoon to find out what went on at the printer. He'd worked in banking before, so I knew that he'd been to the printer. I figured that he'd have the answers.

"Troobie, man, I've got a question for you."

"Yeah, what is it?"

"The printer, I want to know about the printer. Everybody's always going there. What do they do there?"

Troob was quiet for a minute. "You know. They go to the printer. They print up the prospectuses there. Why are you asking me?"

"I'm asking you because everybody's always talking about the printer. I want to know what happens there. What do you mean, they print up prospectuses? Why don't the lawyers just print them out at their office and get the copy center to make copies?"

"Because they need the copies to look really good. They want to have a professional print them out. You know, so that they can print it on that really thin paper, the stuff that's like toilet paper. That way the investors can at least use it to wipe their ass since they're not gonna read it. You have to be able to have some glossy color pictures up front. The copy center can't do those copies on the glossy paper. You know how shitty their color copies always look. That stuff is important. How can you sell a deal with shitty color copies?"

"OK, I'm with you, but what do we do there? I mean the bankers. Do we go to the printer, put on work aprons, and turn a big steel crank to help print the prospectuses? I just don't get it. Are we like those old Chinese guys with big racks of steel alphabet characters? Do we help load them into the printing presses? Why do we have to go?"

"The bankers don't do the actual printing. The bankers go there and they sit around doing the drafting that they should have already done at the lawyer's office. Then they shoot pool and drink beer and proofread each draft as the changes get put through by the guys who work there. You do the same shit there that you do at the drafting sessions, except at the printers you have free beer, free food, a pool table, cable TV, and Nintendo."

"How can all that stuff be free?" I asked Troobie.

"It's not really free. The company doing the offering is paying for everything. If you look at the cover of the prospectus it says something like '. . . expenses related to the Offering payable by the company estimated at $1.5 million.' That $1.5 million is mostly the printer fees, the drafting sessions and the travel expenses. They're the long-distance phone calls we make, the beer we drink, the sushi we order, and the word processing changes we put through. They're the color printing on the front cover and inside cover of the prospectus and the special tissue-like paper we use for the rest of the prospectus. They're the cost of the 30,000 prospectuses we print up when all we really need is a third of that amount.

"It's all about excess. We always have to order more food, drink more beer, and print more prospectuses than we know we're gonna need. Most of the extra prospectuses end up on our office floor and on the office floor of the CFO from the company doing the deal. It usually makes him really happy that he has an extra 10,000 copies of the prospectus for a bond underwriting deal that's causing him ulcers because he can hardly pay the interest expense. It's a constant reminder to the CFO that he over-leveraged the company."

"I still don't think I get it. If we're just drafting at the printer, then why don't we do it at the lawyers' offices during the drafting sessions?"

Troob gave me one of those "You're a total frigging dumb-ass" looks and said, "What the hell do you think? Have you ever drunk beer and shot pool at the lawyer's office? I don't think so. That's why you do it at the printer, so you can drink beer and shoot pool. Stop bothering me."

Troobie was only partly right. Thirty years ago there was a legitimate reason for the bankers to be at the printer. The printing actually got done on site, and the bankers had to be close to the guys with the ink-stained aprons who were cranking copies off the printing press just in case there were any last-minute changes to be made. Now, though, it's all electronic. There are no more ink-stained aprons. There are no more printing presses on-site. The guys who work for the printer wear ties and sit in front of a computer screen and when the final prospectus is ready to be printed they press a button and some printing plant in the middle of a field in Pennsylvania or somewhere starts spitting out copies.

So why do junior bankers continue to show up at the printer? Tradition. It's because printing the prospectuses is a milestone in the deal process. It's a sign that the associate has actually done something besides blow hot air for six months. Going to the printer is symbolic because it means that the associate is actually getting close to producing something that the outside world is going to see. An associate might bust his ass for a couple of months to jump through all the hoops he has to jump through to make a deal happen, but nobody outside his deal team really has any idea what he's been doing. As far as everybody else is concerned, he's just disappeared into a smelly black hole for three months. For all anybody else knows, he could be down in that hole procreating with goats. Parents and friends don't know why little Johnny is working all the time.

At the end of the day, there's nothing tangible except the prospectus to show for the numerous all-nighters and those dark months of toil that go into a deal. The prospectus usually sucks, and nobody ever reads it cover to cover, but the prospectus and a Lucite deal toy is all the associate has to show at the end of a deal. It's not like they're building houses or making widgets. The prospectus and deal toys are the associate's stone tablets, like the ones that Moses had with the Ten Commandments on them. They're the evidence, and without them the associate might start to wonder whether their agonizing existence is anything more than just a bad dream.

Managing directors rarely go to the printer. Normally, the highest-ranking banker that ever makes an appearance at the printer is a vice president. Vice presidents usually show up for a few hours in the morning when everybody first gets to the printer. They glad-hand the lawyers and the CFO, they eat a doughnut and drink some juice, and then they leave. On their way out they tell the associate "use your judgment," and then they laugh because they know that the associate has lost the capacity to have any independent judgment.

This gives associates a passing opportunity to play grown-up. They believe that for that one magical day they're no longer the peon. They're in charge. They're the man. For most of them, it's the next best thing to a free massage—with release—from the women at the Asian Surprise Palace. Every senior banker who's ever been an associate remembers his or her first experience at the printer. The heady sensation of absolute power. The surge of energy that courses through the body as the associate barked his or her first order at a balding lawyer. They all recall the thrill of telling the printer's client service guy, "The macaroni in the dinner buffet is cold. Can you freshen it up for me?"

The associate takes control. The associate tells the CFO that as the underwriter they've mobilized their huge investment banking organization to get the deal sold; the associate has got salespeople calling on accounts, capital markets people lining up the underwriting syndicate, and the road show crew lining up venues for group meetings with buyers. All of this to get the deal teed up for the announced pricing date. If things get off schedule because chores don't get finished up at the printer in time, the whole deal could get scuttled. The associate tells the CFO that this is called "market risk," and that to avoid the market risk the associate is going to have to take charge of the process. The CFO rolls his eyes, and decides to humor the associate.

Unfortunately for the associate, realization soon

strikes that a king in name only is nothing more than a fool. It only takes about fifteen minutes for everybody on the deal team to realize that the emperor has no clothes. The associate realizes that there are certain tasks that need to be accomplished; there's an expensive clock ticking, and the associate has no idea how to get any of the stuff done that needs to get done. The associate realizes that he is good at taking orders but not very good at giving them. The associate sucks it up and turns the process back over to the CFO.

The CFO then sends the accountants off to go work on the financials; sends the lawyers off to go work on the underwriting, tax, and legal sections of the prospectus; and then buckles down on the management section. Basically, the CFO sends everybody but the associate off to work on the sections they should have gotten done at the drafting sessions but that they failed to finish because they were so mired in their own piddling bullshit. This leaves the associate with nothing to do but pick dingleberries or play pool.

The first time I ever went to the printer was for the IPO for Ventotronics, a paging company that told the world it could provide faster and more reliable paging service than its competitors. All morning long I sat in the lounge watching game shows and playing pool. When that got boring, I called in to DLJ to see how hard all my buddies were working and to let them know that I wasn't doing a thing. They called me an asshole and told me to fuck off. They didn't want to talk to me. Troobie was different, though. He tolerated me because he knew that the next time he was at the printer he'd probably want to be able to rub somebody else's nose into his temporary pursuit of leisure. He knew that I'd owe him.

"Hey Troobie, it's Rolfe."

"What's up?"

"I'm at the printer, man. Everything's on autopilot. I don't have anything to do."

"Nothing new there. How many games of pool have you played?"

"Six or seven. I've seen all the talk shows. *Sally Jesse Raphael, Ricki Lake, Jerry Springer, Geraldo,* and *Jenny Jones.* I can't remember which was which but one of them had guys who only like fat women. Another had kids who are kleptomaniacs. Jerry Springer had his usual fight-a-thon. This time the fisticuffs were between two men who love the same woman who is sleeping with another woman. However, the one that took the cake was about a guy who had a sex change and a woman who had a sex change and they're now married and both want to switch back. Jesus, I thought I had problems."

"That's great, Rolfe. Now you know what the printer's all about."

"Am I ever gonna have to do anything here, or do I just sit around and do nothing until the final shit gets printed?"

"The only thing you've got to do is check the style. Make sure that all the summary financial tables have underlines in the right places, and don't fuck up the headings. All your second-level subheadings have to be both bolded *and* italicized. And make sure the third-level subheadings are indented. Most important of all is that you have to make sure the 'Donaldson, Lufkin & Jenrette Securities Corporation' name isn't screwed up on the front or back cover. The 'S' from 'Securities' has to be lined up right under the space between the 'd' and the 's' from 'Donaldson,' and the 'n' at the end of 'Corporation' has to fall directly between the 'J' and the 'e' at the beginning of 'Jenrette.' If you only do one thing right, make sure that's it, 'cause if you fuck the name up you might as well kiss this job good-bye."

"Get outta here, man. Stop lying."

"I'm serious, man. Serious as a heart attack. I was at a drafting session once where an Alex. Brown associate had a conniption fit because the 'Alex. Brown' name wasn't being presented correctly. It was supposed to be 'Alex,' then a period, then 'Brown.' 'Alex. Brown.' It was all screwed up on one of the drafts that came back, and the associate just kept yelling 'Alex period Brown, Alex period Brown,' over and over like a frigging maniac. He wouldn't shut up until the printer guys fixed it."

"All right. I get the point. What else?"

"Once you've done all that, the only other thing you've gotta do is check the blue line."

"The blue line?"

"Yeah. It's the final copy of the document that comes out before they push the button."

"Push the button, what do you mean?"

"Push the button. They have to push the button to start printing out the final copies of the prospectus."

"Where's the button?"

"I don't know, man. Nobody knows. It's a big secret. It's like one of those detonation buttons that the bad guys in the James Bond movies always have. Only the head honcho at the printer knows where it is."

"Thanks for the counsel, man."

"Whatever."

"I've got one other question for you. I was just in the kitchen and there's all this beer in the fridge. Can I drink it or what?"

"Yeah, you can drink it. You might want to take it easy until closer to dinnertime, though. Everybody usually starts to get tired after dinner so nobody really notices if you start drinking then. You don't want to be too blatant about it. Some clients get sensitive to their bankers pounding down too many beers on the job, especially when things are coming down to the wire."

Troob's advice was good. My judgment wasn't. By late afternoon I was already well into my second six-pack of Lone Star. There was some upside. The whining company counsel was no longer annoying me as much as he had earlier in the day.

The deal team worked feverishly into the evening. Everybody, that is, except for me. I continued to drink. At one point, underwriter's counsel pulled me aside after he caught me in the lounge adorning a reproduction of a famous Remington sculpture with broccoli florets.

"Take it easy, man," he told me, "we're almost there."

Fifteen minutes later I returned the favor. At 9 P.M. sharp, underwriter's counsel and company counsel came within a hair's breadth of coming to blows. They were actually up, leaning over the table, in each other's faces. The reason? Disagreement over the placement of a comma in a sentence from the Prospectus Summary section. I'd never seen anybody fight over a comma before. I suggested that if they each had a few Lone Stars things might go a little more smoothly. They ignored my suggestion.

An hour later I wandered in to the buffet. It didn't look so good so I ordered up some steaks from Peter Luger. I couldn't decide between the T-bone and the filet, so I ordered one of each. I washed them down with a few more Lone Stars. I was bored. Really bored. I called Troobie.

"Troobie, hey, it's Rolfe."

"What's up?"

"Nothing, man. I'm still at the printer."

"Well if nothing's up then I gotta go. I've got Gator on one line gobbling like a Thanksgiving turkey and Marjorie on the other. She's pissed at me 'cause I have to cancel my trip to Chicago this weekend. I'm gonna be here doing some shit for the Widow. I was supposed to spend time with her parents. Man, this job is really fucking things up. See you later."

Ten P.M. passed, midnight passed, 2 A.M. passed. I remember thinking to myself that maybe the reason associates couldn't ever remember what happened at the printer was because they always got bored, ate too much food, and passed out. I called up Troobie again to see what he thought. He was still at the office.

"Hey, Troobie. Two A.M.—nice life. Gator must have found a way to stuff that turkey."

"Fuck off."

Troob hung up on me. I sat down on the couch and I passed out. Two hours later, underwriters' counsel woke me up. I had a bad case of cotton mouth, and the blue line was ready. I looked at it carefully. The "S" from "Securities" was lined up right under the space between the "d" and the "s" from "Donaldson." The "n" at the end of "Corporation" was directly between the "J" and the "e" at the beginning of Jenrette." The font was correct.

I gave the order, "Push the button."

My job was done.

Travel

I just flew in from Chicago, and boy are my arms tired.
—Anonymous Joke

Once the associate is finished at the printer and the prospectuses are in the works there is only one thing to do. Sleep. However, this blissful sleep doesn't last for long. The next step in the process of completing a deal is right around the corner. The deal team has to put on a road show. This means travel. A ton of it.

Rolfe and I were told that one of the most glamorous aspects of investment banking was the opportunity it would provide us to travel all over the country and the world. We used to dream of jet-setting off to Paris and then Rome—selling deals, collecting fees, drinking fine wines, and living in the lap of luxury. I told all my friends that I would buy them Hermès and Ferragamo ties at discount prices in the duty-free shops in France. I looked forward to the time that I would have to absorb the world's great cultures. Rolfe told me that he wanted to work on deals in California. He said that he wanted to spend some time out there, and that by working in the Communications and Entertainment Group he would get the chance to get out West as much as possible. Traveling meant freedom, relaxation, and fun. Wrong.

Traveling is a bitch. It gives every young banker multiple ulcers. The pressure of catching planes, hailing cabs, carrying a ton of useless shit, and never ever checking any baggage can drive even the calmest banker bat shit. One-day trips to Dallas from New York are the norm. Taking the red-eye back from California, crammed into coach class, is standard practice. Prop planes are commonplace when the clients are in the middle of nowhere. Rental cars are a part of everyday life.

We used to call one of our good buddies, Mike Roganstahl, "Wings" because he traveled so much. He racked up over 250,000 American Airlines miles in one year and a host of additional miles on other airlines. He was American Airlines Platinum, Hertz Club Gold, tired, haggard, and miserable.

There is no relaxation when traveling. Voice mail must still be checked, work must be done on the plane, and the normal stress of airports and flight times must be battled. Rumor had it that on a flight from JFK to Chicago a senior banker from New York City couldn't fit his bag into the overhead compartment. The flight attendant told him that she would check his bag and that he could get it in Chicago from the baggage carousel after the plane landed. He went ape shit. He told the stewardess, "Sorry, but fuck you, miss. This goddamned bag will fit up here one way or another. This deal I'm working on is important and I don't have time to wait for the fucking carousel." After about ten minutes the banker still couldn't fit the bag into the overhead bin, so he slyly tried to leave the bag in the bathroom before takeoff. He figured that by the time they found it, it would be too late to stow it underneath. The flight attendant caught him and two security guards came to take his bag away. He cussed the security guards while they gave the bag to the baggage handlers. As we said, travel is stressful.

The normal routine for investment bankers includes constant travel. Bankers travel to pitch new business and they travel to meet with existing clients. They travel to visit a company's operations in between drafting sessions so that they can kick the tires and make sure that the company has a real business. These kick-the-tire visits are called "due diligence" sessions, and their purpose is to ensure that the company isn't pulling a scam over on the investing public.

While normal banking travel is a one-day trip to Pittsburgh or an overnight excursion to San Diego, the road show is a whole different animal. If normal banking travel is a watered-down well drink, then the road show is a beer bong full of pure grain alcohol. A normal road show lasts about two weeks, makes its way through at least three countries, and covers a minimum of fifteen domestic cities. In the course of this two-week marathon the banker will rarely spend an entire afternoon in the same city. On one road show, I covered London and Paris in a single day. I saw the Eiffel Tower, the Louvre, Buckingham Palace, and Trafalgar Square. The only problem was that I saw them all from the back of the limousine. It was real culture. It was glamorous.

A road show is exactly what it sounds like. It's a show that the bankers and the company take on the road to the investors. The show is well rehearsed. There are directors, producers, costumes, and props. Sometimes there are videos or product demonstrations. The road shows are a lot like the infomercials on late-night TV that tell you how to get rich and be your own boss. A slide show is created to make the presentation more user friendly. A finely scripted monologue is written for the company executives who are doing the presentation. The monologue is synchronized with the slide presentation.

The whole show is rehearsed, over and over again. The bankers ask the company executives mock questions to make sure that the company executives will be ready with any and all the answers. No stone is left unturned. Every detail is covered. Each of the potential investors will get no more than an hour with the management team, so the bankers have to make sure that the song and dance will go off flawlessly.

Meanwhile, as the show is being rehearsed, a whole cast of salespeople and professional travel planners in the investment bank are scheduling the meetings with potential investors. The associate is their ringleader. The associate has to book plane flights, hotel rooms, limousine pickup times, and dinner reservations. The associate is the pack mule. The associate has to carry extra prospectuses, the slide-show presentation, and all the audiovisual equipment. The investment banking travel department will help set up some of the details, but if there's a fuckup it's the associate's fault and the associate's responsibility to fix it. Sometimes, if the road show schedule gets tight, a private jet gets chartered. That can take a major burden off the associate's back. A good associate, however, will have a backup jet available, ready and waiting just in case the first one has a mechanical problem. Every base must be covered—once, twice, three times. At times, associates feel not like they're going on a road show to sell a deal to investors but like they're astronauts planning man's first mission to Uranus. Meals are planned, backup meals are planned. Hotel rooms, backup hotel rooms. Limousines and backup limousines.

The problems with travel, especially road show travel, get even worse when you have to go overseas. It's not easy to be a mule when you can't understand the language. But that's not the only problem. The time zones are all messed up, everybody who's French hates everything American, and the Germans eat sausage for every meal. Talk about your harrowing experiences: try having a bratwurst at 7:30 A.M.

Rolfe did a lot of international travel. Instead of spending time in California, the way he thought he was going to, he ended up making a whole lot of random trips to Europe. He didn't like them much. There was good reason why.

My first experience with international travel at DLJ was just a primer. It was a harbinger of much worse, and much uglier, things to come. I popped my cherry on the European leg of a road show for a junk bond offering. A storm trooper in managing director's clothing called me up and barked into the phone: "Rolfe, you're gonna cover Europe on this road show. Pack your fuckin' bags!" I was thrilled. I was going to Europe. I was the big man, heading over to the Continent to sell alternative investment products to Europe's landed aristocracy. It seemed sexy. I was an international playboy. It was the '80s all over again.

It didn't take long to shatter the illusion. I was midway through my first foray to the Old Country when I realized how much international travel sucked. The time changes completely fucked me up. The institutional accounts in Europe were all grade B—the bastard stepsons of their U.S. counterparts. Europe was just a backup in case we couldn't rustle up enough demand back home. I was a pitiful schmuck, baby-sitting a management team and peddling junk bonds to marginal European accounts. It was exactly the kind of assignment that was custom made for an associate.

The European institutional investors were all based out of either London or Paris, so just about every road show DLJ did made a stop in both cities. Typically, we'd take the management team on a red-eye out of New York that would get us into London just as the day was starting. A limo would pick us up at the airport and we'd spend the morning visiting British asset managers, all badly in need of dental work, who spent more time worrying about getting their tea "just so" than they did listening to us make our pitch for the crap we were trying to sell. We'd then jump an early-afternoon plane to Paris, where we'd spend the next few hours trying to sell the deal to small groups of gamey Frogs who made their Brit counterparts look like rocket scientists.

After we'd finished up with our meetings in Paris, we'd jump a plane back to New York, which would get us back home just a little over twenty-four hours after we'd left. That usually meant that we would arrive just in time for me to put in another eight hours at work before I finally

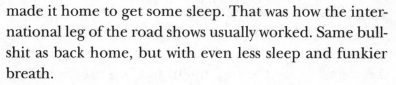

made it home to get some sleep. That was how the international leg of the road shows usually worked. Same bullshit as back home, but with even less sleep and funkier breath.

As it came to pass, though, the Paris-London road shows were just scrimmages in my international travelogue. They were warm-ups for the big game, the game where I'd get my butt reamed out like a sclerotic vein undergoing balloon angioplasty.

The Big Kahuna turned out to be a due diligence trip I had to take for a co-managed IPO. It was for a company called Global Wireless Assets (GWA). The deal looked soft and pretty from afar, and I wanted to take it to the dance. The closer I got, though, the nastier it started to look. I turned to run, I tried to scream, but it was too late. I couldn't turn back. I was obligated to boogie.

GWA was a "story" stock. That meant that there were no fundamentals to support valuation. It was the kind of investment opportunity that would have made Ben Graham, the father of value investing, turn over in his grave. The company had no earnings. It didn't have any cash flow. Its assets consisted primarily of equity stakes in a bunch of wireless communications properties all over the world. Its cash was heading out the door quicker than a greased pig in a Kansas City slaughterhouse, and it needed to get to market fast before it went broke.

GWA's business development director was running the capital-raising effort for the company. He was an ex-Goldman banker, which automatically meant that Goldman was leading the deal. SBC Warburg had been added to the underwriting lineup as a co-manager due to its significant European presence, and CIBC Wood Gundy was on board as the Canadian representative. That left DLJ, the final leg of the underwriting stool. DLJ didn't really belong, but GWA management was worried that the money from the IPO might not be enough to tide them over. If that happened, they figured that they'd need to issue some junk bonds. And if that happened, they wanted the DLJ franchise around so that they could jam some of those junk bonds down the throats of the hungry DLJ customers.

GWA's ownership interests were far-flung. The company had interests in telecommunications operations in Canada, Ireland, France, Austria, Poland, Mexico, Pakistan, and Hong Kong. In order to underwrite the deal, tradition had it that the bankers needed to see the company's operations. That was so that we could represent to the potential investors that the deal wasn't a complete scam. The ironic thing was that they could have put any of us bankers in any room, anywhere, full of beeping metal boxes with blinking lights and we would have given the thumbs up. We didn't know any better. It was like asking Ray Charles to opine on the authenticity of a Rembrandt.

Since the company was so hard up for money the deal was on a fast track. That meant that we were going to have to do our diligence on the operations in record time. It was decided that we'd visit all the regions, with the exception of Pakistan and Hong Kong, in the course of a one-week diligence marathon. We were going to have to pass up the curry and the chop suey for the sake of expediency.

Monday, 8 A.M.—We all met in Toronto on a Monday morning at GWA's world headquarters. The one-hour,

MONKEY BUSINESS

350-mile trip from New York to Toronto was the first small step in our diligence marathon. I was the sole DLJ representative. Co-managed deals generally didn't merit the presence of anybody over the rank of associate on diligence trips and this one was no different. I alone would bear full responsibility for DLJ's potential legal exposure. I wasn't sweating the details. I viewed it as a boondoggle.

The day in Toronto had been planned as an overview of all the company's operations. It was supposed to set the stage for the coming week's activities. We sat in a room with no windows, eating finger sandwiches and listening to the company's business development director run through his descriptive analysis of the various properties. He talked for six hours straight without taking a break. I don't even think that he took a sip of water. He had a glassy-eyed manservant who circled the room nonstop handing out reams of paper that were covered with details and numerical analyses. By lunchtime of that first day I was already thoroughly confused. I couldn't get straight whether the paging operations were in Austria or Paris. By late afternoon I'd completely given up. There was just too much stuff to remember.

At 5 P.M. we got into some limos and headed out to the airport. We were short one seat, and I somehow managed to get elbowed up front to sit with the driver. It was my first clue that the other underwriters viewed my presence as an annoyance. They viewed DLJ as the unclean freak, and as the sole DLJ representative they looked upon me as the freak incarnate who was responsible for taking fee dollars out of their pockets. That didn't bother me so much. The limo driver was a good guy, and on the way to the airport we talked about his new Lincoln Continental while the other bankers sucked up to the company guys in the back. I could have sworn that I heard some slurping noises.

Monday, 7 P.M.—Our British Airways flight departed Toronto International Airport bound for Dublin. The lady banker from Goldman was sitting next to me. She wouldn't even talk to me. She answered every question I asked her with a one-word reply. What a bitch. I took the pair of earplugs out of the travel packet that the stewardess had given me, stuffed them up my nose, and pretended to go to sleep. I knew that would bother her. Thirty-five hundred miles and six hours later, we touched down in Dublin.

Tuesday, 6 A.M.—We lost five hours on the trip over, so we arrived as the sun was coming up. We were scheduled to stay at the St. Rugala hotel and our meetings for the day had been scheduled in one of the hotel's conference rooms. The St. Rugala hotel was a fancy one. In Europe, that meant that it was in a really old building with small rooms and crappy plumbing, and that it cost a boatload to stay there. Once we were checked in, we had a half hour to blow before our meetings with the management team from GWA's Irish operations were set to begin. That was just enough time for me to figure out that the hotel's cable system had a free soft-porn channel. Maybe that was what made it a luxury hotel, no extra charge for porno. I called my voice mail back at the office. I had fourteen messages.

The meeting was a farce. We had traveled 3,500 miles to do diligence on the operations, and all we did was sit in a hotel conference room and listen to a bunch of suits tell us about what a great business they were going to build. We could have done it over the phone and saved the airfare. Company management viewed the Irish business as a major piece of the overall value, but the operations hadn't yet been built and the plans were for implementation of an untested technology. They didn't even have an antenna to show us. They had nothing.

By late afternoon I was dragging hard. I'd been up all night and my body couldn't figure out what the hell was going on. For lunch we'd been served cucumber sandwiches and flat orange drinks that just hadn't done the trick.

I figured that I could slip upstairs to my room for just a couple of minutes to lie down. I wouldn't be gone long, and I wouldn't miss anything important in the diligence meeting. I'd pretend that I was leaving to make a phone call. I could close my eyes for just thirty minutes. Nobody would even notice.

I left the conference room and made my way upstairs. The bed felt so good. I was so tired. I'll just relax for a minute, I told myself.

I woke up, rolled over, and looked at the clock. Fuck. My thirty-minute snooze had turned into a two-hour nap. I ran down the stairs and back into the conference room where the diligence meeting was taking place. The other bankers were taking a quick recess, working the phones to their offices back in New York and Toronto. The SBC

Warburg banker spotted me as I entered and made an exaggerated stage whisper, loud enough for everybody present to hear. "Oh, and where have *you* been?"

"My apologies," I replied, "one of my other deals blew up. I've been trying to salvage it."

I didn't realize that my hair was standing straight up in the air, my shirt was untucked, and that everybody in the room knew I was lying.

I took a seat. The useless diligence dance continued, on into the night.

Wednesday, 5 A.M.—After four hours of sleep, we got on the earliest possible flight headed to Paris. Another 190 miles. Another hour time change. GWA operated a dispatch radio business in Paris. They owned a few big antennae that sat up on top of hills around the city. Truckers and cab drivers bought radios from the company and used them to talk to each other through the antennae. GWA had given up trying to convince the bankers that the business was a sexy one. Instead, they told us it would be a "solid business." In banker language that meant that it wasn't a hot prospect and that it didn't have any good marketing potential.

Once again, we sat in a room and listened to one of the general managers tell us about the business. Like most French people, he hated us for being American. That was OK with me. To amuse myself, while the other bankers were asking legitimate questions about the operations I asked him stupid questions like, "If one of the cab drivers spills a cup of coffee into the radio, will it stop working?" When the meeting ended, the Goldman and SBC Warburg bankers got into a fight over whether we should spend the night in Paris and head out for Innsbruck in the morning or whether we should go to Innsbruck that night. The Goldman vice president wanted to go shopping in Paris and get Hermès scarves. I told everybody that they could do whatever the hell they wanted but I was going to Innsbruck. I called my voice mail back at the office. I had seven more messages.

Wednesday, 7 P.M.—We got on the puddle jumper from Paris to Innsbruck, Austria. Another 190 miles. By this point, I'd only had six hours of sleep in the prior sixty hours. I fell asleep before the stewardess even got to me with the cocktail peanuts.

Wednesday, 11 P.M.—Innsbruck was a welcome change from France. Then again, a kick in the head would have been a welcome change. Everybody spoke English. Our cab driver was named Max Van Weezel. GWA, who had been responsible for booking all the travel arrangements, had booked us into the Innsbruck Holiday Inn. The Goldman bankers weren't too hip on that. They didn't think that "Goldman Sachs" and "Holiday Inn" belonged together. Four Seasons, definitely. Hilton, maybe. Holiday Inn, no way. It didn't seem to matter that the rooms were twice as big as they would have been at one of the classy hotels. It didn't seem to matter that there was a swimming pool, which the classy hotels never had. It was still a Holiday Inn and that didn't cut the mustard with Goldman bankers.

I called my voice mail back at the office. I had four more messages. I accidentally erased three of those before listening to them.

Thursday, 8 A.M.—We began our meetings with the operating managers of the Austrian paging operation. The Austrians served us fish for lunch. I fell asleep during the meeting and drooled on my tie. I learned nothing about the paging operations that day.

Thursday, 6:30 P.M.—We got on a plane bound for Warsaw, Poland. Another 1,100 miles. We lost another hour in the time change. I had a banking dream on the plane. I dreamed that one of my managing directors, dressed in a black leather dominatrix outfit, was flagellating me with a whip made of Twizzlers. I may have been delirious.

Four hours later we landed at the Warsaw International Airport. The airport had no lights, the runway was covered with snow, and there were wild dogs running alongside the plane as it landed. None of it fazed me. All I wanted was a hot shower and a warm bed.

Thursday, Midnight—It was midnight by the time we got to our hotel. I was now 5,000 miles away, and seven time zones removed, from DLJ's headquarters back in New York. I was in snowy Warsaw inside the former Eastern Bloc. I actually started to feel as if I'd left it all behind. I could disappear into the Polish countryside and become a potato farmer. I was tired and disoriented but felt better than I'd felt in months because I knew that nobody could touch me. No managing directors. No vice presidents. I was flying solo.

As it turned out the only place I was flying was right into the eye of the storm. I was a pitiful fool to think that I was beyond the iron clutches of my superiors. There was no escape.

I was standing at the check-in counter when the phone behind the desk rang. The clerk picked it up. Somebody on the other end was speaking. The clerk appeared puzzled. He looked up.

"Is there a Mr. Rolfe here?"

I couldn't believe it. It had to be a coincidence. There had to be another Mr. Rolfe. There was no way that I'd come this far to be tracked down in the lobby of the hotel. I spoke up: "I'm Mr. Rolfe."

"You have a phone call." The clerk handed me the phone.

"Hello?"

"Hey Johnny, it's Melba." Melba was one of my BAs.

"How the fuck did you find me here? I'm standing at the check-in counter."

"I called GWA in Toronto. They told me where you were staying. I figured that you'd be in your room."

"Unbelievable. Why are you calling?"

"It's Bubbles. He's going nuts. He's been down here all afternoon screaming at everybody. He needs to talk to you about the Woodpecker deal. He said that he's been leaving you voice mails for the last two days and that you haven't returned any of them. He said that he left you one last night telling you that it was urgent, that you needed to call him."

Uh-oh, I thought. That must have been one of the messages that I'd accidentally erased the night before in Innsbruck. "All right, look," I told Melba, "tell him that my plane got delayed and that I just got into Warsaw. I'll call him in a couple of minutes."

My peace was shattered. Not even the tattered remnants of the Iron Curtain could keep my managing directors at bay. There was to be no peace. I trudged up to my room, head held low, and put in a call to Bubbles. First he ripped me a new bunghole. Then he proceeded to generate enough demands related to Project Woodpecker to keep me working frantically for the next four hours. When I was too tired to work any more I called my voice mail back at the office. I had nine new messages. I didn't listen to any of them. I didn't care any more. It was 4 A.M.

Friday, 5 A.M.—I woke up an hour after I'd fallen asleep. I was dazed. I stumbled into the bathroom and, in my confused state, mistook the bidet for a toilet. Why couldn't the Europeans have just one big porcelain throne in the bathroom like the Americans did? I didn't get it. They refused to shower regularly, but wanted to have the cleanest asses in town.

Friday, 12 Noon—Friday morning was free. It had been scheduled that way to give us time to do some sightseeing around Warsaw. But that was a pipe dream. I sat in my hotel room instead and did some cleanup work on Project Woodpecker.

MONKEY BUSINESS

The diligence sessions on the Polish cellular operations began at noon. Poland was GWA's crown jewel. A big chunk of the expected offering proceeds had been earmarked to pay for the buildout of the Polish system. We had to pray that the money from the offering would actually be used to build the system and wouldn't end up in an anonymous bank account in the Cayman Islands. It was now Friday afternoon and I'd only had fourteen hours of sleep since the previous Monday morning. The chairs were comfortable and there was no way to keep my eyes open. I fell into a deep sleep. Diligence be damned.

Friday, 7 P.M.—GWA had planned a special dinner for us. Some dignitaries from the Canadian embassy showed up. I sat across from the ambassador. He was a big, fat jolly guy who looked a lot like Santa Claus. He spent most of the dinner drinking plum wine. I didn't want him to feel alone so I joined in. Before going to bed I called New York and checked my voice mail. I had six new messages.

Saturday, 12 Noon—We got on a plane and chased daylight for twelve hours. Warsaw to Frankfurt to London to New York, 5,000 miles. It was 5 P.M. Saturday—New York time—when we finally landed. I thought about bending over to kiss the ground when I got off the plane at Kennedy International Airport, but my back was really killing me from all the hours that I'd spent in plane seats that week, and the ground didn't look so clean.

Sunday, 9 A.M.—I spent three and a half hours responding to the forty voice mails I'd gotten during my previous week's absence. I did it from home because I didn't want anybody to see me in the office and know that I was back in the country. That could spell trouble. I held a cloth over the phone as I returned each voice mail so that it would sound like I was far away.

Sunday, 8 P.M.—The trip wasn't over yet. We still had to go to Mexico City. Another 1,900 miles. Another five hours. We didn't get into our hotel until about 2 A.M. By the time we finally walked into the lobby, we all looked like such pieces of dung that I swear I saw the lady behind the front desk grab for the Bat Phone to call security. I wouldn't have cared. I could have slept anywhere, even in a Mexican jail.

Monday, 8 A.M.—We sat in a room, listening to guys with heavy Mexican accents talk about how great their business was, and looking at metal boxes with blinking lights on them. I can't even remember what GWA owned in Mexico City. I think that it was either paging or cellular or dispatch radio. Maybe it was a grocery store or a whorehouse. It didn't really matter. I was a robot. I was a dog. I was dead tired.

Monday, 9 P.M.—Home for good. Finally. The diligence was finished. I fell asleep in my suit.

I'd spent eight days doing diligence on GWA's foreign

operations. I'd traveled 12,000 miles through seven countries and eight time zones. I was now the sole fount of DLJ's institutional knowledge on GWA's operations. I'd slept through a few diligence sessions and zoned out through almost all of the others. All I had to show for the eight days' work was a page and a half of notes and a headache. DLJ was going to attempt to sell GWA's equity to their best institutional accounts based on my assertions that the deal was a good one. I hoped that somebody, somewhere, had their fingers crossed.

Bonuses, Reviews, and Compensation

Me want cookie!
—Cookie Monster

"He's a fuckstick. A complete fuckstick."

Troob and I were sitting in the back of the biannual analyst review session. Andrew Gold, a second-year associate, was giving his assessment of one of the first-year analysts, Carl Kantor. Doug Franken, the managing director in charge of all staffing matters for investment banking, didn't understand what Goldy was trying to say. He asked for some clarification.

"Goldy, what's a fuckstick? I don't know what a fuckstick is."

Goldy clarified. "A fuckstick is a stick that's only good for one thing and that's for cramming up somebody's ass. It's no good as a walking stick. It's no good for stickball. It's only good for sticking into a butt. It's the stupidest, most worthless kind of stick there is. That's what Kantor is. He's a fuckstick."

Franken decided that this one was worth digging into a little deeper. "Give me a little help here, Goldy. What is it that Kantor did that endeared him to you so deeply?"

"He built a merger model for me that left an entire division out of the final roll-up for the merged entity. We delivered a goddamned fairness opinion to the committee based on a model with one of the target's primary divisions missing. It was a disgrace. I can't work with somebody like that. We should fire him."

I looked over at Troob. I knew that we were thinking the same thing. Kantor, the analyst, wasn't the fuckstick. Goldy was the fuckstick. It was basic. You didn't tell a monkey to make a merger model for you and then expect that there wouldn't be any mistakes. You had to check the monkey's work, because monkeys were always liable to leave a few banana peels lying behind. We knew that Goldy was lazy and that his laziness had finally caught up to him on this one. He just didn't want to go down alone. He wanted to take Kantor down with him.

Troob and I had to come to Kantor's defense. He was a good kid. Overworked, but good. He'd done a lot of work for both me and Troob. We'd promised him that we'd go to bat for him during the review. Troob spoke up.

"Kantor's a good man. Goldy's rap is bullshit. The kid's here twenty-four hours a day, seven days a week. He's walked through walls for me. The wrong walls sometimes, but he's walked through walls. We're not training brain surgeons, we're training apes. Kantor's a good ape."

The room was quiet for a minute. The other associates didn't know what to do. As associates, nodding our heads in agreement was an involuntary reflex. We'd been taught to always concur. Conflict was confusing. Finally, somebody else spoke up.

"Yeah, I think that Kantor's good. He's always done good work for me. I like him."

The tide had turned. The associate gods were now smiling on Kantor. His review would be favorable. He'd get his bonus.

Twice a year all the DLJ associates piled into a conference room. We sat in padded chairs and ate macaroni salad. Managing Director Franken and the senior associate in charge of analyst staffing sat at the front of the room like two Indian chiefs. They read the names of the analysts off one by one in alphabetical order. As each name was read, the associates who had worked with that analyst weighed in with their judgment of the analyst's worth. Those assessments were used, in turn, to determine the analysts' bonuses—bonuses that ranged anywhere from $30,000 for a first-year analyst to $100,000 for a third-year analyst. We were all sworn to secrecy regarding the review session's proceedings. We were told that if word ever got out that we had divulged details of the review session's proceedings the repercussions would be fast and furious. It was our own little Star Chamber. We were horse traders, checking out the teeth and gums of the old nags to determine their health before we sent them packing to the glue factory. For a few short hours we had the power.

There were two problems with these review sessions. The first was that outside of the review sessions we'd been conditioned to always tow the party line. Independent thought wasn't valued. We were processors. We weren't allowed to have our own opinions; we were only allowed to have our managing directors' opinions. So, when they locked us into the room twice a year for these analyst review sessions and asked for our opinions most of us didn't know what to do. We usually panicked and fell back onto our instinctive reflex—nodding in agreement.

In practice, what this meant was that there was generally complete unanimity on every analyst's review. If the first associate to speak gave a glowing review, then all the other reviews that followed would glow like kryptonite. If the first associate to speak trashed the analyst, forget about it. Resurrection was unlikely, and the offending analyst could end up with $30,000 less than his more fortunate counterparts. The tide, once it began to ebb or flow, was difficult to stem. The associates at the review session all wanted to be on the same helicopter out of Ho Chi Minh City, whether it was headed deeper into the jungle or back to the DMZ. That's how we'd been trained.

The other problem with the analyst review sessions was that they inevitably degenerated into outlets for the months of frustration that we ourselves had suffered at the hands of our vice presidents, senior vice presidents, and managing directors. They'd spanked, whipped, and bludgeoned us and we had to pass those beatings along to help clear our anger. If our rite of passage was going to be difficult, we were surely going to make the analysts' rites of passage that much more miserable. The biannual review sessions were the only opportunity that we had to inflict that abuse in front of an audience. Beating the dog was a much more satisfying exercise with people watching. Our mothers would not have been proud.

As we sat in these reviews, there was an unspoken concern in the back of all of our minds. We all recognized that the reviews were bullshit. We knew that the reviews didn't do a good of job rewarding the analysts who deserved to be rewarded and canning the ones who didn't. We knew that an analyst's reviews depended on what kind of a day the associates who had worked with that analyst were having. We also knew that if Franken, the senior banker taking notes on each analyst, had an itch on his ass when a good comment was being made about one of the analysts, then that analyst could be shit out of luck because Franken wouldn't write it down. We also knew that a roomful of vice presidents, senior vice presidents, and managing directors were reviewing us the same way that we were reviewing the analysts. We knew that the process wasn't any more equitable for us than it was for the analysts. We knew that for us the stakes were higher because the bonuses that were on the line were that much bigger. There was that much more to worry about.

At DLJ, the culmination of reviews came in early February each year with the announcement of bonuses. DLJ was late in the process. Bankers at Goldman and Morgan got their bonus numbers in late December. Most of the other investment banks gave out their numbers in January. Not DLJ. DLJ waited to see what kind of bonuses the other banks were giving out, and then they figured out how much they'd have to pay to keep the golden rats from jumping. The upshot was that there was a six-week period every year between late December and early February during which we began hearing stirrings through the grapevine about what the other banks were paying out. As the six weeks passed, we worked ourselves into an increasing state of agitation. Work slowed to a crawl. Bonuses were all we thought, talked, and cared about. We could have been diagnosed with a terminal case of rancid halitosis and it wouldn't have mattered. We'd spent twelve months busting our humps and kissing the ass of the institution with the expectation that we'd be well compensated. If our counterparts at the other banks ended up making more than us, we figured that we might as well be kissing ass there. After all, at the end of the day it wasn't like a DLJ ass was any tastier than a Morgan Stanley ass.

Every associate who knew an associate at another investment bank became a potential source of intelligence. Rumor ran rampant. We would all get on the phone and begin calling people whom we hadn't spoken to since business school.

"Hey, man, it's Johnny Rolfe calling. Do you guys have your nums yet?"

"Yeah, we got them."

"What's the range?"

"Eighty thousand on the low end, $110,000 on the high end."

"Shit, that's not bad."

"What have you heard?"

"I heard that Goldman was $90,000 to $130,000. They're the best so far. Bankers Trust came in $70,000 to $100,000. Cheap bastards."

That was the extent of the conversation. No formalities. No "Hi, how have things been since business school?" The nature of the call was clear, the need for information was accepted. The ritual was embraced by associates at every bank. We were on a mission.

As soon as one of us got a new data point, it was instantaneously disseminated among our classmates. It was like magic, we could smell the money. We approached the information-gathering task on comparable company bonuses with more zeal than any of us had ever mustered for a deal. This was our bank account that we were talking about. There could be no secrets. We knew that if the investment banking department had an unusually profitable year the bonuses might go up modestly, and if the year really sucked they might drop a bit. In general, though, the size of our bonuses was much less affected by the bank's profitability than it was for the more senior bankers. What really mattered was how well we were paid in relation to our peers at other banks.

DLJ had always had a reputation for paying top dollar. For a second-year associate that could mean an incremental $30,000 in the bonus over what associates at the other banks were getting. The only other bank that consistently had payouts equal to DLJ was Goldman, so the first numbers that we always tried to get were the Goldman numbers. Those set the hurdle for us. Some banks like PaineWebber ended up at the bottom of the payout scale every year. Troob and I were never able to figure out what the associates at those places used as their yardstick. As far as we were concerned, if our payout from DLJ wasn't one of the top three on the Street, then we might as well be working for Dairy Queen. We didn't have any other way to measure our success. It wasn't the money. We needed the bragging rights.

After six weeks of obsessive focus on what we were

going to get paid, it was inevitable that when we actually got the number it would be a letdown. Regardless of what the bonus number was, if fireworks didn't go off with a brass band playing "Stars and Stripes Forever" in the background it would seem like our obsession had been misplaced. We'd spent close to two months puffing up like peacocks to convince ourselves that we actually deserved a cash bonus that, a year and a half out of business school, would take our total compensation for the year close to $200,000. By the time judgment day rolled around we were damned sure that if we only ended with total comp for the year of $180,000, we were getting raped. We weren't about to take that shit lying down.

Jim Firestone, the head of my group, called me on the phone.

"John, why don't you come down to my office for a couple of minutes. We need to talk about your bonus."

I walked down the hall toward Firestone's office. What awaited me? Would it be fame and fortune? Humiliation and ruin? I'd soon find out.

As I entered Firestone's office he motioned me toward the sofa. So be it. Firestone handed me a piece of paper. It was a memo addressed to me from Steven Tolls and Brock LeBlank, the chairman and vice chairman of the Banking Group. At the top, it said "Annual bonus and compensation."

Firestone began to speak. "John, we've been extraordinarily pleased with your performance this year. The firm has also had a great year. Your bonus reflects all of that. . . ."

I didn't hear a single word he was saying. I began to

scan the memo, frantically looking for numbers. They
were not hard to find; they were in the first paragraph.

> We are pleased to inform you that you have
> been awarded a cash bonus of $125,000 . . . you
> also received $19,000 in special incentives for
> your role in lead-managed IPOs . . . together
> with your salary . . . your total compensation . . .
> is $209,000.

There it was. That was it. The anticipation was over.
The number was pretty good, as good as Goldman's
numbers. I'd just made over ten times as much money
as I'd made in my last year of full-time work in advertising before going to business school. The more successful managing directors whom I was working for would,
in turn, make ten times as much as I had. That was a
steep income curve. That was what awaited me if I could
just tough it out. I couldn't be happy just yet, though. I
didn't know what my classmates had made. Even though
I'd just made $209,000, there was a possibility that my
classmates had all made $215,000. If that was the case,
then I was either a guinea pig, an idiot, or chopped liver.

Firestone, meanwhile, was still droning on in the background. He was reading excerpts from some of the written reviews that the vice presidents and managing
directors whom I'd worked with had submitted. He was a
thorough guy and wanted me to hear the whole story.

". . . John's a real team player, a valuable asset to the
Communications and Entertainment group."

". . . he shows great maturity. He can always be relied
on to get the job done."

"... I really enjoy working with John. The clients all speak highly of him."

"... John shows great promise as a banker. He has the potential to be a real star."

I wasn't listening. All the excerpts that Firestone was reading to me were generic. I began to suspect that the vice presidents, senior vice presidents, and managing directors each had a drawer full of Xerox copies of their associate review sheets, fully prepared except for the "name" slot. They each probably had three different sheets; "Good," "Average," and "Crap," which they affixed names to each year when reviews came due.

Firestone was just finishing up.

"John, you're at the top of your class this year and your bonus reflects that. You're almost in a league of your own. It's very important that you don't discuss your compensation with any of your classmates. That information is nobody's business but yours and we expect it to stay that way."

I stood up to go. I was thinking about what Firestone had just said, the part about not discussing my compensation with any of my classmates. I'd been expecting something like that. I'd been warned by others. Their rationale was transparent. That information was power and if none of us told each other how we'd been compensated, then they could tell each of us whatever they wanted to and we'd all be happy clams. They could pay each of us the same amount and then tell each of us that we were at the top of the class. Our egos would remain intact and there'd be no dissension. We were too smart for that, though. We had a plan.

My classmates and I had devised a plan to circumvent

the call for secrecy. We all felt a little gun-shy about telling each other what our actual bonus numbers were, so we had come up with a system beforehand that would protect our anonymity while still giving us the strategic advantage of full disclosure. We'd all agreed to meet in a conference room, write our bonus numbers down on a piece of paper, and throw them into a hat. One of us would then take all the pieces of paper, write down the numbers from highest to lowest, and distribute copies of the list to everybody. That way, we'd all know where we really panned out in the hierarchy among our class-mates. If anybody thought that they'd gotten fucked, they could bitch and moan about it to the higher powers. They could make their dissatisfaction known. The bal-ance of power would shift from them to us. We'd hold the cards.

I got back to my office and called Slick.

"Hey, Slick, it's Rolfe. I got my nums, how about you?"

"Yeah, I got 'em. When are we meeting?"

"That's what I'm calling to find out. Round up the troops. Let's get this over with."

"OK."

Ten minutes later, Slick called me back. "Rolfe, you're not gonna believe this."

"What?"

"Everybody's bailing on us. Nobody wants to do it any-more."

"Why the fuck not?"

"I don't know. Nobody's being straight with me. They've all got bullshit excuses."

It didn't take a rocket scientist to figure it out. Each of us had been told that we were at the top of the class.

We all had a pretty good idea that we were being given a line of crap, but nobody really wanted to find out that they weren't, in fact, the best. Investment banking had a way of attracting arrogant fuckers like us, and that was our Achilles' heel. The big boys knew that. They knew us better than we knew ourselves. We were screwed.

"Slick, what was your total comp number, man? Did it have a two in front of it?"

"Yeah, it did."

"Did they tell you that you were at the top of the class?"

"Yeah."

"Me too."

"You don't figure that we're really the best, do you?"

"No way. They must have told everybody the same thing. I'm gonna call Wings. He's still in for figuring out where we stand. I'll find out what he got."

I called Wings. His number had a two in front of it also. They'd told him that he was at the top of the class. There was a pattern. It was no coincidence. They'd played us like a shopworn fiddle. We were hopeless amateurs. My phone rang. It was Gator.

"Rolfe, I've got a high-yield pitch that needs doing. I'm gonna need to see a draft by tomorrow morning because the pitch is on Thursday. Why don't you come up to my office so that we can talk about exactly what we're gonna need for this thing."

Fuck. That meant that an all-nighter lay ahead. Reality hit me like an acute case of Montezuma's revenge. The evanescent joy of my big payday exhaled its final gasp and was no more. I'd worked for a year, obsessed for six weeks, and enjoyed the fruits of my labors for ten minutes. Now it was back into the dark underbelly of my investment banking existence. I remembered that I was nothing but unwanted garbage. I took a deep breath and headed for Gator's office.

The Epiphany

The good thing about masturbation is that you don't have to dress up for it.

—*Truman Capote*

The dream. Was it worth it? Was big money by thirty the goal, or would we rather enjoy our lives? Could you have both and still be an investment banking associate? You can be rich at thirty, forty, or fifty, but you can't recapture your youth. You can't buy time and you can't buy happiness. Time marches on. The DLJ annual report said "Have fun." We weren't.

During our first few months at DLJ the dream was still alive and well in our minds. We didn't take notice of the sorry state of our lives. We didn't realize that we no longer had a life at work and a life outside of work. All had become one. At some point, though, as the numbing months of toil rolled on, our views began to change. For Troob, the change was gradual—a nagging periodic sense that he was missing something, that something wasn't right. Troob was still in his relationship with Marjorie, his beauty from Chicago. Things had been rocky for them at times, but I could tell that he wanted to make it work. He had taken it to the next level, and was now professing his undying love for her. He was worried because he had seen Slick and other colleagues break off their impending engagements due to the pressures of the job. His life was deteriorating and it bothered him. He was a guy who used to work out every day. He had once been lean and mean. Now, when he put a swimsuit on, he looked like a big pink piece of Spam in a can. His negative feelings, only occasional at first, began recurring with increasing frequency until the dull buzz couldn't be ignored any longer.

Things were different for me. The feeling was more than a nagging sense; it was an epiphany. It was a thunderbolt from the blue.

I am a man. Like other men, I have needs. I need women to tell me that they like me. I crave the company of women. I desire their pleasures.

When my classmates and I began our journey through the web of DLJ, most of us had significant others. We were all fresh out of business school. We had all landed sought-after positions as investment bankers with the mighty DLJ. We all had high opinions of ourselves. We had taken a giant first step toward establishing ourselves as players in the financial fast lane. For most of us, an indispensable square on that quilt of plenty was our significant other. As our first year wore on, however, the devotion to the job that was required of us began to wear on many of these heavenly matches. One after another, my classmates got dumped, thrown out, and had engagements broken off by mates who concluded that a healthy paycheck wasn't nearly enough compensation for a partner who was never there.

Not me. I didn't have a girlfriend to begin with so there was nobody there to dump me. I had become quite accustomed to pleasuring myself, and while my classmates searched for enough free time to make it to the gym to work out, I had no need for such common pursuits. Due to my natural ardor, and my need to satisfy that ardor through self-gratification, I was now sporting some of the strongest forearms in the banking division. Popeye had nothing on me.

It wasn't long after my banking career began that an irrepressible urge for self-gratification at the workplace first hit me. I haven't seen many published statistics on this sort of contemptible behavior, but I think that most people have enough self-control to resist whatever urges may traverse their loins. Unfortunately, while most people can waylay their needs for several hours and, upon returning home, achieve momentary nirvana, the task isn't so easy for a lecherous young banker. If the urge to indulge hits at 4 P.M., chances are that there are another good ten hours of work ahead before you're going to be able to take care of business.

At least that was how I justified it to myself the first time I slunk into the DLJ men's room in search of pleasure.

The problem with breaking a taboo is that, once you've broken it, there's no turning back. My forays into the men's room became more and more frequent, my lust for life more unquenchable. I was a super sperm dynamo and nobody was going to stop me.

One thing led to another. I became emboldened. One

night, in the wee hours of the A.M., the urge settled in as I sat at my desk. I was so tired. I didn't want to move. Just one lone act of passion couldn't hurt.

I poked my head out into the corridor. It was 3 A.M., there was nobody around. I can do it just this once, I convinced myself, then never again. It's not like it's going to take me long to close the deal. What are the chances of getting caught? Who's even around to catch me? I didn't care if I was going to go blind and get hairy palms. I was out of control.

And so the action for satisfaction began. I didn't get caught. It didn't take long. And when the dirty deed was finished, I sat back to bask in the momentary glow of a job well done. I craved a cigarette, but had none. It was during this moment of reflection that I had my epiphany.

In my pre-performance haste to ensure that none of my colleagues were still around, I'd forgotten about the thousands of potential spectators who lay directly across the street. My life was DLJ. Only the DLJ people mattered. Others were irrelevant.

One entire wall of my office was glass. It looked out onto two adjacent office buildings. At 3 A.M. most of the offices in my building were dark. Any offices that were still lit up at 3 A.M. demanded the attention of anybody who happened to be looking out a window in one of the adjacent buildings. To break it down, I was spanking off on a Broadway stage and everybody in the two adjacent buildings was my audience. Did any of my neighbors watch my performance? Was it worthy of a Tony? I don't know. If they did, their image of investment bankers must have been permanently disfigured. It was 3 A.M., I was sitting at my office desk, and I'd just finished spanking. I was worthless and weak. There was no longer any life outside the office. That was my epiphany, and it was the beginning of the end of my life as an investment banker.

My public stroke-a-thon in the office might not, by itself, have been enough to turn my career tide against investment banking. I might have surveyed my sorry display but concluded that my perversities were mine alone and would persist regardless of the career venue in which I was placed. Fortunately, I was able to look around at DLJ and see the remains of age-old bankers who had probably once been like me. I could see the guys who'd been bankers for twenty years, had never been married, and were as perverted as Pee-Wee Herman in a raincoat. Banking was their life, and banking had been their death. I could see these people, and take hope that maybe it was banking that had made them the way they were. If it was banking, I reasoned, escape might provide me with an opportunity for redemption.

The textbook example of one of these filthy career bankers was Kirk Flynn, aka Captain Kirk. He was a senior vice president. He was a pervert. He was a teacher. He was a friend. Most of all, though, he was my eye-opener—the guy who made me realize what I didn't want to become.

Everybody, everywhere has a friend or relative who they keep quiet about. Usually, it's because that person says and does things that are so incredibly egregious, outrageous, and patently unacceptable that their behavior is inevitably going to end up serving as a source of total embarrassment. What most people fail to admit, even to themselves, however, is that they enjoy that person's company. The next time that the drunk guy at the party calls the pompous bastard's wife a fat pig, open your eyes. The signs of public outcry that follow generally mask twinkling eyes and barely concealed signs of genuine mirth. After all, chances are good that the pompous bastard's wife is indeed fat, and chances are even better that if she wasn't a bitch the drunk guy wouldn't have called her out on it. It's just that nobody else has the nuts to say it.

Captain Kirk was the drunk guy at the party. He was like my perverted uncle who has to stay out back in the woodshed during Thanksgiving dinner. He was a good guy to go out on a weekend bender with, but his real intrinsic value lay in his filthy, lecherous mind.

The Captain was a senior vice president in the Consumer Technology Group. We worked on more than a few deals together.

I had heard rumblings regarding Captain Kirk's reputation while I was still a summer guy at DLJ. Kirk was a lifelong DLJer. After twenty years with the firm, he was a member of the Old Guard. He'd been a senior vice president for as long as anyone could remember. He had a few clients of his own, but not enough to get him the bump to the next level. He had long ago stopped fretting about the fact that he was never going to get promoted to managing director, though. He didn't care anymore.

Captain Kirk was forty-seven, long since divorced, and he was as horny as a bullfrog.

Often, when people met the Captain, they'd wonder

why he wasn't married. Occasionally, the brave ones would ask him outright. He never minced words.

"Why the fuck would I want to be married?"

"Don't you ever want to have kids?" they'd usually follow up.

"Kids? My sister's got three kids. She lives an hour away from me. I can visit the kids anytime I want. Meanwhile, I can keep on fucking the twenty-five-year-olds."

There was no question that Kirk loved the ladies. Demonstrating that love was a Captain Kirk specialty. Many of the women, whether they were social or professional acquaintances, were treated to the lip-smacking Captain Kirk kiss upon introduction.

The Captain knew that he wasn't supposed to be smooching his female colleagues. As long as they would tolerate it, though, he'd keep it up.

Captain Kirk's sexual peccadilloes weren't limited to occasional indiscretions with the female employees. The fire in his loins burned far too bright for that. When it came to the lust in his heart, the Captain was like a bull in a china shop.

Captain Kirk's lack of technical knowledge was mythical. This was a man who worked in the Consumer Technology Group, yet he had to write step-by-step directions on the plastic casing of his computer monitor so that he wouldn't forget how to activate his automated stock quotation system. The Internet was a foreign concept to Kirk. He didn't know what it was, he didn't know what it was capable of, and he would have gone on in perpetual blissful oblivion if it hadn't been for an offhand comment I made to him in the hallway one afternoon.

The Captain and I were walking to a conference room

to meet with the management of SharpSound, a manufacturer of high-end audio speakers. I was giving the Captain a primer on the Internet.

"Kirk, did you know that with DLJ's new high-speed Internet connection I can download full-motion porno videos off the Internet while I'm sitting at my desk? It doesn't cost a penny."

Free porno! That was enough to grab his attention.

"What're you talking about, John?"

"It's like this, Kirk. If I get bored, I click my mouse a few times, and before you know it I'm watching first-class porn."

We had reached the conference room, and SharpSound management was waiting. I could see that the Captain had many questions to ask me, but they'd have to wait.

We were halfway through our pitch with SharpSound and I could see that the Captain was having a difficult time focusing on the business at hand. He was still thinking about those dirty videos. Fortunately, he knew SharpSound management well. They were a longtime client of his, and they were well versed in the particulars of his fetishes. So it really came as no huge surprise when, during a momentary lapse in the conversation, Kirk suddenly blurted it out.

"John knows how to get free porno on the Internet!"

Nobody said anything. We all looked around at each other. I smiled.

"Kirk's just learned of the power of the Internet. He's looking forward to exploring its offerings," I offered up to everybody.

Everyone laughed.

MONKEY BUSINESS

Captain Kirk beamed at me. I was his protégé, and my client management skills were coming along fabulously.

Following our meeting, the Captain and I headed back toward my office.

"John, you've got to show me some of that porno. I won't believe it till I've seen it."

We hunkered down in my office in front of the computer monitor. I began to introduce the Captain to the wonders of free porno, Internet-style. I pulled up a long list of potential fantasy sites and directed Kirk to take his pick. His first selection was a dandy: "Asian Babe Extravaganza." We accessed the site, and within seconds we were staring at leggy Asian women giving us private beaver screenings. The Captain couldn't believe his eyes.

"Oh my God. This is incredible. Can I do this on my computer? Can you show me how to do this?"

"Absolutely, Kirk, we all have access now. Technology's a beautiful thing. This is going to change the complexion of the next generation."

A voice spoke up behind us: "What are you guys looking at?"

I turned, and there was Diane, one of my associate classmates. She was Asian, she was female, and I wasn't sure that she'd appreciate the gynecological specimen so prominently displayed on my monitor. I made a lame effort to stand up and conceal our evil goings-ons, but it was too late. The beaver had been witnessed.

"Well, well, well, Diane. Look's like we're caught in the act!" the Captain proclaimed. "Boys will be boys, you know."

Diane looked at me. Diane looked at the Captain. It

wasn't a battle worth fighting. She sighed, turned, and left.

I thought about the whole thing later. It was pretty damned funny. Looking at porno on the computer with the Captain was a decent job perk. I thought about it a little bit more later that night, though, and I started to worry. It wasn't that I felt guilty. As far as I was concerned, the PC Nazis and their sexual harassment allegations were mostly a crock of shit cooked up by overzealous trial lawyers to generate free business for themselves. What I worried about was becoming like Captain Kirk. I thought that the Captain was funny because he was still so damned horny at the age of 47 and he didn't give a fuck what anybody thought. That didn't mean that I wanted to be like him. Forty-seven and never having been married because investment banking had consumed my life. Forty-seven and still spanking the monkey in my office at 3 A.M. That was scary. What was I becoming? I began to think that maybe it wasn't worth it. I wasn't living the dream. I wasn't having any fun. Maybe there was more to life than whatever the hell I was running after.

The Last Straw

*He's turned his life around. He used to be
depressed and miserable. Now he's miserable and
depressed.*

—David Frost

Unlike Rolfe's epiphany, which hit him like a ton of
bricks, my realization that banking wasn't for me crept up
on me more slowly. I'm not even sure when it first began.
Maybe the seeds of doubt were planted during a four-day
pitching marathon with only six hours of sleep. Maybe I
first started questioning my career choice after one of my
colleagues called me a "fat little fuck" for the fifty-seventh
time. Maybe it was the recurring nights at strip clubs that
got me thinking. Was I nothing more than a filthy little animal who had so little time to enjoy the pleasures of life
that I had to resort to stuffing a ten-dollar bill into a neon-
yellow G-string for satisfaction? Would I ever have time to
have a lasting relationship? Marjorie and I had gotten engaged and she was planning on moving to New York in a
couple months. I loved her and wanted things to work
out, but I was never around. I had no time. While Mar-

jorie knew I spent a lot of time at work, the entire time we had been dating she had lived in Chicago, so she'd never really experienced the whole investment banking routine. How much of my lifestyle could she take? Would my only skills after twenty years in the business be a proficiency at inventing creative excuses for my loved ones to explain my perpetual absence and the ability to immediately identify the raunchiest strip clubs in every major city worldwide? I wasn't so sure that I wanted that to be my legacy.

I don't think the bare reality of the situation really hit me, though, until I realized that I was actively recruiting other young suckers to follow in my footsteps. I was like the crackhead who starts dealing to support his habit, and then realizes one day that he's selling dime bags of the rock to elementary school kids. Wow. It didn't make me feel so good.

I got a call one afternoon in early January. MBA recruiting season was in full swing. One of the managing directors in charge of Harvard recruiting was a-jingling on my phone.

"Hey, Troobie, we need you to go to Harvard and help recruit some new meat. We need you to be part of a panel discussion. You can fly up to Boston tonight and have a good old time up there. Live large on the firm's nickel. Tomorrow is an open house where all the MBAs get to ask questions of all the panel members. Afterwards, there'll be a reception and you'll stand at the DLJ booth handing out annual reports and talking to the students. All the usual suspects will be there: Morgan, Goldman, Merrill, and Lehman. You have to try and sell the kids on DLJ. You know the drill. Thanks for the help. I've already booked plane tickets and a hotel room for you. This is top priority. You've got to do some recruiting. Tell your other deal teams that you'll be out of commission for a day."

Yeah, I knew the drill because I'd been through the drill for the last two years. I was supposed to tell the young, impressionable MBAs that being an investment banking associate was fun, exciting, and rewarding. I was supposed to tell them that being an associate was a thrilling job and that only the best of the best ever made it to showtime. I was supposed to pump them up with all the jive hype that I had been pumped up with just a couple of years before.

I went to Harvard, put on my name tag, and sat at the little DLJ booth. MBAs swamped me. One woman literally ran up to the booth clutching her résumé and started speaking before I could even introduce myself.

"Mr. Troob, I really want to work at DLJ. Here's my résumé and my husband's résumé. We'd love to be able to work together. We know we'll work hard and we don't mind the long hours. We know what banking is all about and we want to work for DLJ. Do you like it there? Is it as awesome as I've heard? Are you doing deals all day?"

I came back with the party line. "Yeah, I like it there. It's an awesome place to work. And, yes, I'm doing a lot of deals. I'll take your résumé and see to it that it gets to the right person. You have the right level of enthusiasm to work for DLJ. Thanks for showing interest." It was hard to sound enthusiastic. I was getting tired of all the brow-beatings, the long nights, and the never-ending day-to-day grind. I was at the end of my rope.

With my comments and compliments still ringing in her ears, she glowed and floated away. If I allowed this woman and her husband to come work for DLJ I would effectively be breaking up their marriage. DLJ would kick her eager ass all over the place. DLJ would chew her up and spit her out, and she'd end up a shell of her former enthusiastic self. Screw it. Who was I to care? I was there to fill the pipeline. I was there to get some fresh bodies down below me so that it wouldn't hurt so badly when I fell. So I smiled and went on.

A guy named Ernie stopped at the booth. I'd worked with Ernie while I was an analyst at Kidder Peabody. He recognized me right away. "Hey, Pete. I hear DLJ's the place to be. The money is supposed to be great and the work is interesting. You guys do great deals—high-yield, merchant banking, all the fun stuff. It's not like Kidder, is it? If I'm going back to the Street I want to work at DLJ. Can you help me out?"

I bit my tongue and resisted the urge to tell him how much life as an associate really sucked and how unhappy I really was. I took a deep breath. "Ernie, absolutely. I can help you out. First, the money is great. Think about what we made at Kidder and multiply it by five or six. Second, it's not like Kidder. It's fun. Even the pitches are interesting. The deals are the best, interesting and challenging. You should work at DLJ. I'll definitely help you out."

He thanked me and left. I saw him go to the Goldman, Lehman, and Merrill booths. I sold him down the river. I helped him get a job at DLJ and he accepted it. I heard that he quit about a year later.

As I boarded the plane on my way back to New York I saw another old friend, Danny, who had become an associate at Merrill Lynch at the same time I had joined DLJ. He was the guy that I had sat with in the steam room two years earlier at Harvard. We had sworn to each other that we wouldn't go back into banking. I yelled his name and he came over. He told me how his job sucked and how he never had time for anything and how he needed to get out and find a more rewarding job. We got on the plane and sat next to each other. Two losers. Two guys that all the MBAs thought were big winners sitting there miserable and just wanting out.

I was everything that I didn't want to be. I had lost the one thing that I needed most. I had lost my pride. If a senior banker asked me to spit-shine his shoes for an extra-good review at bonus time, I would hock a loogie and start scrubbing.

When I got off the plane my beeper was beeping. I called into the office to check my voice mail. There was a message: "Peter, I need you to come into the office and help the analyst run a couple of models, and then I need you to start writing the equity underwriting committee memo. It has to be done by tomorrow afternoon. The vacation's over. Back to work." FUCK. I looked over at my friend Danny. His beeper had gone off too and he was checking his messages. Some senior Merrill Lynch banker had left him a voice mail with marching orders that were going to keep him at the office all night. We wallowed in our misery together for a few minutes, and then both of us had to get back to the office.

Danny and I had each called our firm's car service from the plane. We both jumped into our cars and told the drivers to get their asses moving back to Manhattan because we had important banker stuff to do.

Things had changed at DLJ. The place had grown from around 325 bankers when we had first started to over 600 a couple of years after that. I think the mandate was to get to 1,000 bankers by the year 2000. That just meant more people to boss me around. It seemed like every day more lateral hires were announced—more bankers coming in over the transom from other investment banks. It was like that old saying about knowing your enemies. At least when there were only 325 bankers I knew who my enemies were. Six hundred bankers was too many to keep track of, and 1,000 would be out of control.

Life went on and time marched by. I fell into the black hole called work. The next thing I knew, it was time for Marjorie to leave Chicago and move to the Big Apple. She called me and asked if I would pick her up from the airport. I promised that I would. She was moving to a new city. She was leaving her family, friends, and career in Chicago. She needed my support. When she stepped off the plane in La Guardia all she got was a guy named Gupta standing at the baggage carousel holding a sign that said "TROOB." I couldn't make it to the airport because an uptight manager director was busting my hump over some word processing document. When he angrily said, "Jump," I politely replied, "How high, sir?" Marjorie went back to our apartment and cried herself to sleep. I was ruining the best thing in my life.

I thought about quitting, but what else could I do? How could I ever find the time to look for another job? And then it struck me. I was supposed to take a vacation to Greece in another two weeks. I figured that would give me the time I needed to clear my head and think. Maybe I could handle this banking stuff if I had a strategy. This vacation would give me the time to develop a game plan.

Marjorie was going to leave ahead of me with a girlfriend. They were going to spend some time in Turkey, then Marjorie was going to rendezvous with me in Greece. Wow, was I excited. I told all my deal teams that I was going on a vacation. One of my managing directors smiled mysteriously.

Two days before I was supposed to leave for Greece the managing director with the mysterious smile decided that I couldn't go. He told me, "One of the deal team members has to cover the road show in both Kansas City and Seattle. We need somebody out there with management. Both me and the VP on the deal are busy. You've got to take one on the chin for the team. It happens to all of us. It's part of the job."

Part of the job? FUCK YOU, MAN! There was a pounding in my head that I couldn't control. I wanted to pull a Wile E. Coyote on him and drop a big iron anvil on his head.

I was crushed. I asked the VP why he couldn't go. He told me that he was having trouble with his girlfriend and that he needed to spend some time with her. He told me, "Don't worry, it's happened to me too. Welcome to investment banking."

I had to call Marjorie in Turkey and tell her that I wouldn't be meeting her in Greece. She was pissed, really pissed. There was nothing I could say to make her happy. How many more times could she forgive me? How many more times could I tell her I was sorry? This wasn't the dream. I had thought that I would have more time and more fun. What was at the end of the desert anyway? An oasis? A mirage? Maybe I wasn't in a desert after all. It seemed more like a never-ending jungle. I didn't care anymore. Whatever I was in, I wanted to be airlifted out.

I was upset that I had missed my vacation, and I didn't like the fact that I'd pissed Marjorie off, but neither of those was the deciding factor. When I looked in the mirror, I didn't like the person I saw in the reflection. I was disappointed in myself. I had no dignity. Greece would have been a break in the action but not an end to my misery. I wasn't the man I wanted to be. I only had one thought: "Fuck this. No more."

It was the last straw. There was no more fire in my belly. There was no more spark in my eyes. I had to get out.

Liberation

*Beam me up, Scotty. There's no intelligent life
down here.*

—Captain James T. Kirk

I had to find a new career. I did the only thing I knew
how to do. I called a headhunter and I didn't tell a living
soul. Not even Rolfe. Any leak of information that I was
trying to leave the bank and I would either be immediately fired or summarily castrated. Neither of those options struck me as particularly attractive. In order to find a
new job I had to be ultrasecretive and move like a stealth
bomber. I went on interviews in the mornings at 7:00 A.M.
before work. I interviewed on the weekends and did interviews by phone. Months went by and nothing seemed
to pique my interest.

Finally, I met a group of guys through a headhunter and
coincidentally, through one of the deals that I was working on. They were value investors of distressed bonds. I
liked the guys and they liked me. They had a good setup.
They had six people with north of $400 million dollars in
their fund. They were doing research, thinking, and mak-

ing decisions about how to invest the money. The concept of actually using my brain intrigued me. They were looking for another guy to help them invest the money. They made me an offer. I didn't have to think about it for very long—I accepted.

Now came the hard part. I had to tell DLJ that I was quitting. Whom should I tell? Whom did I really work for? None of the senior bankers dealt with personnel issues. The head of the whole shooting match, Gary Lang, didn't know me from Adam, and even if he had, he probably wouldn't have given a rat's ass that I was quitting. So I called up Rolfe and told him. He was surprised and he seemed a little pissed off. I couldn't worry about that, though. I had to figure out who else to tell.

I told Brock LeBlank. He was the vice chairman of the investment banking division. I liked Brock and respected him. He was a good guy. He had worked hard, caught some breaks, and had moved up the DLJ ranks in short order. He was one of the chosen ones, and he'd always treated me pretty well. I told him that I was leaving because I didn't see a fruitful future for me at DLJ. He smiled. It was a crooked smile, though. There was a glint of evil in his eyes and I wondered momentarily whether he might throw a stapler at my head.

"Peter, you're one of our superstars. I mean that. You could really excel here. Anyway, Peter, do you know those large houses in Greenwich on the water? Bankers own those houses. DLJ gives you the opportunity to have more money than you could ever dream of, and to have the biggest house in the neighborhood. This hedge fund you're going to won't ever give you that opportunity. The Street is cluttered with hedge funds. The one you're joining could fail. And then what do you do? I think that you're making a big mistake and I think you should reconsider. You have a bright future here. You're well regarded and if you stay here you can succeed beyond your wildest dreams. DLJ isn't going to fail. I'd like you to reconsider. I'd like you to talk to Nussbaum and Weinstein. I'll set it up."

What a bunch of phony baloney. I knew that the biggest house in the neighborhood usually belonged to a construction contractor or the guy who invented the paper clip. He couldn't fool me. Still, I had to give Brock credit for acting like he was truly concerned. He also had my hot buttons down pretty well. The guy knew how to stroke my ego.

I went to see Nussbaum. He was the head of High Yield Banking, the group that I worked for. I told him about the job I had found. I told him that I wanted more free time, that I wanted a life. He was quiet for a minute, then he spoke.

"Peter, you'll have plenty of free time later in life. Look, Peter, you have to pay your dues now but later you'll reap the benefits. That's how it is in life, trust me. Anyway, this job you're thinking about taking, it seems like it sucks. You might get screwed by the partners. It's too risky. I think that you're making a big mistake. We'll take care of you here. We'll do anything that has to be done in order to keep you. Is there anything we can change for you? If there is, then we'll change it. We want to keep you."

They'd take care of me? Sure, just like a wise guy "takes care" of a guy who gets caught with the wise guy's wife. I figured that I'd humor Nussbaum. I'd see what I could get out of him. I told him that I didn't want to work for Gator anymore, and that, in fact, I didn't want to work for any of the vice presidents in the group. He said, "Done." I knew it was bullshit. He was a good guy. He was trying to be helpful. However, he was a senior guy and he didn't understand that there was a mass of investment banking humanity between the two of us and there was no way for him to control it all. I would continue to get crushed. He could see that I wasn't coming around, so he decided to send me to Weinstein's office to get the final once-over.

Weinstein. The Black Widow. I'd interviewed with him while I was at business school. He was a little pit bull. He stood about five foot six and was pissed about it. He was going to beat the tar out of me and scare me into staying at DLJ. I walked into his office and he immediately launched into his tirade.

"Well, well, well. So little Peter thinks that he's going to a hedge fund to make lots of money. No way. You're going to fail. I hope you have a backup plan because you won't succeed. Your best chance of succeeding is by staying here. You're naive and you don't know what you're doing. I hear that you want to enjoy your life and have more free time. Well, if that's what you want, then you're a pansy and you may as well go into the advertising business. C'mon, Pete, you know that you're not ready to leave. I assume you're staying. Now tell Brock you are back on the DLJ team."

The Widow was shaking my confidence. It hadn't broken yet, but it wasn't exactly sturdy. I steeled myself. I was leaving. That was it.

I had just gone through the three-step banking process. These three steps are used in banking whether a banker is pitching a deal, executing a deal, or attacking a colleague

who's thinking of quitting. *Greed, Fear, and Abandon.*
Those are the three steps. First, persuade by talking about
money and success. Greed and the pursuit of money is
the banker's ultimate aphrodisiac. Stroke the ego and tell
the clients what they want to hear. Act sincere. If this
doesn't work, move to the second stage of the process—
fear. Scare the shit out of the clients and shake their confidence. Tell them that if they don't join the bank in a
deal, then they'll fail and be miserable. If the banker can't
entice the client with money, then maybe they can use
fear to achieve the desired result. Finally, if this doesn't
work the banker will abandon in an unusually rapid fashion. If there's no deal, then there's no need to continue
any discussion.

I called up Brock LeBlank the following day. His secretary said he wasn't in. Maybe he just didn't want to take
my call. I left him a voice mail. I told him, "Brock, thanks
for taking the time to talk to me. I've thought about my
decision and continue to believe that I'll be happiest if I
take this new job. Thanks for your support. I hope to keep
in touch. Good luck." I never heard from Brock again.

I called Nussbaum and told him I'd made up my mind.
I told him that I was leaving for sure.

"I've got to go to a meeting," he said. "Good luck."

Finally, I called the Widow. "Hey, Greg, it's Pete. I'm
going to take the job."

The Widow said, "You're making a big mistake."

"I think that things will work out," I told him.

"They won't," he said. "I hope your dad has money."
The Widow had dug his stinger deep into my mind. Fuck
him.

The phone rang one last time. It was someone from

personnel. "Hey, Peter," he said. "Say your good-byes to everyone and get your stuff together. There's a lot of proprietary information lying around here and we can't have you around it. Your computer's been shut off, your ID card has been deactivated, and I've sent boxes down for your files. Good luck. Bye."

I called Rolfe and told him that I was getting booted. In forty-eight hours I had announced my resignation, spoken to the head of the bank, and been put through the wringer with the top guys in my department. They had tried to persuade me to stay. They had tried to scare the bejesus out of me. Then, they abandoned the ship and told me to get the hell out. It was that quick. I had been hired in a seventy-two-hour time frame and was out the door in forty-eight. On to something new.

"You're bailing on me," Rolfe said. "How can you do that?"

"I just can't take it anymore," I told him. "There's gotta be more to life than this crap."

That was it. I was free. Really, really free. Rolfe was pissed, but I could deal with that. He got pissed a lot and he usually just needed to kick and scream a little before he came around. He made me suffer a little bit, though, before he forgave me. He made me feel like I'd abandoned my only brother in the orphanage.

You're damn right I was pissed. When Troobie first called me and told me he was leaving I was ripshit. My boy was leaving. Leaving me hanging. We'd clawed our way up the bloody beaches of Iwo Jima together and now, when I needed him most, he wasn't going to be there. There'd be no one to watch my back.

Troobie's decision to leave was more than just me losing my buddy, the guy whom I could always rely on to go down to Shenanigans with me at 2 A.M. to grope naked ladies. I mean, I couldn't go down there *alone*. I'd feel like a frigging pervert, and none of my other boys were as reliable in the search for diversion as Troobie.

Troob's decision to leave was significant because as long as none of the associates in our class had left we'd been able to convince ourselves that at least part of the dream was still alive. Regardless of what went on around us, regardless of the depths of our despair, regardless of the degree to which everything we were doing seemed counter to what we'd hoped for, our unwillingness to break ranks kept us all sane. We bitched and moaned. We told each other that we were jerkoffs with no lives. But there was no way that we could all be idiots. And if we weren't all idiots, and none of us had left, then there had to be a reason to believe. We couldn't all be stupid enough to stay locked into a no-win situation.

That all changed when Troobie walked out. The doubts became real. Maybe we were idiots after all. Maybe it really wouldn't ever get better. Maybe we were doomed to a life of perpetual pitching, making copies, and endless rounds of word processing. Maybe there really was something better out there that the rest of us were missing out on. But then maybe Troobie was wrong. I was confused.

Troob called me every day from his new job. After the first week, he told me that one of the partners at his fund had yelled at him when he found him in the office at

8:30 P.M. one night. "You're not a banker anymore," the guy told him. "We're paying you to think, not to stay here all night."

Troob said that it took him a few weeks to remember how to use his brain. He didn't make pitch books anymore. He didn't have to bribe a bunch of guys at the copy center. He spent all day thinking about companies and whether it made sense to invest money in them. He was the guy on the other side of the table now, the guy with the money. He was looking for the right answer, not just the answer that he thought the guy upstairs wanted to hear. He was making decisions, not chugalugging the last remaining vestiges of his pride. He'd gone from happy to angry. Now he was happy again.

It didn't take long for me to make the decision that I had to get out, too. Even after the initial excitement of leaving DLJ had died down for Troobie, he was still jazzed up about his new job. It wasn't just that he was glad to be gone. He actually looked forward to going in to work every day. I couldn't remember the last time that I'd felt like that. I wanted to feel that excitement again. I wanted to walk into work in the morning with a big smile on my face.

I got the names of a bunch of headhunters who specialized in the financial services industry. I put all their names into a spreadsheet and began to call each one. I took a lot of notes. I met with most of them and learned what each of them specialized in. I told them why I wanted to quit banking and what I wanted to do. They all told me that I was a smart guy with a good résumé and finding a new position shouldn't be difficult. Every once in a while one of them would call me up and tell me about the latest position they were trying to fill. Most of it was garbage. I got more and more frustrated.

Then, one day in early December, I got a call from Slick. He'd talked to Troob earlier that morning and Troob had mentioned that he'd heard about a small hedge fund that was looking to add somebody. It wasn't the sort of thing that Slick was interested in but he knew that I was looking. He gave me a phone number. Troob, who had abandoned me in mid-battle, was throwing out a lifeline. If I held on tight enough maybe he could help pull me out.

I dialed the number Slick had given me. A guy answered. I told him that I had heard that his fund was looking to add somebody. He said, "Come on over and meet us. Tell us why we should hire you." I did.

The guys I met with had $100 million. They were looking to add another guy. That guy was me. They wanted somebody who could think, somebody who could help them make money.

They told me that they were worried that I might have been brainwashed by DLJ. They weren't sure if I still remembered how to reason. I told them that it might take a couple of weeks but I would remember how to use my mind again. We had a deal.

All that was left to do was quit.

I walked into each of my managing directors' offices and told them that I was quitting. I told them that I couldn't take it anymore, that I didn't want to be a banker, that I wanted to do something different. They told me that I was a nice guy and a good associate. They asked me if there was anything they could do to get me to stay. I thought about revenge. I thought that maybe if they allowed me to first pour boiling oil over them and then stretch them out on a rack for a couple of weeks I might start to feel better. Maybe then I'd want to stay.

"No, there's nothing you can do," I told them.

Later that day I got a call from Brock LeBlank. "I hear you're leaving," he said. "I want you to come up and talk to me."

I called Troobie at work. I knew that he had talked to Brock when he was leaving. "What's Brock gonna say?" I asked him.

"He'll tell you that you're making a big mistake. He'll tell you that you're a superstar and that you can excel at DLJ. He'll tell you that all the guys up in Greenwich with big houses are bankers. He'll tell you that hedge fund managers are a dime a dozen. He's not a bad guy, but he doesn't understand that the place has changed and that there's a big difference between being on the top and being on the bottom. Remember: greed, fear, and abandon."

"OK, I gotta go."

I walked up to Brock's office. He was on the phone. He made me sit and wait for ten minutes. Maybe he thought that by making me feel small I'd want to stay.

Brock started, "So I hear that you want to leave us."

"Yeah, Brock," I said, "I got a job with a hedge fund."

"You're making a big mistake, John. You'll never find another job where you get as much responsibility as you've got here. You get to travel all over the world. Heads of the world's largest corporations will look to you for advice. No other job is going to give you that. Hedge fund managers are a dime a dozen."

That's funny, I thought, I never *feel* very important

when I'm doing my job here. The only thing a leader of industry has ever looked to me for is to pass him a pitch book. I feel small. I feel like a gnat.

"You know, John," Brock continued, "ten years from now you could be sitting in this chair." He motioned to the chair he was sitting in. "You're one of our superstars. I mean that. You could excel here at DLJ."

I started to laugh. Where the hell was he going to be in ten years? How was I going to get his chair? Maybe he'd be supervising the new addition to his house in Greenwich to ensure that it was bigger than the house next door that the hedge fund manager had just bought.

When I walked out the doors of the DLJ building for the final time later that week I felt no remorse. It was two years and nine months after I'd walked through the doors for the very first time as a summer associate. My buddy Troob had been gone for about six months. DLJ had taken their pound of flesh, but I was off to something new.

The dues we paid took their toll on us. We felt ten years older. Our rite of passage may not have been complete according to the Investment Banker's Code, but we had cut it short. Maybe the dues-paying part of any job doesn't stop until you decide to take a stand and stop it. Maybe we weren't up to the task. Either way, we were out. The beginning of something good was finally stirring inside us again. Maybe there was another dream out there that we could chase. There was hope yet.

Epilogue

What's the use in running if you're not on the right road?

—German proverb

Rolfe and I saw each other a lot after we left DLJ. Our old buddies back in the DLJ purgatory were still spending every waking hour tied to the job, so we didn't get to see too much of them. It wasn't for a lack of trying, though.

A couple of months went by and we decided to round up some of the old crew. The plan called for a 7:00 P.M. rendezvous down in Little Italy with me, Rolfe, Slick, Big Man, Wings, and Tubby. Well, 7:00 came and 7:00 went and the only ones at the reunion dinner were Rolfe and I.

Slick rolled in about half an hour late, smiling like the Cheshire Cat. It was obvious that he had something he wanted to tell us.

"What's up, you smug bastard?" Rolfe asked him.

"I'm leaving, man. I'm done," Slick replied.

Rolfe and I looked at each other. We knew what he meant. He was leaving DLJ. We were shocked. Honestly, truly shocked. Slick and Wings were the last guys that we ever thought would leave. They'd always bitched and moaned as loud as the rest of us but we had figured them for lifers. We thought that the cache of being investment bankers was enough to keep them happy.

"What are you going to do?" I asked him.

"Risk arb. There's a group of guys over at Attica Capital who are doing merger arb and special situations investing. It's mostly equities. I think it'll be good."

Rolfe was laughing. "You're unbelievable! We never thought you'd leave. Troobie and I figured you were in for life."

"You guys don't know shit," Slick said. "I want a life too. I've been looking around for months."

"Well, get ready, man," I started out, "'cause you're gonna have to talk to Brock. He's going to tell you . . ."

"I know," Slick said, "Rolfe already told me about the houses in Greenwich speech, the song and dance about being an indispensable associate, and all the rest of that horse shit. I'm ready for it. I'm gone."

A waiter stopped by the table. "You gentlemen ready to order yet?"

I looked over at Slick. "What about the rest of the guys? They coming or not?"

"No way, man," Slick said. "Big Man's getting his clock cleaned by the Widow and Tubby's tap dancing all over a merchant banking deal like Fred Astaire in an MGM musical. I don't think that either of them'll hit their balls out of the bunker in time to meet us here. I'm not sure about Wings, I think he's flying back in from Mexico City later tonight. Maybe he'll show up eventually. Let's go ahead and order."

Slick turned to the waiter. "I'll have the artichoke heart

appetizer and the shrimp scampi. Also, I'll have the apple pie for dessert, OK? Thanks."

Rolfe and I stared at each other, dumbfounded. There was absolutely no question that we were thinking the same thing: Slick had not ordered his customary penne bolognese, tira misu, and two small bottles of San Pelegrino sparkling water. Things were changing indeed.

By 10:00 P.M. Wings had shown up, but Big Man and Tubby were nowhere to be found. When Slick told Wings that he was leaving, I thought Wings was going to cry.

"What?" Wings said. "You're leaving me, man? Who will I eat dinner with every night? Tubby's always too busy and Big Man's already out searching for the escape hatch. He'll be gone within a couple of months. Ahhh, shit. This sucks."

It was like watching two lovers part. Wings was brokenhearted.

By 11:00 P.M. Wings had to leave. He told us, "I'd like to stay, but tomorrow I have to get up at five A.M. to catch a flight to Dallas. Another deal, another dollar. Good luck, Slick. I'll talk to you later. Troobie and Rolfe, nice to see you guys, and if I don't see you sooner, I'll see you at Troobie's wedding. I gotta go. I'm tired as shit."

Wings was always on the run, but I think he liked it that way.

"So," Rolfe ventured to Slick after Wings took off, "do you figure that they'll miss you as much as they missed Troobie and I when we left?"

Slick looked at Rolfe like he was a three-eyed hyena. "Are you kidding? They'll slot a couple of lateral hires from some second-tier bank in on my deals. Maybe they'll even pull some gung-ho first-year into one of them. He'll probably bust his ass and put me to shame. Don't get any demented ideas about how much they missed you guys when you left, either. It wasn't like that."

Rolfe looked confused and concerned. "You mean, it didn't create any turmoil when we left? We didn't leave a legacy? They didn't miss us at all?"

Slick laughed. "Don't fool yourself, man. It was like taking a teaspoon of sand off the beaches in Rio. Nobody missed a beat. We're all commodities. Completely replaceable."

I thought about it. Slick was right. DLJ and most of the other investment banks are big places. Everyone in the institution is readily replaceable. We exited, and immediately a new, fresh-faced young banker replaced us and nobody missed a beat.

Rolfe, Slick, and I all sat back in our chairs and were quiet. The wine and the pasta had taken its toll. We were all full, tipsy, and talked out. The silence was welcomed. I looked at Rolfe. Rolfe looked at Slick. Slick looked at me.

"You know what?" Rolfe asked.

"What?" Slick and I replied.

"I hope we know what the fuck we're doing."

"So do I," I said. "So do I."

When we originally entered the investment banking world we thought that we were standing on the edge of a desert. We believed there was an oasis on the other side of the blistering sand, and if we were willing to withstand the heat we would eventually be given the opportunity to drink from a magical spring. What we learned, though, was that investment banking wasn't really a desert. It wasn't what we thought it would be. Investment banking was a lot more like a jungle.

We learned that there wasn't a straight shot across an arid landscape to reach the promised land. Instead, we found ourselves in a big, confusing place with lots of tall trees, ferocious tigers, and big hairy jumping spiders that looked like they wanted to bite us. The signs in the jungle were all pointing in different directions and we had no idea which way to go.

Eventually, though, we looked up into the canopy. High above in the lush foliage there were branches laden down with bananas, mangoes, and plantains. We liked what we saw. So we learned, first, to climb, and then to swing on vines in order to grab the fruit. We swung from vine to vine, all day and all night, and filled our arms with the tasty morsels. At first we had a good time swinging around, but eventually we began to feel like we were moving in circles. Every day we saw the same vines and the same trees. Every day we had the same dung beetles crawling up our legs and the same annoying baboons swinging behind us barking orders. Ultimately, we realized that while we had an armload of fruit, we had no time to eat it and nothing much else. The more we swung, the more the jungle seemed to expand. Our arms were tired.

And so, we decided to get out. We cut down a rubber tree and made ourselves a dugout canoe. We made some paddles out of warthog horns. We navigated our canoe down the river and out of the jungle. We broke free.

There's still a bunch of guys back there in the jungle swinging, arms full of fruit. Some of them like being swingers, but we chose to plant our feet on the ground.

MONKEY BUSINESS

Sometimes we wonder if we should have continued swinging. When you leave something behind that you've poured so much of yourself into, it's tough not to second-guess your decision at times. Every once in a while, as we ponder the path we've taken, Rolfe and I think about what we may have left behind. We wonder, are we missing out on something?

Our lives are a seesaw and what we strive for is some sort of equilibrium. When we were investment bankers, there was always a fat, greasy angry guy on one end of the seesaw and a happy little wood fairy on the other end. The fat guy didn't look like he was going anywhere, and we didn't see how we'd ever reach a balance.

Miss it? Like a cannibal misses a side order of vegetables.

Afterword
Getting the Band Back Together

I knew I was going to take the wrong train, so I left early.
—Yogi Berra

When we first wrote *Monkey Business,* we thought that it was a snapshot of an industry in transition. It was clear that changes were afoot, but we knew that the investment banks would fight hard to protect their gravy train, so we expected those changes to come about gradually. We had no idea that through a toxic combination of greed, stupidity, and mismanagement the banks would blow themselves to smithereens less than a decade later. As we look back now, *Monkey Business* seems not so much like a snapshot of an industry in transition, but a whole lot more like the final coda on an industry that once was. But more on all that later. First, let's go back to the months right after we left the DLJ Mother Ship . . .

Initially, when we left DLJ we stayed pretty tight with a bunch of the guys from our old crew. A lot of calls went back and forth between those of us who had left and those who had stayed behind. For those of us who had left, we wanted the guys on the inside to know that there was indeed a life after investment banking. A more balanced life, a satisfying career, and decent comp weren't necessarily mutually exclusive, and we wanted the guys back in the trenches to know that they might need to step off the one-hundred-hour week treadmill to get some perspective. A lot of the guys back in banking were still in denial, so they didn't take much of what we told them to heart, but they were happy to take the occasional break to listen to us pontificate. At that point, hedge funds hadn't yet exploded onto the scene, and the guys were curious to find out what it was that Rolfe and I actually did.

After the dinner in Little Italy, the next time I got a chance to see most of the crew again was at my wedding. Love is a funny thing, and when you get ensnared you just have to go along for the ride. Rolfe, Slick, and Wings all made the trip out to my fiancée Marjorie's hometown, Chicago, to see me tie the knot. We had a great time all weekend eating hot dogs at Wiener Circle and spent plenty of time discussing our future plans, most of which involved finance, making money, and searching for the time to enjoy it.

I was obviously busy making the rounds during my wedding reception and saying hello to all the guests. While I trailed behind my beautiful new bride, however, I could have sworn that at one point I saw Rolfe seated at a table with the tablecloth over his waist and a look of relief on his face. I assumed that some lucky guest at my wedding was going to have speckled shoes by the end of the night.

Marjorie and I settled down in New York City in a two-bedroom apartment on 86th Street: Yorkshire Towers. Actually, my parents had lived in the same building when I was born. Although that was an interesting tidbit to tell people, what it really meant was that I lived in an old building with poor plumbing that needed a new paint job and carpeting. One thing led to another and we had our first child, Rachel, about a year later. A couple of years after that, our little boy, Benjamin, was born. We moved to the suburbs in Westchester, and now I coach soccer and Little League games just like my dad did for me. And yes, it is a cliché, but having children changes everything, and they have brought more joy into my life than I ever expected. Having time to watch them grow up and to spend time with them is priceless. One of my biggest concerns is that, as my children learn to read, they will pick up a copy of *Monkey Business* and read it and ask Daddy what all those four-letter words mean.

Rolfe, meanwhile, against all imaginable odds, ended up getting engaged soon after leaving DLJ. Not only did he get engaged, but it wasn't even to a midget hooker or other garden-variety deviant; it was to a chick who was not only smart, but hot. In a grand bit of DLJ irony, Rolfe had asked Veronica, the Wharton girl who'd been instrumental in helping him land his DLJ summer offer, to marry him. Shocking her friends, parents, and not least of all Rolfe, she said "yes."

Rolfe was convinced that this was a match made in heaven. Not only was he crazy about her, but as he put it to me: "Veronica was directly responsible for getting me my summer job at DLJ, which meant that she was *indirectly* directly responsible for me going there full-time after business school. So I figure, she's the one who steered me into two of the most painful years of my life. Since I'm still in love with her after all of that, I figure I can tolerate just about anything she can do to me till death do us part. That's a recipe for a great marriage."

In another twist of fate, Rolfe had asked me to score his engagement ring for him. He knew that my family had roots in the jewelry business, so he told me to go out and get him the best deal that I could. Well, the night I was driving down to his apartment to deliver the goods, I ended up in a bit of a pickle. I had to get the ring to him before he was set to head out to dinner and pop the question, but I'd gotten a late start on my way home from work and, to add insult to injury, I got stuck in a massive traffic jam on Second Avenue. As I finally came up alongside the triple-parked car that was causing the jam, my road rage took hold of me and I flipped the person inside the bird, because that's what I felt he deserved. Unfortunately, it was an undercover police officer, so he felt that I deserved a ticket. As he peered into my window, I told him that, in fact, I was getting engaged that evening and that I was pretty stressed out, and I showed him the engagement ring as proof that I was about to tie the knot. The cop said, "Welcome to hell," and let me go. Rolfe had saved me.

In a fitting footnote to Rolfe's engagement, Yves Des-Champs, the other key player in Rolfe's summer job offer, had the final word. Veronica had stayed in occasional contact with Yves after Rolfe had joined DLJ, and she had run into him on the street in New York about a month after getting engaged. She told Yves that she and Rolfe had gotten engaged, expecting at a minimum to be congratulated. Yves' response? "Jesus, and I never got a chance to fuck you." Wow, what a class act.

Rolfe and Veronica were married in Puerto Rico, and Marjorie and I were there for the big event. I wasn't sure who the Justice of the Peace was, but he had a striking resemblance to Ronald McDonald. I think in Puerto Rico he was known as "Juanald McDonald." Rolfe ended up getting Veronica knocked up soon after getting married, although not soon enough to raise any real suspicions among their parents. He ended up having two daughters, Carolina and Savannah. As the only man in a house of four, he now claims to be thankful for the way DLJ prepared him to endure a constant barrage of mental abuse.

So both personally and professionally, Rolfe and I were doing OK. We felt like we were finding some balance in our lives, and we weren't turning into the angry, money-obsessed bankers we had feared we might become. We each spent the next couple of years working at the hedge funds that we'd joined out of DLJ and things were going well. We were learning a lot and the guys we were working for had given each of us plenty of rope to hang ourselves. We felt like we were developing a set of skills that we would actually be able to use as we grew old and decrepit, as opposed to just shuffling paper and making sure we had the font sizes right. Neither of us had so much as laid eyes on a pitch book in the years since we'd left banking. That alone was worth a lot.

As for the other members of our class, well, not a lot changed. At least for a little while. After Rolfe, Slick, and I bailed, there was no stampede for the doors. Most of our other classmates put their heads down, sucked up their pride, and told themselves that the dream was still alive. Although we harbored secret hopes that our departures would be the spark that would light the slaves' palace revolt, it wasn't to be. As we'd suspected, we were nothing but replaceable cogs in the giant investment banking machine.

DLJ continued to grow after we left. The place became more institutionalized, but the changes were gradual. Then, in August 2000, things changed abruptly. DLJ announced that it was being acquired by Credit Suisse First Boston (CSFB). The press release announcing the merger crowed about how the new merged firm would be a "tremendous new force in the investment banking industry" with the "intellectual capital to rival any financial services organization in the world." It also asserted that "Credit Suisse First Boston and DLJ complement each other ideally in culture and market strength." Wow. It all sounded fantastic, at least on paper.

Those of us who'd spent time at DLJ, though, had a sneaking suspicion straight out of the gate that CSFB might be biting off more than it could chew. The entire history of Wall Street mergers was a case study in failure, so the CSFB bankers were facing some long odds right off the bat. Plus, for those of us privy to the true DLJ culture, we couldn't believe that DLJ was agreeing to get gang-banged by a bunch of stuffed-shirt Swiss bankers. The Swiss were known for their spit-and-polish, discreet approach to financial services. The DLJers, on the other hand, were a bunch of hyperaggressive, hungry, independent tough guys who ran their own fiefdoms like a federation of Afghani warlords. Where was this complementary cultural fit that the press release was talking about? God almighty, this was no marriage made in heaven. It was Prince William of Wales and Amy Winehouse getting hitched.

The DLJ bankers may have been tough sons of bitches, but they were savvy. So when CSFB announced that it would be funding a $1.2 billion "retention plan" for DLJ employees, we started wondering exactly who was getting fucked, and who was doing the fucking. Basically, CSFB management was offering huge incentives to DLJ employees in order to get them not to jump ship. The Swiss knew that the allure of working for a legion of buttoned-up Swiss wasn't going to be enough to keep the DLJ hoi polloi from dashing for the exits, so they opened their wallets. The employment contracts they offered reached all the way up and down the investment banking food chain. Since it's unlikely that there were specific performance guarantees in the contracts, that meant that midlevel guys would get paid millions of dollars to sit tight for a few years, bang out some deals at a leisurely pace, and polish up their résumés until the contracts expired.

Many of the DLJ bankers did exactly that. They signed the guarantees and bided their time. The merger's timing was spectacularly bad: It had been announced in August 2000, within two days of the S&P hitting a peak that it would not regain for nearly seven years. By the time the merger closed three months later, the market had already begun a tailspin that would continue through late 2002. Investment banking revenues dried up and banking salaries all over the Street dropped faster than a frozen turd from an airplane lavatory. But the DLJ bankers were fat and happy, with their guaranteed bonuses, making about 50 percent more than what they could have been making at most other firms.

Almost immediately, CSFB management knew that it was screwed. In fact, the new management team went on bended knee to many of the DLJ bankers and asked them to voluntarily agree to a reduction in the level of their guarantees. In the classic spirit of camaraderie and "one for all," many of the DLJ bankers said, "Thanks, and we appreciate that we need to do this for the good of the team, but fuck you." CSFB management got so desperate that it paid some of the DLJ bankers their guarantees, and then told them to leave. That's right. Here's your seven-figure guarantee, now get the fuck out.

Meanwhile, as expected, the DLJers started to chafe under the oversight of the Swiss bureaucrats. They began plotting their escapes, and as soon as the employment guarantees expired the exodus began in earnest. Many who didn't leave voluntarily were shitcanned. There were nearly ten separate rounds of layoffs in the investment bank over the next few years.

After all was said and done, the decimation of the DLJ franchise was nearly absolute. CSFB ended up with little to show for their $13 billion outlay but a high-yield capital markets group, a merchant banking operation that was a shell of its former self, and a few other odds and ends. Poof. DLJ was no more. The guaranteed bonuses had caused comp costs to balloon and had been responsible for two years of heavy operating losses at the investment bank. Virtually the entire cadre of DLJ bankers and traders had moved on to other shops, and many were now competing against their former employers. Pockets of guys had ended up at UBS, others at Blackstone. Some ex-DLJers started private equity funds or hedge funds. The senior DLJ guys had clearly known when to sell. The merger went down in history, as Rob Cox wrote in the *New York Times,* as "the mother of all bad Wall Street takeovers."

Despite the demise of DLJ, Troob and I were happy to see that just about everybody we had known managed to land on their feet. Even our friends who were canned managed to keep their heads up, and continued to project the confidence that was so critical to landing another overpaid position. If DLJ had taught us all one thing it was how to take a licking and keep on ticking, and that lesson came in handy for those still around when things got squirrelly after the merger.

By this time, it had been nearly five years since Troob and I had left DLJ for the hedge fund world. We didn't get to see the old crew nearly as often anymore as we had right after leaving. DLJ was the glue that held us all together, and as DLJ shrank further into the past we naturally grew apart. On top of that, our family and work obligations often made it difficult for all of us to get together. So it was a surprise when Troob called me at the office one afternoon and told me that he'd gotten a call earlier that morning from Wings.

"Wings called me earlier today," Troob began. "He says he wants us all to get together like the old days. He wants to grab dinner. He told me to round you and Slick up. Tubby's in, too."

"I'll be there," I told him. It had been a long time since I'd seen Wings and Tubby. It would be fun to catch up with everybody. "Where are we gonna meet?"

"I told Wings to make some reservations," Troob said. "He's gonna let us know once he has it nailed down."

"I say we skip dinner and just hit Shenanigans," I told him. "We can get a plate of chicken fingers there. I'm sure they're tasty."

"First of all," Troob replied, "Shenanigans has been shut

for at least two years. There's a sushi restaurant where it used to be. Second, we all have kids now, and some of them are uncomfortably close in age to the girls at these places."

"Fine." I said. "Let Wings figure out where he wants us to meet."

We should have known better than to leave the reservations up to Wings. Wings chose TAO, which was twice as pricey as it should have been and way too crowded. You see, Wings was a private equity guy now; a self-professed "civilized" member of the Ape Battalion. Actually, Wings and Tubby were both private equity guys. When the DLJ recruiting machine had originally promised all of us that we'd be taken care of, and that we'd get to work in the Merchant Bank, it had been only a partial lie. Although the only time most of us got to see the Merchant Bank was in the glossy pictures in the annual report, Wings and Tubby had actually made it onto the hallowed ground. After toiling in the salt mines for a couple of years, they'd both been promoted into DLJ's Merchant Banking Group, and they'd been practicing their private equity chops ever since.

Being private equity guys, Wings and Tubby were both making investments like the rest of us, but were doing it in private deals. So instead of just buying an investment in the market when they found something that they liked at the right price, they had to go out and find a business they liked, convince the owner that he should sell it to them, and then negotiate the terms of the sale. And instead of just selling an investment they owned into the market when the price was right, they had to figure out how to extricate themselves from these deals—through an IPO, or a sale to another private equity guy, or perhaps a sale to a strategic acquirer.

To us public market guys, private equity seemed like an awful lot of work for no real incremental benefit. The private equity guys liked to crow about how their business model was superior, since they didn't have to mark their portfolio to market every day and they were able to buy whole companies and have a significant say in how those companies were managed. From our perspective, though, it stank too much of investment banking. Everything still revolved around the deal. Whenever we talked to our private equity buddies, they were always negotiating a deal, or getting financing for a deal, or putting their deal in triage, or exiting a deal. And for those of us scarred by our investment banking experience, the mere whisper of the word "deal" gave us cold sweats and panic attacks. Deals meant deal teams, hierarchies, and weekends spent in the office. They meant lawyers, pitch books, and all manner of irate assholes telling us how we had fucked something up. Even if you were the senior guy on a deal, this stuff was unavoidable. Basically, although the private equity guys weren't technically still investment bankers, they were some sort of odd investment banking mutation. That was scary shit.

Although Wings and Tubby were both private equity guys, the similarity ended there. Wings had eventually left DLJ's Merchant Banking Group and joined a start-up private equity firm with a few other guys. Unfortunately, like a doctor in an Ebola ward, he'd also eventually succumbed to the disease-ridden surroundings that he had been operating in. Instead of using his knowledge of what it was like to be at the bottom of the slag pile in order to improve life for those underneath him once he'd risen a few rungs, over the years he'd become increasingly determined to dish the shit out three times as hard as he'd ever received it. He lived high, and stooped low. To the junior guys underneath him he was, simply put, a douche bag. He'd become like one of those guys whom many of us had bitched about during our bull sessions at dinner.

Tubby, on the other hand, had kept his head down and stayed humble. Of the two dozen or so members of our starting associate class, he was the sole survivor, the only one who was still working at what remained of DLJ. Granted, he was tucked deep inside the CSFB mind-fuck machine, but he was still there. And by keeping his head down, by answering the call of duty day after day, month after month, and year after year, Tubby had done what very few of the rest of us actually had the fortitude to do. He had gotten all the way across that burning desert and had finally reached the oasis. Tubby was now one of the most senior guys in the Merchant Bank. He had the big house in Scarsdale and the managing director title. Surprisingly, he still had his integrity intact and he seemed happy.

Troob, Slick, Tubby, and I had been at the bar eating wasabi peas and drinking fancy drinks for about forty-five minutes when Wings finally rolled in. I could see him from where we sat, surveying the room like a German field marshal. It had been nearly five years since I'd last seen him, and boy had he aged. He looked like he had been in a stockade for the entire time, receiving weekly beatings about the head and shoulders. All the deals, all the late nights, and the millions of miles on airplanes had clearly taken their toll.

"Wings!" I screamed across the bar. He caught my eye. "You look like shit!"

He laughed and yelled back. "Fuck you, Rolfe." He made his way over to the table and sat down. "Sorry I'm late, guys." He looked at Troob, Slick, Tubby, and me. "You know, we don't all have it as easy as you guys, cutting out every day when the markets shut down."

"Well that's funny," Slick chimed in, "because Tubby got here on time. Last I checked he was a private deal guy too, aren't you Tubby?"

"Yeah, that's right," Tubby responded. "I'm a fucking private deal machine. Some of us just know how to manage our time better than others. So why the fuck are you so late anyway, Wings?"

Wings smiled a big, shit-eating grin. "I just got done canning the entire senior management team for one of my portfolio companies."

"Sounds like fun," I said, trying to inject a note of irony into my voice.

"Oh yeah," said Wings, "that's what it's all about. Had to chop out the dead wood, man. They just weren't delivering. I gave them a chance to redeem themselves but they fucked it up. They asked for more time, but time is one thing that I haven't got. I've got to get this business back into shape so that I can sell it, or at least pull enough out in dividends to get my bait back."

"So were they upset?" I asked him.

"Well hell, I don't know," Wings answered. "I'm not their shrink. I'm the guy who owns the equity."

Wings still had a smile on his face. He didn't seem bothered in the least. He'd just canned a bunch of guys. Guys who probably had families. Guys who had probably been counting on this LBO to take them to the Promised Land. I mean, business is definitely business, and if somebody isn't pulling their weight you've got to cut them loose, but maybe at least show a shred of remorse in the process. It was all a game to Wings. He was probably going to go home that night and spank off to his collector's edition DVD of *Wall Street*. Greed is good!

So we sat around for the next few hours, pounding down overpriced Scotch and undoubtedly annoying everybody within earshot. After the first few rounds, it didn't feel all that different from our dinners from five years earlier. We bitched and moaned and gossiped: about other members of our class, about the senior guys we'd known from DLJ and what they were doing, and about how we still spent too much time every day dealing with jackasses and cretins. We were five years older, a little bit wiser, and we were higher up the ladder, but we still weren't in any mood to blow sunshine up anybody's ass.

There was one guy missing from the old dinner crew that night: Big Man. Big Man was an enigma. Although the rest of us didn't all see each other that often anymore, at least we always had a pretty good sense of what each of the other guys was doing. Not so with Big Man. Big Man had gone AWOL. He was off the grid. Big Man, like Troob, was a Harvard alum, so Troob was best positioned of any of us to track him down. Even the famed Harvard alum network wasn't a lot of help in this regard, though. Troob had heard through some intermediaries that Big Man, after leaving DLJ, had relocated to Chicago and was working for a nonprofit. When this information was reported back to the DLJ troops, it was like the guy was a leper. People just didn't understand it. They figured that he must have cracked under the pressure. The implicit assumption was that if you weren't doing something for profit, if you weren't teabagging the balls of capitalism, than you must be a retard. Fact was, Big Man had done two tours of investment banking duty—one prior to B-school, and then DLJ following B-school. He knew what it was all about, and he had decided it wasn't for him. He had decided that there was something out there in life that mattered more to him than maximizing his paycheck. Good for him. He had truly broken free.

The dinner at TAO was the last time we all saw one another as a group. It has been almost five years since that dinner, and maybe we'll all get together again at a ten-year reunion to reminisce. That would be nice. Sometimes doors open in life and sometimes they shut. That night the door swung a little more shut, but it is still ajar.

Indigestion

I just wish I had time for one more bowl of chili.
—Kit Carson

Rolfe and I, meanwhile, continued to work at the hedge funds that we had moved to and continued to enjoy our jobs. We both had a nagging suspicion, though, that we might like things even *better* if we were doing it for ourselves. The hedge fund industry is full of guys who have spun out of other firms, raised a small grubstake, and bootstrapped themselves up to build larger investment funds. So we started talking about what it would take to launch our own fund. There was just one primary impediment. Since leaving DLJ, I had been focused primarily on debt investing, while Rolfe had been focused on equities. From our perspective that wasn't a hugely material difference. Regardless of where you are in the capital structure, you're still trying to identify value, do your due diligence, and buy assets at a discount. The problem, as we saw it, was that the outside world didn't necessarily see it that way. A lot of hedge fund investors aren't interested in the old, classic model of a hedge fund that can go anywhere and do anything. They want specialization; narrowly focused funds that do only one thing and do it well. If we tried to combine our styles and launch a fund with a broad mandate, we would be trying to jam a square peg into a round hole. The marketing headwinds would have been significant, and we decided that it wasn't workable.

So instead, I ended up launching a debt-focused fund with my brother, and Rolfe ended up launching an equity-focused fund with Slick. We both started small with some money from friends and family and grew our businesses from there. It was hard work. Sometimes we caught breaks, but we also had our fair share of challenges.

Although we hadn't gone into business together, Rolfe and I still spoke constantly. We talked about investment ideas, and we helped each other out on the business side. We were both in start-up mode, so we were facing many of the same issues when it came to structuring our funds, investing, marketing, and dealing with an army of lawyers, brokers, and investors. If one of us was facing a business issue, there was a good chance that the other guy was facing it too. We were able to piggyback on each other, which worked out well for both of us. Ultimately, we both got our funds off the runway and into the air.

Coincidentally, Rolfe and I also both used Bear Stearns as the prime broker for our respective funds. That meant that our funds kept most of their assets parked with Bear, and Bear provided custody, trading, and financing services for the funds. In addition, Bear ran a steady calendar of conferences for the benefit of the funds that were under its wing.

In late 2006, Rolfe and I were both at one of these conferences in New York City. The purpose of the conference was to give Bear an opportunity to show its prime brokerage clients the huge panoply of services that it could provide. At the conference, we listened to the prime brokerage bigwigs explain how the House of Bear was client-focused. James Izro spoke and he was a jolly, good-natured, Jewish guy with a wicked afro. Everyone called him Jizro because his name and his hair fit so perfectly, and also because everybody thought it was funny to call a guy something that had the word "jizz" in it. He discussed the access to leverage that hedge funds could tap into at Bear, to help us magnify the effect of the implicit bets we were making. Then, we listened to other Bear guys discuss how they could provide us preferred access to the growing collateralized debt obligations (CDO) and credit default swap (CDS) markets. We listened to lots of propeller heads with crazy math minds and round glasses, who looked like they had never attended any fraternity parties in college, discuss Greek letters like beta, alpha, and theta. A Theta was a hot girl in college, but not to these guys. These guys thought about regression and yield curves for fun and got boners when they heard the words "standard deviation."

Rolfe and I listened, but we figured that we were just fundamental investor types and these math geniuses were the next generation of investors. Most of the stuff they discussed didn't make much sense to us, but these guys made it sound so hedged and wedged up that you could invest with enormous leverage and create a portfolio that had very little risk and lots of reward.

After the conference, Rolfe and I went out to dinner with a couple of our relationship guys from Bear. It was the classic broker quid pro quo, where they figure that if they buy you a fancy meal you're going to do some extra trading with them. Rolfe had a meeting up in Stamford the next morning, so he had told me that if I let him sleep on my couch he'd give me a ride home. I told him that was fine, as long as he behaved himself and didn't say anything to my kids that I wouldn't want them to repeat in school. Little did I know that I shouldn't have been concerned with what would happen after we got to my house, but what would happen on the way there.

So Troob and I went to the dinner after the conference. I watched Troob as he yapped it up with the Bear guys and kept pouring wine and food down his maw. He knew that I was driving him home, so he had his chauffeur and didn't need to worry about tying one on. There were some really funky dishes at dinner, and Troob is slightly lactose intolerant. That didn't stop him, though, from having a cream-based soup as an appetizer and apple pie à la mode for dessert. When dinner was over, Troob and I walked to my car and we started driving up to Westchester. When he should have stopped eating, he kept eating, and what he was eating was actually toxic to his system. By the time we hit the Bronx, Troob had shooting pangs in his side, was sweating profusely, and was begging for me to pull into the nearest gas station so that he could relieve himself.

The problem was that there wasn't enough time between his stomach pangs starting and our arrival at the next gas station. I kept telling him, "Hold on, there's gotta be a place to pull off soon," but we were on one of those stretches where there just wasn't. Eventually he told me, "Pull over to the side. Do it now, or I'm going to shit all over your car." That was all I needed to hear, so somewhere between the Bronx and Westchester I pulled over to the shoulder. Troob stumbled out, grabbed the hood of my car, whipped his pants down, and let loose. He had no choice. He had gorged and not paid attention to what he had been putting in his body. He overdid it and he was paying the price. He was thirty-seven years old, knew better, and was bare-assed somewhere on the shoulder of the Major Deegan taking a crap because he had eaten so recklessly. I love the guy, and I laughed so hard watching him that I nearly had to get out of the car to join him, but he had brought it on himself.

We were both still laughing about Troob crapping himself out on the highway by the time we went to bed later that evening. Little did we know that night how steep the precipice on which Wall Street stood was. Sure, we knew there were some excesses, but that was nothing new. The Street had always had a way of separating the winners from the losers and working those excesses out over time. This time, though, things were different. Within a few years Wall Street would begin a cataclysmic process of unraveling, and at the center of that process would be the very investment banks that had birthed us all. Like Troob's shitfest, the banks would gorge themselves on huge amounts of fancy eats at what they thought was a free dinner. And by the time they finally realized what they'd done, it would be too late. They would have to pull over on the side of the highway and explode in plain view for everybody to see.

The Mess

If stupidity got us into this mess, then why can't it get us out?
—Will Rogers

Wall Street has gotten itself and the global economies into a pretty pickle these days. The smooth-talking bankers aren't going to able to sweet-talk themselves out of this mess. Our revered financial institutions have taken yards of dental floss and made thousands of tiny, tight little knots and double knots, and after the dental floss has become completely mangled, they've dropped it on the government and taxpayers' doorstep and screamed "mea culpa" and "please help." The root of the problem? Those old Wall Street standbys: greed and fear.

Greed
Nothing, and we mean nothing, on Wall Street is as deeply ingrained as greed. Greed is what makes Wall Street tick. If money is a drug, then Wall Street is the great enabler. If you want money, then Wall Street has the one-hitter to smoke it, the needle to shoot it, or the grinder to snort it. Heck, they even have the safe house to go to with nice rooms and

maid service. Actually, not only do they enable the potential user, they lead the user to the source and then help the production cartel create even more of the product.

Wall Street's addiction to greed reminds us of the old parable about the scorpion and the frog. The scorpion and the frog are both on one side of a river, and that side of the river is about to be engulfed by fire. The scorpion says to the frog, "Please, I cannot swim and I have to get to the other side of the river." The frog says, "If I let you get on my back, you will sting me and I will surely die." The scorpion promises, "If you save my life and bring me to the other side of the river, I will not sting you." So, the frog allows the scorpion to jump on his back and he swims him over to the other side of the river. As the frog is letting the scorpion off his back, the scorpion stings him. The frog cries out, "What the fuck! Why did you do that? I am going to die now and I just saved your life!" The scorpion replies, "I could not help myself; it is just in my nature." Greed is in Wall Street's nature.

To feed the greed, Wall Street has to sell constantly. It is essentially a selling machine. Bankers sell companies on raising money, then they sell their capital markets departments and research and sales departments on the idea. After that, the sales force sells the idea to mutual funds, pension funds, hedge funds, and individuals. If a company is thriving because Wall Street raised it money, then the hungry banker will be in the face of every other company in that industry espousing the benefits of raising money and showing them that they could be as rich and successful as the other company if they only raised some much-needed funds for expansion. There is so much selling going on all the time at a Wall Street firm that sometimes the bankers, traders, and salespeople lose sight of what they are selling, and are just selling for selling's sake, because they can't help themselves.

This sales machine needs a constant flow of product, and that product comes from one of two wellsprings. The first wellspring is old product. Take equity or bonds. Equity and debt have been around since capitalism was first invented. There are always new companies that need to issue equity or debt, and existing companies that need more equity or debt. The bankers are happy to go out and sell these securities, and each time they sell it they get a fee.

The real juice for the mighty sales machine, though, comes from the second wellspring: new products. Bankers are always thinking up new securities to sell. The Super Banker is the one who thinks up not just a new twist on an old type of security, say preferred equity, but a way to open up an *entirely new* securities market. For instance, in the 1980s, Michael Milken and Drexel Burnham Lambert created the junk bond market. Bond buyers have always generally been a conservative bunch, and prior to the creation of the junk bond market they had been focused solely on buying debt from financially sound companies. What Milken did was to allow these investors to believe that by running a diversified portfolio of credits from less financially sound companies, they could actually generate better returns than from their investment grade portfolio without taking on appreciably more risk. It sounded counterintuitive, but he had the historical data to back it up, and he did a bang-up sales job. The junk bond market was born.

An even more important new market, though, was created over the last few decades with the arrival of asset-backed securities. An asset-backed security is a piece of debt that represents a claim on a large collection of much smaller, asset-backed loans. Historically, commercial banks provided most types of consumer loans. If the consumer needed a mortgage on their house, a car loan, or even a credit card loan so that they could buy some Sham-Wow towels, then they went to their local bank and got the loan. Each of these loans had risks, and each borrower was a unique risk to the bank making the loan. The investment banks didn't get involved in these kind of loans, because the dollar amounts were too small. Wall Street had no interest in trying to sell a $200,000 mortgage secured by a house in Indianapolis because it was small potatoes, and Wall Street's customers needed to buy in much greater amounts. Mutual funds and pension funds needed a minimum of million-dollar-sized bites or it just wasn't worth their while.

So Wall Street came up with a solution: asset-backed securities. It worked like this. Wall Street told the banks, "Don't worry. Sell us your consumer loans, and we'll take care of you." What Wall Street did was to buy enormous buckets full of these small loans, package them together, and "tranche" them out. So, for example, they'd buy 1,000 loans, each of which was for $100,000. That made $100 million worth of total loans. They'd break this loan pool into four parts, with each part having a successively lower claim on the assets of the underlying loans: For instance, $40 million of first priority, $30 million of second priority, $20 million of third priority (or mezzanine), and $10 million of equity.

Once this Frankenstein had been created, the sales machine leapt into action. The sales pitch, fueled by wildly optimistic projections from the ratings agencies, went something like this: "Well, if you buy into the first priority then you are basically completely safe. 60 percent of the borrowers will have to default before you are impaired. So, you are like fucking gold and you are gonna get paid a very, very low interest rate because you are taking on such puny risk. If you buy the second tranche you are still taking on a small risk because 30 percent of the borrowers will have to default before you get fucked. Thirty percent defaults has never happened, so you're going to get a pretty small interest rate too, but larger than the first lien guy. If you take on the mezzanine piece, your risk still isn't too bad. It's not often that we reach a 10 percent default rate, and as long as we don't go above that rate your money is good. If things really go to hell in a handbasket, though, you may see some impairment, so we're going to pay you a reasonable interest rate to compensate you for this possible risk. Last of all, if you take on the equity tranche, you're taking on the most risk. We'll pay you for this risk, and in addition we (the bank) are going to hold on to part of this tranche as well because we think it's a great investment. You should be comfortable, because if we are taking it on our own books, and then issuing the paper, it must be good." This is where the banks stepped over the line of being just drug pushers and became users as well.

What the bankers didn't remind their customer of, though, was that the bankers were making a 3 percent spread on the $100 million deal. So even if they had to turn around and put $2 million back into the deal by purchasing part of the equity tranche, they still came out free and clear with $1 million of risk-free fees. The $2 million equity tranche, which gave the customers "comfort" that the bank knew what it was doing, was nothing but free up-side if things eventually worked out. Not a bad business.

The reason that this asset-backed market was so impor-tant to the investment bankers was its sheer size. Let's put things into perspective. The U.S. junk bond market, which could be considered the greatest "new" securities product of the late twentieth century, is roughly a $1 trillion market today. The U.S. residential mortgage market, on the other hand, is nearly ten times that size. And don't forget: Mort-gage-backed securities are just one piece of the asset-backed market. In addition, you've got auto loans, credit card loans, and student loans. The Wall Street banker never forgets one thing: Each sale creates a fee, and the more you sell, the more fees you generate, and the more fees you generate, the more you get paid.

Fear

Fear is the other great motivator that the consummate Wall Street salesperson understands. Wall Street is a clearing-house for risk, and different investors have different levels of risk tolerance. Wall Street investors have long been able to either mitigate or magnify the risk in their equity invest-ments by using options, but until recently fixed income in-vestors weren't able to do the same. As we said before, bond investors are, relatively speaking, a risk-averse group. So as the proliferation of asset-backed securities created more "risky" tranches of debt, the fixed income investors started to get a bit nervous. Wall Street, not surprisingly, had the answer: a new product called credit default swaps (CDS). CDS were sort of like methadone for the heroin ad-dict. You could buy insurance on a company if you were an owner of its bonds (i.e., you could mitigate the risk). If the company defaulted, and you had a CDS contract on that company's credit, then you would get paid out in full on the company's bonds. This was good insurance for anyone holding the bonds who wanted to make sure they had protection against default.

The CDS market quickly became a huge success. Not only did holders of the underlying bonds begin buying credit protection, but the Wall Street salespeople started pitching CDS to investors who didn't even own the underlying bonds. For many investors, CDS simply became a convenient instrument to bet on a company's future solvency. The bets that Wall Street advocated were similar to the bets on Super Bowl Sunday. You could bet on who would score the first touchdown, or who would fumble first, or who would run for the first first down of the game. In this environment, the game becomes just a side note within all the bets about the game. Wall Street whipped up such a frenzy in its sale of CDS that in five short years the CDS market dwarfed the actual bond market that it was protecting. Along the way, it created massive counterparty risk. Many buyers never bothered to consider that the insurance being sold was only as valuable as the seller's ability to make good if things went awry. And, as usual, the investment banks were there to pick off their commission on each and every CDS sale they made.

The Beginning of the End

The concurrent rise of the asset-backed market and the CDS market ushered in a decade-long wet dream for Wall

Street. Fees were exploding and everybody was getting rich. There were a few lone voices of caution, but they were roundly ignored. Wall Street had the game completely knocked. They were selling like whirling dervishes and feeding the beast of greed. Wall Street told the lending institutions, "Keep making loans. And fast! The more loans we have, the more of these securitizations we can sell!" So the lending institutions went out far and wide, and made loans to people who needed the money and to people who didn't need the money. They made loans to people who could pay the interest on the loans and to people who could not. When any investor got cold feet, they could remind them that they were not alone. By putting everyone together in the same room through securitizations, even the most uncomfortable investor would feel warm and cozy. And if somebody really got out of line and started rousing the crowd, well then they would sell them some protection through CDS, and shove their fear so deep into the closet that it would keep the party going without any worry of an impending hangover.

Eventually, it got so good that the creative Wall Street bankers figured out that they could raise large funds called CDOs (collateralized debt obligations) to buy corporate bonds and tranche the risk out in the same way that they were tranching out asset-backed loans. Then, an even more ingenious banker figured that he could take the equity tranches of these CDOs, merge them together, and tranche those equity interests out. Hence, the CDO squared was born. Soon after came the CDO cubed. Hedge funds were created just to invest and trade in CDOs, and companies were created to be managers of these CDOs. For all intents and purposes, bankers had discovered that they could mush enough of just about any shit together, tranche it out, and convince investors that the top tranches were perfectly safe. The CDO market became so intoxicating to the investing community that it was like sex in a public place (that is, exhilarating until you get nabbed by the police and your mug shot for indecent exposure ends up on the Internet).

There were just a few problems lurking.

First, the incentive system for everybody who was running the game in the investment banks was completely fucked. The bankers were getting paid every year based on their production. The investment banks kept a percentage of every deal they underwrote, and the bankers in charge of that deal kept a percentage of the bank's fee. Since everybody in the food chain was getting paid purely on volume, there was no incentive to monitor the quality of the paper that was being underwritten. The banker got paid the same amount for underwriting a cubic zirconia as he did for underwriting the Hope diamond. Moreover, once a banker got his year-end bonus, who cared if a deal subsequently blew up and the investors who had bought the deal got hit with losses? Fuck the customer; the banker had already gotten paid. Back in the pre-asset-backed days, when commercial banks had been underwriting the $200,000 mortgage on the house in Indianapolis, that loan had stayed on their books. If the loan subsequently self-destructed, the banker or loan officer who had made the original loan would be held responsible. So they had an incentive to make sure that the homeowner had a solid ability to pay off the loan, and that the value of the underlying house could cover the full loan amount. Not so once Wall Street took over.

Second, the asset-backed market impaired the banks' ability to do due diligence on the underlying assets. Each asset-backed deal included loans on thousands of underlying small consumer loans. There was no way that the banks underwriting the deal were about to go out and check on the actual collateral backing those loans. That would have entailed traipsing around muddy construction sites and getting their Ferragamos dirty. Instead, the banks told their pimply faced associates to gin up spreadsheets detailing what the payouts on the various tranches would be under certain default scenarios, and then they told the customers, "Don't worry, defaults have never been greater than X, so you're in like Flynn." And then to top off the delicious hot fudge sundae they'd created, they had the rating agencies "bless" their securities with investment grade ratings. The idea of a banker being the primary line of defense in assessing risk was thrown out the window, then trampled by an unruly mob in search of bigger bonuses than they'd gotten the year before.

And lastly, there was a sole, underlying premise that the entire house of cards was built upon: Nationally, average home values in the U.S. had never, not even once, declined year over year. This was important, because home prices were the ultimate foundation of the collateral that was backing the mortgage-backed securities that, in turn, comprised what was by far the biggest piece of the asset-backed market. Sure there were certain local markets where things had gotten dicey from time to time, but these were isolated pockets. Nationally, through good times and bad, average home values had always risen. And of course, that meant they always would. Never mind the fact that something smelled funny when you read the

MONKEY BUSINESS

newspaper stories about waitresses buying condos in South Beach on spec and then flipping them for $100,000 in pure profit before they were ever built. This was a sure thing, and nobody wanted to kill the golden goose. It wasn't just the bankers. It was the buyers of the asset-backed securities. It was the entire American public. Home values were soaring, and everybody was raking in the dough. So what if a lot of the newest buyers wouldn't even have enough income to cover their monthly mortgage nut once the introductory teaser rates expired? As long as home values kept going up, they'd always be able to refinance into a more attractive mortgage. And, well, if they could always refinance, then the asset-backed securities that their mortgages were now a part of were definitely money good.

These three fundamental problems are what, eventually, led to the collapse of the entire system. Wall Street didn't just drink its own Kool-Aid, it wrapped its lips around a fire hose full of the stuff. The bankers believed that they had fully mastered risk and had truly created a perpetual money machine. They put their global presence to work, jamming these sure-thing, super safe, senior tranche asset-backed securities down the throats of every buyer they could find. They didn't stop with their traditional customers: pension funds, mutual funds, and hedge funds. They went into the Outback of Australia and plumbed the depths of China, Japan, Western Europe, and Latin America, and sold them to localities that were looking for something with just a little bit of extra yield to pad their municipal budgets. They sold them to absolutely anybody who would listen to their sales pitch. Meanwhile, they continued to gorge themselves on the equity tranches and ignore all the counterparty risk they were creating. The $2 million of equity they had to put into each deal to get the buyers comfortable wasn't much on a deal-by-deal basis, but when you multiplied it by the hundreds of deals and billions of aggregate dollars that they were underwriting, it started to add up. And because this was a can't-lose proposition, they kept borrowing more and more money to fund bigger and bigger deals and buy more and more equity tranches and lend more and more money to counterparties and therefore create greater and greater leverage and counterparty risk, all the while standing in the middle of the road assuming that none of the cars on either side of the highway would cross the median. They ended up turning themselves into what were effectively massive, leveraged hedge funds with a single, directional bet: that U.S. housing prices would go up, and up, and up forever. Wall Street had turned itself into an eighteen-wheeler carrying a load of toxic nuclear waste, hurtling toward a brick wall.

The End

If you want a happy ending, that depends, of course, on where you stop your story.

—Orson Welles

When the End arrived, the worm turned quickly. The implosion of two Bear Stearns hedge funds in July 2007 was the canary in the coal mine. The hedge funds, run by a couple of well-regarded senior Bear guys, blew themselves up and wiped out their investors. For those who were watching it was a shot across the bow, because the Bear funds were effectively microcosms of all the investment banks themselves. The Bear funds were trading exactly the kinds of securities that the banks had been gorging on, and they were heavily leveraged. Clearly, some part of the fundamental premise that the U.S. housing market was impregnable was dead wrong.

Things quieted down for a couple of months after the Bear funds blew up, but as the U.S. housing market continued to deteriorate, more people began to sit up and take notice. Investors started to pull their heads out of the sand and question what they had previously taken for gospel. Ironically, investors began to use the very CDS that the investment banks had created to bet against those same banks' solvency. The tail started to wag the dog. Equity investors saw the price of default insurance for the banks going up and told themselves, "Something must be wrong." They started dumping their shares.

As the market value of the banks began to shrivel, trading partners got antsy. Nobody wanted to trade with a counterparty that might not be there to settle the trade in a few days. As rumors started to circulate about trading parties pulling back, the hedge funds that had assets parked at the banks decided they didn't want to be left holding the bag and they started pulling their capital out. This further crimped liquidity, sent CDS prices up, freaked out equity holders even more, and so on and so on. The downward spiral had begun, and it had become clear that the investment banks weren't just houses of cards. They were houses of cards built on foundations of sand. When that foundation of sand—counterparty confidence—disappeared, they were as good as dead.

The first domino to fall, Bear Stearns, was forced into a shotgun marriage with JPMorgan by the Federal Reserve. That move didn't sit too well with a lot of folks, who were understandably not too happy that the U.S. government had stepped in to backstop a bunch of Wall Street fat cats. So, after getting an earful, the Fed decided to let the second domino, Lehman Brothers, fall. Big mistake. Lehman's trading counterparties and debt holders, of whom there were plenty, got seriously fucked. The entire credit market froze up. Nobody would lend to anybody else, not even overnight, because nobody knew who might be next to give up the ghost. The federal government knew that it was staring into the abyss, and it blinked. It stepped in to try to arrest the downward spiral. The Treasury forced the largest of the remaining national commercial banks and investment houses to accept direct equity investments from the U.S. government, and began twisting arms to force marriages among the survivors quicker than a preacher in a polygamist compound. The banks weren't the only culprits. Fannie Mae, Freddie Mac, and AIG were all nationalized; each was seen to be such a basket case that a direct equity investment wouldn't even do the trick. In these cases, nothing short of a complete government takeover could stem the bleeding. Although they weren't banks, in many ways they had become just like the banks: leveraged investment funds with huge, implicit directional bets on the U.S. housing market.

That left just two remaining stand-alone bulge bracket investment banks: Goldman Sachs and Morgan Stanley. They didn't stand alone for long. Both of them quickly tucked their tails between their legs, cried "Uncle!", and converted themselves to bank holding companies. Being an investment bank had gotten just a little too scary, and they were desperate for the security blanket that comes with federal oversight. Going forward, Goldman and Morgan will be collecting deposits and letting the Feds into their shorts to keep a close eye on things. What a turnabout. Just a few years ago, Goldman was the shining house on the hill, the gold standard that all the other investment banks strove to emulate. Now, well, there are apparently going to be Goldman bankers manning teller windows to collect deposits from grandmothers and orphans.

Rolfe and I left DLJ just a little more than ten years ago. During that decade, the investment banking industry didn't just party hard and give itself a hangover. No, it partied so hard that it blacked out, woke up naked on Madison and 57th, got its picture splashed on the front page of the *New York Post*, and landed in jail with no near-term chance for parole.

Wall Street not only stung the frog but also stung every animal on the other bank of the river, every freaking animal on Noah's Ark, and then, in truly grandiose manner, it stung itself.

Wall Street, for now, is officially dead. The investment banking industry is looking like a morbid band of flesh-eating zombies from a 1950s horror flick. Will the zombies rise again? They may; we don't know. Money is a powerful motivator, and we don't underestimate the Street's ability to reinvent itself. But for the foreseeable future, Wall Street is screwed. To try to salvage our economy, the U.S. government has had to attach itself to Wall Street's face like the space creature in *Alien*, and it's busy laying its eggs. With the U.S. government as Wall Street's largest shareholder, the Treasury will now be calling the shots. The taxpayers have said enough is enough. Payback is hell and, well, Wall Street's now getting paid back in spades.

As for Rolfe and me? We can't complain. Being an investment banker was bad enough when times were good, and now it's much worse. Forget about the pain of making pitch books; now every taxpayer in the country wants to make your nut sack into a hacky sack and mount your head on the wall in their rumpus room.

We left banking because we wanted more balance in our lives, and as investment bankers we didn't have it. As we said, if you have one foot on a block of ice and the other on a hot stove, the average temperature may be okay, but you'll still have two blistered feet at the end of the day. We've tried to balance our lives. Leaving investment banking helped in this regard, but it wasn't a cure-all. We still work hard, and our family and friends take a lot of time and effort, but they're worth it. We now have one foot in lukewarm water and the other in chilly water. It isn't always terribly comfortable, but the seesaw is more balanced than it used to be and we consider ourselves lucky and blessed.

We talk to each other a lot, and help keep each other from getting too seasick from life's bumpy ride. Having a friendship like this makes life's journey worth the trip.

About the Authors

JOHN ROLFE graduated from Virginia Tech, the University of Florida, and Wharton Business School. At Wharton, he was the editor of *The Wharton Vulgarian*. Following his sentence with DLJ, he spent several years working at a private investment fund. In 2001, he cofounded an equity-oriented money management firm, and today manages the firm from a top-secret location deep in Vermont. He lives with his wife and two children, and is currently attempting to learn how to produce maple syrup.

PETER TROOB graduated from Duke University and Harvard Business School. At Harvard, he was the humor editor for *Harbus*. After a gross error in judgment caused him to return to the investment banking world at DLJ, he left for the greener pastures of distressed debt investing at a private investment fund. In 2002 he cofounded a debt-oriented money management firm, which he continues to manage today. He lives with his wife and two children outside of New York City, where he can often be seen limping around the neighborhood and complaining about his bad knees.